THE TEMPLE OF APOLLO.

Engraved by William Woollett from the painting by Claude Lorrain, 1760.
Museum of Fine Arts, Boston, Massachusetts.

ITALIAN LANDSCAPE
IN EIGHTEENTH CENTURY
ENGLAND

A STUDY CHIEFLY OF THE INFLUENCE
OF CLAUDE LORRAIN AND SALVATOR ROSA
ON ENGLISH TASTE
1700 – 1800

BY

ELIZABETH WHEELER MANWARING, Ph.D.

ASSOCIATE PROFESSOR OF ENGLISH COMPOSITION
IN WELLESLEY COLLEGE

THE WELLESLEY SEMI-CENTENNIAL SERIES

NEW YORK
OXFORD UNIVERSITY PRESS
AMERICAN BRANCH: 35 WEST 32ND STREET
LONDON, TORONTO, MELBOURNE & BOMBAY

1925

PRINTED IN THE UNITED STATES OF AMERICA

PREFACE

The idea that the eighteenth century, until the last two decades, was generally blind to natural beauty is probably no longer current. But aside from several glancing hints, there has been no consideration of the part played by painting in developing the love of landscape in England. Yet the landscape which was taken as a model by Thomson and Dyer, by Kent and Shenstone, by Mrs. Radcliffe, was Italian, the landscape of the seventeenth century painters, Claude Lorrain, Salvator Rosa, the Poussins, and the long line of their followers and imitators, French, Dutch, and English.

This relation of poetry and painting in the eighteenth century has been noticed by several critics, but only briefly. The Greek poets, says Thomas Twining, in one of his dissertations on Aristotle's *Poetics* (1789), " did not *describe* the scenery of nature in a picturesque manner, because . . . those beauties were not heightened to them, as they are to us, by comparison with painting — with those models of *improved* and *selected* nature, which it is the business of the landscape painter to exhibit. They had no Thomsons, because they had no Claudes." And he contrasts the effect of landscape on the peasant with its effect on the person of culture, used to pictured scenes: " such beauty does imitation reflect back upon the object imitated." Alison in his *Essays on Taste* (1790) attributes the creation of English landscape gardening to admiration of Italian scenery, and " the difference or inferiority of the scenery of our own country." This admiration was founded, he thought, partly on the study of the classics, and the strong prejudice which " we so early and so deeply feel, in favour of every thing that relates to Grecian and to Roman Antiquity "; and very largely on landscape painting. " Our first impressions of the Beauty of Nature had been gained from the Compositions which delineated such scenery; and we were gradually accustomed to consider them as the standard of Natural Beauty."

Some later critics refer to, but do not examine, the relation of landscape painting to the view of nature in the eighteenth

iii

century. In *Landscape Art before Claude and Salvator* (1885)
Josiah Gilbert hints that literature has owed more to art than
art to literature in respect to appreciation of nature; and that
" the great expression of delight in natural scenery which we find
contemporaneously in Gray and Rousseau may . . . much of it
have been due to the abundant landscape art then in existence."
Miss Myra Reynolds in *The Treatment of Nature in English
Poetry between Pope and Wordsworth* (1896) briefly notices the
influence of painting on the Picturesque School, especially in
gardening, and refers to both Dutch and Italian influences on
English painting, especially " the atmospheric effects, the wide
landscapes, and the ruined temples of Claude." In his chapter
on Thomson in the *Cambridge Modern History of English
Literature,* Mr. A. Hamilton Thompson observes " the tendency
inherent in the later seventeenth century to group details in
broad masses of colour and striking contrasts of light and
shadow," and to the influence on Thomson of the painters.
" Those who began to revolt against trimness," says Mr. Irving
Babbitt in *Rousseau and Romanticism* (1919), " turned at times
to painting — as the very word picturesque testifies — for the
encouragement they failed to find in literature." " The real dis-
coverer of the picturesque, the first enthusiast for the savage aspects of nature," according to Mr. Frank Jewett Mather, in his
History of Italian Painting (1923), was Salvator Rosa. " These
forests, cascades, evening seaports, and ruined sites were freely
bought by the English, greatly admired, and had their part in
producing the literary enthusiasm for wild nature in the eighteenth century."

More emphatically than any of these, though still but briefly,
Sir Walter Raleigh, lecturing on *Romance* at Princeton in 1915,
asserted the connection of the pictorial arts with the development of regard for nature. He especially noticed the part played
by the print, besides giving due weight to the landscape gardener
(" If the house was set in order, the garden broke out into a
wilderness ") and to the Reverend Mr. Gilpin, as precursors
of romanticism.

That the seventeenth century saw a radical change in the
emphasis on landscape in painting is a sufficiently familiar idea.

Interest in mere landscape had been foreshadowed, it is true, by Titian and the Caracci, in the sixteenth century, and by Paul Bril and Elsheimer in the late sixteenth and early seventeenth. But not till about 1640 was landscape fully established in the lay mind as a separate and important branch of painting. By that year both Claude and Salvator were well on their way to being the fashion, and the fashion they remained for a hundred and fifty years. From 1640 on, they could not satisfy the commissions which poured in upon them from prelates, princes, and nobles, and until they died, Salvator in 1673, Claude in 1682, their pictures were sought for, extravagantly valued, copied, imitated, forged.

Two great contemporaries, Nicolas Poussin and Rubens, contributed to strengthen the taste for landscape painting; but as they were accounted history painters, their influence is less important. Gaspar Dughet, called Poussin, brother-in-law of Nicolas and associate of Claude, was enormously admired by the English, and much collected by them. His pictures show the training which he received from both Nicolas and Claude, and even at times, in his scenes of wild nature, have a suggestion of Salvator. Ruysdael and other Dutch and Flemish artists, though often admired, were generally classed below the painters of Italian landscape, as following nature slavishly, rather than selecting and improving her scenes.

Of all landscape painters, Claude and Salvator are named most often by the English of taste in the eighteenth century. The very contrast between them helped to associate them as examples of the two sorts of scenery which had most impressed the English visitor to Italy. Contrasted as they were in subjects and manner, they were akin in possessing literary and poetic appeal. The visitor least a virtuoso could discern something of what they were trying to say. For his better enlightenment there was usually some title, — a *Cephalus and Procris*, a *Repose in Egypt*, an *Annunciation*, or a *Job*, a *Diogenes*, a *St. Jerome*. Title and figures, however slight their importance, helped to make connection with the more familiar art of history painting, which was easy for the novice in taste to value, because of the story told. But Claude and Salvator gave what even Raphael, so effusively admired, could not give in the same way — the pleasure of recognition. On their canvases the English visitor saw a powerful representation of scenes already in his memory. What he had felt at Frascati, the Virgilian tranquillity, the evocation of a Golden Age, had been felt with infinitely more dreamy sweetness by Claude Lorrain; the awe, which he called horror, that had stricken the traveler as he crossed the dizzy crags in his journey, the sense of the might and vastness of nature and the littleness of man, the thrill of the wild and untamable, Salvator Rosa had felt more passionately.

The value which modern criticism assigns to these artists is not important for a study of their influence in the eighteenth century. What that influence was; what were the early traces of its appearance; what the men of that time supposed they knew about these artists; by what means their influence spread; the conceptions of landscape beauty which it established for a hundred years in literature, in gardening, in general taste: something of these it is the business of this study to present.

Forced to choose between a close study of some period or phase of this influence, and a view more extended in both time and content, I have chosen the second, from a conviction that any division I might impose would be but arbitrary, and that only a multitude of instances, ranging through the century, can adequately reveal the extent to which general taste was affected and ideals of beauty and sublimity were formed by the landscape painters. The result is naturally too often a tissue of citation. To have burdened the pages with the appropriate footnote references for all these would have been grotesque; I have kept therefore only such as cannot be supplied with the help of the text. For a like reason I omit the bibliography; given with anything like completeness and with suitable annotation, it would have required disproportionate space. The index in some measure supplies a bibliography.

In its original form, this study was presented to the English Faculty of the Graduate School of Yale University in candidacy for the degree of Doctor of Philosophy. The greater part of the material is derived from the Yale University Library, to the officials and staff of which I am grateful for many kindnesses. To the Harvard University Library also I am indebted for courtesies; and to the Metropolitan Museum, the Fogg Art Museum of Harvard University, and the Boston Museum of Fine Arts, especially to Miss Laura H. Dudley of the Fogg Art Museum and Mr. H. P. Rossiter, Keeper of the Prints in the Boston Museum. Besides obligations of long standing to Professor Albert S. Cook, I am specially indebted to him, and to Mrs. Cook, for help in collecting photographs.

For being first made aware of the possibilities of the subject, for unwearied advice and encouragement during its preparation, for suggestions of material, for much practical help in the gathering of prints, and in details of publication, and, finally, for reading the greater part of the first proofs, I am deeply indebted to Professor Chauncey Brewster Tinker, without whose aid this work could scarcely have been prepared.

The honour of inclusion in the Wellesley Semi-Centennial Series, I gratefully acknowledge. The advice and friendly interest of Professor Katharine Lee Bates and Professor Josephine Batchelder of the Semi-Centennial Committee have been very valuable to me.

E. W. M.

WELLESLEY, February 23, 1925.

CONTENTS

ILLUSTRATIONS

ITALIAN LANDSCAPE IN
EIGHTEENTH CENTURY ENGLAND

ITALIAN LANDSCAPE IN EIGHTEENTH CENTURY ENGLAND

I

ENGLISH INTEREST IN LANDSCAPE AT THE OPENING OF THE EIGHTEENTH CENTURY

WHEN Dyer wrote in 1726,

> The quick'ning Sun a show'ry Radiance sheds,
> And lights up all the Mountains' russet Heads,
> Gilds the fair Fleeces of the distant Flocks,
> And, glittering, plays between the broken rocks.
> Light, as the Lustre of the rising Dawn,
> Spreads the gay Carpet of yon level Lawn; . . .

and Thomson the next year,

> . . . Young Day pours in a-pace,
> And opens all the lawny Prospect wide.
> The dripping Rock, the Mountain's misty Top
> Swell on the Eye, and brighten with the Dawn,

it was evident that something had happened to the eyes of British poets since the time of Denham and even of Milton. The nearest intimations of *seeing* landscape in *Cooper's Hill* — published in 1640, the very year which marked the beginning of popularity for both Claude and Salvator — are such vague observations as

> . . . Such an easie and unforc't ascent,
> That no stupendious precipice denyes,
> Accesse, no horror turnes away our eyes. . . .

> While the steepe horrid roughnesse of the Wood
> Strives with the gentle calmeness of the flood . . .

> But his proud head the ayery Mountain hides
> Among the Clouds; his shoulders, and his sides
> A shady mantle cloaths. . . .
> Low at his feet a spacious plaine is plac'd,
> Betweene the mountain and the streame imbrac't,

3

which clearly is not seeing in the artist's way at all. John Scott of Aimwell, a fair representative of the intelligent reader in the middle of the eighteenth century, finds precisely this fault with Denham: " The author one should expect would have painted, as nearly as possible, the appearance of a fine river, amidst a beautiful region of hills, woods and vallies. Instead of this, we are presented with a tedious enumeration of supposed qualities."[1] The difference between Denham and Thomson is the difference between a person slightly used to landscape pictures, and one well used to them. Denham has no sense of composing the parts of his scene into one group, nor does he even see the parts pictorially; Thomson has the sense of composition in a marked degree.

Milton, it may be objected, is pictorial. He does see the parts, in *L'Allegro,* for example, as separate small scenes; but there is no centre, nor is there consistency of perspective in his

> Russet Lawns, and Fallows Gray,
> Where the nibbling Flocks do stray,
> Mountains on whose barren breast
> The labouring Clouds do often rest:
> Meadows trim with Daisies pide,
> Shallow Brooks and Rivers wide,
> Towers and Battlements it sees,
> Bosom'd high in tufted Trees,

nor even in his description of Eden, much commended in the eighteenth century. Dyer and Thomson had read Milton with devotion, as their verbal reminiscences show; but they had something which Milton had not — the landscapes, abundantly multiplied in painting and print, of Claude and Poussin.

It was this new element — the picturesque — which helped to transform the distaste for mountains as things uncouth into a fearful joy at their precipices, crags, and hanging woods. To appreciate this change in view, we need to turn back to Dryden. His famous remark on mountains has been taken as typical of his age, though it may be doubted whether he really knew mountains. " High objects, it is true, attract the sight; but it looks up with pain on craggy rocks and barren mountains, and continues not long on any object, which is wanting in shades of green to entertain it."[2]

[1] *Critical Essays,* 1785, p. 19.
[2] Dedication to *The Indian Emperor,* 1667.

Charles Cotton, on the other hand, who was at least familiar with Derbyshire, and also, it is manifest, with painted landscapes, when he describes Chatsworth recognizes a pictorial value in the crags and wild rocks, — that contrast of beauty and sublimity which was so frequently made in the next age. The palace is girded with " wild Prospects "; its garden " rivals proud Italy."

The *Groves,* whose curled *Brows* shade ev'ry *Lake*
Do ev'rywhere such waving *Landskips* make,
As *Painter's* baffled *Art* is far above,
Who *Waves* and *Leaves* could never yet make *move . . .*
To view from hence the glitt'ring Pile above . . .
Environ'd round with Nature's Shames and Ills,
Black Heath, Wild Rock, bleak Craggs, and naked Hills,
Who is it, but must presently conclude,
That this is *Paradise,* which seated stands
In midst of Desarts, and of barren *Sands?*

John Dennis, crossing the Alps in 1688, showed that he too appreciated the contrast of beauty and sublimity, and was ready to enjoy the picturesque, but lacked vocabulary:

. . . The impending Rock that hung over us, the dreadful Depth of the Precipice, and the Torrent that roar'd at the Bottom, gave us such a view as was altogether new and amazing. On the other side of that Torrent, was a Mountain that Equall'd ours. . . . Its craggy Clifts, which we half discern'd thro' the misty gloom of the Clouds that surrounded them, sometimes gave us a horrid Prospect. And sometimes its face appear'd Smooth and Beautiful, as the most even and fruitful Vallies. So different from themselves were the different parts of it: In the same place Nature was seen Severe and Wanton. In the mean time we walk'd upon the very brink, in a literal sense, of Destruction; one Stumble, and both Life and Carcass had been at once destroy'd. The sense of all this produc'd different motives in me, viz. a delightful Horrour, a terrible Joy, and at the same time that I was infinitely pleas'd I trembled.[3]

He despairs of making his friend at home see Mount Cenis. If the Alps were designed by Nature " only as a Mound to enclose her Garden *Italy:* Then we may well say of her, what some affirm of great Wits, that her careless irregular and boldest Strokes are most admirable."

[3] *Miscellanies in Verse and Prose,* 1693, pp. 133–134. *Cf.* Coryat, who finds in Italy " The Tempe — or Paradise of the world," but ignores the wild scenery. Ed. 1905, I, 238, 245, 264.

I am delighted, 'tis true, at the prospect of Hills and Valleys, of flowry Meads, and murmuring Streams, yet 'tis a delight that is consistent with Reason. . . . But transporting Pleasure follow'd the sight of the *Alpes* . . . Ruins upon Ruins, in monstrous Heaps, and Heaven and Earth confounded. The uncouth Rocks that were above us, Rocks that were void of all form, but what they had received from Ruine: the frightfull view of the Precipices, and the foaming Waters that threw themselves headlong down them, made all such a Comfort [Consort?] for the Eye, as that sort of Music does for the Ear, in which Horrour can be joyn'd with Harmony.

A man who felt thus in crossing the Alps was ready to admire Salvator Rosa when he reached Rome; and on his return journey, to take still greater pleasure from the precipices and foaming waters.

Celia Fiennes, who rode about England on horseback, suitably attended, in the days of William and Mary,[4] makes artless comments which provide a fair notion of the standards of taste in scenery held by a person of quality in that time. Mistress Fiennes viewed with delight the parks and gardens along her way, and never failed to visit each, and to give particulars of its grottos, " squaires " of turf, walks of grass and gravel, " knotts of flowers," trees cut in geometric forms, " vistos," terraces, and especially fountains and water-works, with their surprises and wetting-spots, sudden showers descending from a tree of copper, streams spouted from the mouths of leaden dolphins, and artificial " melody of Nightingerlls " made by waterpipes. Her favourite encomiastic adjective was *neat,* and though she was capable of enjoying a wide prospect or shady grove, these must be in cultivated country. She visited two of the spots later frequented by the pilgrims of the picturesque — Derbyshire and the Lakes. But she thought that steep hills made " travelling tedious and ye miles long ": " Looking upward I was as farre from the top which was all Rocks, and something more barren, tho' there was some trees and woods growing in ye Rocks and hanging over all down ye Brow of some of the hills." Hills interfered with her view, except of " ye Clouds," and were so full of loose stones that it was very unsafe to ride down them.

Her insistence on the discomforts which hills introduced into

4 *Through England on a Side-Saddle* . . . 1888, passim.

travel — and she was a cheerful person, not given to complaining — makes us realize that improvements in roads and means of travel during the eighteenth century had a great deal to do with the increasing enjoyment of scenery. In fact, a large part of what has been considered hatred or fear of mountains was well-warranted uneasiness at discomfort and danger. When to such uneasiness was added the strangeness of such a spectacle as the Alps afforded, and the difficulty of finding anything in one's experience to compare them with, the appellation of *horrid* might seem well justified, even without classic precedent. In truth, however, it often is used to indicate a pleasurable awe, such as Dennis felt.

When, soon after the Peace of Ryswick in 1697, the grand tour became part of a gentleman's preparation for life, pictures, prints, and drawings collected by many a tourist began to pour into England, and to familiarize the eyes of intending travelers with what they were to see in their turn. So young Walpole and Gray, despite the perils and discomforts of their passage into Italy, were able to enjoy the grandeur of the scenery, with an enjoyment which is distinctly reminiscent of the paintings of Salvator Rosa.

For their pictures of landscape the English were not entirely dependent on the pictures which they brought back from Italy in such extraordinary quantities. Walpole mentions in his *Anecdotes* a number of landscape painters (chiefly of foreign extraction, indeed) who were painting in England in the last years of the seventeenth century and the first of the eighteenth. The Dutch Henry Dankers, who had studied in Italy, was employed by Charles II as a topographical artist. John Loten, also Dutch, painted " glades, dark oaken groves, land-storms, and water-falls; and in Swisserland, where he resided too, he drew many views of the Alps." This artist, manifestly an imitator of Salvator or Gaspar or both, died in London about 1680. An English landscape painter, Thomas Manby, studied in Italy, brought back, as the practice was, a collection of pictures for sale, and died about 1690. Gerard Edema came to England about 1670, and took subjects of wild nature from Norway and Newfoundland, to which countries he made voyages; " delighting in rocky views, falls of water, and scenes of horror." Henry

Adrian Coloni, who died in 1701, imitated Salvator Rosa. John Griffier (1645–1718), " the Gentleman of Utrecht," who painted " views of London, Italian ruins, and prospects on the Rhine," came to London soon after the great fire. He was patronized by the Duke of Beaufort, and other noblemen, according to Strutt, who says that his pictures were held in the highest estimation. He was an imitator of great versatility, judging from the pictures sold after his death, which ranged over some ten Dutch and Italian masters, including Salvator; his son John was one of the many copyists of Claude. Other artists of this period include Thomas Stevenson, whose landscapes were apparently scene paintings; Jacques Rousseau, a pupil of Swanevelt, the follower and perhaps pupil of Claude; Philip Boul, whom Vertue reported to have had " a pocket-book almost full of sketches and views of Derbyshire, the Peak, Chatsworth, &c. very finely touched, and in imitation of Salvator Rosa, whose works this person studied "; Henry Cooke, who died in 1700, said to have been a pupil of Salvator himself; and Henry van Straaten, who " resided in London about the year 1690, and afterwards. He got much money here, and squandered it as fast." The predominance of wild scenery in the subjects of these artists is striking.

Besides these, and the innumerable paintings — originals and copies — as well as prints and drawings, which poured into England with returning travelers, and with speculating artists and dealers, the amateur artists also was highly important for dissemination of the painter's point of view on scenery; and the amateur landscape painter had begun to flourish before the seventeenth century closed, and long continued to flourish increasingly. Mistress Anne Killigrew was one, —

> Her pencil drew whate'er her soul design'd . . .
> The sylvan scenes of herds and flocks,
> The fruitful plains and barren rocks,
> Of shallow brooks that flowed so clear,
> The bottom did the top appear;
> Of deeper too and ampler floods,
> Which, as in mirrors, showed the woods;
> Of lofty trees, with sacred shades,
> And perspectives of pleasant glades,
> Where nymphs of brightest form appear,
> And shaggy satyrs standing near . . .

The ruins, too, of some majestic piece,
Boasting the power of ancient Rome or Greece,
Whose statues, friezes, columns, broken lie,
And, though defaced, the wonder of the eye.

As Scott says, the landscapes here described are decidedly reminiscent of Claude Lorrain.

Excellent evidence of increased interest in painting in general, and landscape painting in especial, is gained by comparing travelers' accounts at the close of the seventeenth century with those a few years later. The earlier traveler is absorbed in the social and political life of the places visited, the important buildings and antiquities. He enjoys naïvely the water-works and wetting-spots in Italian gardens, and respectfully admires the terraces and statues. Richard Lassels' *Italian Voyage* (1670, second edition, 1698) was evidently a popular guide-book, and with reason, for it gives much practical advice. He had made the journey to Italy five times, by as many routes, and accounted the passage over Mount Cenis the most desirable for speed and convenience. He well exemplified the usual English opinion. Italy he regarded as " *Nature's Darling* . . . receiving such gracious looks from the *Sun* and *Heaven,* that if there be any fault in Italy, it is, that her Mother *Nature* hath indulg'd her even to wantonness." He liked views. The suburbs of San Pietro, at Genoa, " compos'd of Pallaces and Gardens, such a beautiful Landskip, that the whole Place seem'd to me to be the charming Paradise of the King of the *Mountains* anciently, and I was almost going to say, that we durst not bless ourselves, lest this enchanted place should have vanish'd." The view from the Carthusian monastery at Naples, a favourite point of description with travelers, he considered " as fine a Prospect as Europe can afford, excepting that of *Greenwich,* thought by *Barclay,* the best Prospect in Europe." His interest in painting was less than that in jewels, but interest he had, even if his comments are of childish simplicity. Though he refers in a casual contemporary manner to " the Judgment of *Monsieur Poussin,* a famous Painter," he says nothing of landscape painting. Nor does E. Veryard, whose *Account* was published in 1701. He too was pleased with Prospects, and enjoyed the sight from a hill overlooking Bologna of the adjacent plain and the snow-crowned Alps, "seeming to hang in the Air like Clouds at a great distance." But he gives more time than Lassels does to enumerating pictures in galleries. W. Bromley, whose *Travels* appeared in 1702, noticed the landscape painters; at Florence, "many Pictures of the best Masters; four battles of *Bourguignone*, some by *Salvator Rosa*"; but oddly classes Salvator among "the most antient." He names Giovanni da Udine as "the first Inventor of Landschapes." Though he does not refer to "Landschapes" by Claude or Salvator, he mentions pictures by "*Gasparo Poussin,* a Frenchman," and by Paul Bril.

Addison, as a more cultivated person, has more intelligent remarks to make on art, though he is mostly preoccupied with the art of the ancients. His *Letter* to Lord Halifax suggests the landscape painters; but Raphael's is the only name he chooses to use:

> For wheresoe'er I turn my ravish'd eyes,
> Gay gilded scenes and shining prospects rise.

The glamour which classic scenes held for the Englishman he well expresses, — that glamour which, captured by Claude, made a great part of Claude's charm for the English. The ancients, says Addison, had pleasures beyond ours in reading their poets; for "they liv'd as it were on *Fairy Ground,* and convers'd in an enchanted Region, where every Thing they look'd on appear'd Romantic, and gave a thousand pleasing Hints to their Imagination." [5]

Just once in his *Remarks on Several Parts of Italy* (1705), which seemed to the immediately succeeding generations such an unsatisfactory account, does he refer to the landscape painters, and then it is with swift return to the classics, — that description of "a beautiful Prospect that none of 'em have mentioned" near Tivoli:

It opens on one side into the *Roman Campania*, where the Eye loses it self on a smooth spacious Plain. On the other Side is a more broken and interrupted Scene, made up of an infinite Variety of Inequalities and Shadowings, that naturally arise from an agreeable Mixture of Hills, Groves, and Vallies. But the most enlivening Part of all is the River *Teverone*, which you see at about a quarter of a Miles distance throwing it self down a Precipice, and falling by several Cascades from one

[5] *A Discourse on Ancient and Modern Learning*, 1739, p. 14.

Rock to another, 'till it gains the Bottom of the Valley, where the Sight of it would be quite lost, did not it sometimes discover it self thro' the Breakings and Interstices of the Woods that grow about it. The *Roman* Painters often work upon this Landskip, and I am apt to believe that *Horace* had his Eye upon it in those Two or Three beautiful Touches that he has given us of these Seats.

His pleasure in prospects was more exquisite and frequent than that of preceding travelers; but not expressed with fulness, it is to be noted, till after he had been at Rome, where the largest collections of landscape paintings were to be found. It is hard to understand why Addison should be cited as an example of the dislike of mountains supposedly prevalent in the Augustan Age, except that he remarks, not unnaturally, on the discomforts of traveling over them. As parts of a landscape he had a high regard for them, — especially after he had been in Rome. Thus he found the fatigue of crossing the Apennines "very agreeably reliev'd by the Variety of Scenes we pass'd thro. For not to mention the rude Prospects of so many rocks rising one above another, . . . we saw, in Six Days Travelling, the several Seasons of the Year in their Beauty and Perfection." He paints a Claudian landscape, with amphitheatre form, from the Capucins' garden at Albano:

It takes in the whole *Campania,* and terminates in a full View of the Mediterranean. You have a Sight at the same time of the *Alban* Lake, that lyes just by, . . . and by reason of the continu'd Circuit of high Mountains that encompass it, looks like the *Area* of some vast Amphitheatre. This, together with the several Green Hills and naked Rocks, that lye within the Neighbourhood, makes the most agreeable Confusion imaginable.

The Alps about Geneva " make an Horizon that has something in it very singular and agreeable." He enjoys the contrast of the hills " cover'd with Vineyards and Pasturage " on one side, with the " huge Precipices of naked Rocks rising up in a Thousand odd Figures " on the other, " cleft in some Places, so as to discover high Mountains of Snow that lye several leagues behind 'em. Towards the South the Hills rise more insensibly, and leave the Eye a vast uninterrupted Prospect for many Miles." In another " Prospect " near Geneva the Alps " are broken into so many Steeps and Precipices, that they fill the Mind with an agreeable kind of Horror, and form one of the most irregular misshapen Scenes in the World."

The few letters that we have from Bishop Berkeley, describing his impressions of Italy in 1714, show appreciation of scenery. We cannot blame him for being more preoccupied with his safety, crossing the Alps in January, than with sublimities; he thought himself lucky to have come off with but four falls, and the breaking of sword, watch, and snuff-box. But writing to Pope later, he seems to feel that something was gained even from these perils, and thinks it may

. . . be worth a poet's while to travel, in order to store his mind with strong images of nature. Green fields and groves, flowery meadows and purling streams, are no where in such perfection as in England; but if you would know lightsome days, warm suns, and blue skies, you must come to Italy; and to enable a man to describe rocks and precipices, it is absolutely necessary that he pass the Alps.

He went out of the regular tourist's track to visit Imarime, and had a full sense of its

. . . wonderful variety of hills, vales, ragged rocks, fruitful plains, and barren mountains, all thrown together in a most romantic confusion. . . . Several fountains and rivulets add to the beauty of this landscape, which is likewise set off by the variety of some barren spots and naked rocks. But that which crowns the scene is a large mountain, rising out of the middle of the island . . . from which you have the finest prospect in the world, surveying at one view, besides several pleasant islands lying at your feet, a tract of Italy about three hundred miles in length . . . the greater part of which hath been sung by Homer and Virgil. . . . The islands . . . the bay of Naples, the promontory . . . and the whole Campagna Felice, make but a part of this noble landscape, which would demand an imagination as warm, and numbers as flowing, as your own, to describe it.

Berkeley developed something like a painter's eye. When he visited Rhode Island he was impressed by " many delightful landscapes of rocks and promontories, and adjacent islands." He was so much interested in painting, as his letters show, that we are surprised to find no intimation of his joining his wife and children in amateur practice of the art, which he commended as a source of wealth to the nation.

What differentiates Berkeley and Addison from the later picturesque tourist is not only the rather small proportion of their interest in scenery, compared with their interest in other things, but their apparent failure to connect agreeable scenes of nature with paintings of landscape. Yet their descriptions are unmistakable evidence that they were influenced to find beauty in a particular sort of landscape — elaborate, wide-spread, greatly diversified, and having classical association — the landscape, that is, of the seventeenth century Roman landscape painters.

II

THE REGARD FOR THE PICTORIAL ARTS IN EIGHTEENTH CENTURY ENGLAND

I

ALTHOUGH English amateur artists and collectors of prints, drawings, and to some degree, paintings, were multiplying before the close of the seventeenth century, acquaintance, real or pretended, with the graphic arts had by no means become, as it had by 1750, an essential part of a gentleman's social equipment. Thanks partly to the work of such engravers as Faithorne and Hollar, and partly to continental example, print collecting was fashionable to some extent following the Restoration; but the landscape print — Hollar's cannot be counted as landscape in the later sense — was not at this time important.

Several works on art published in England before 1700 indicate the growing interest in drawing, painting, and etching. The quack doctor William Salmon's *Polygraphice* ran to eight editions from 1672 to 1701. A reason for its popularity is no doubt its comprehensiveness; it gave receipts for cosmetics and perfumes as well as instructions in all the graphic arts. The remarks which it offers on landscape painting and etching are very brief; but the domination of Italian forms is clear, though there is some reference to Dutch. " Landskip is that which expresseth in lines the perfect vision of the earth, and all things thereupon, placed above the horizon, as towns, villages, castles, promontaries, mountains, rocks, valleys, ruines, rivers, woods, forests, chases, trees, houses and all other buildings both beautiful and ruinous." [1] The instructions for the landscape painter certainly suggest Claude, still living at this time: " Always express a fair horizon . . . And if you express the Sun, let it be as rising or setting, and as it were behind or over some hill or mountain. . . . Make your Landskip to shoot (as it were) away, one

[1] A sample " landskip " is given, mostly buildings. (Ed. 1673.)

14

part lower than another . . . Let every site have its proper
parerga, adjuncts, or additional graces, as the Farm-house, Wind-
mill, Water-mill, Woods, Flocks of Sheep, Herds of cattel, Pilgrims, ruines of Temples, Castles, and Monuments." " If you
draw a Landskip from the life, you shall take your station from
the rise of ground, or top of a hill, where you shall have a large
Horizon, marking your tablet into three divisions downward."
    The chief critical work on art (if it may be called critical)
published in England before Richardson's *Essay on Painting* was
Dryden's translation of Du Fresnoy's *De Arte Graphica*, in 1695,
with Graham's " Short Account of the most Eminent Painters "
appended. Hack work as it was,

> Yet still he pleas'd, for Dryden still must please.

It was not of his own choice that he undertook the work, Dryden
says. " Not but that I understood the *Original Latine* and the
French Authour perhaps as well as most *Englishmen;* But I was
not sufficiently vers'd in the *Terms of Art:* And therefore thought
that many of those persons who put this honourable task on me,
were more able to perform it themselves." He is vague in his
references to painting, has not many examples at hand, mentions
no landscape painters at all, and inclines to let his parallel become chiefly a discourse on his own art. " 'Tis sufficient if I
bring a Sample of some Goods in this Voyage. It will be easie
for others to add more when the commerce is settled."
    The rise of a new interest is discernible in this last sentence;
and the growing importance of the collector in another: " Many
of our most skillful Painters, and other Artists, were pleas'd to
recommend *this Authour* to me, as one who . . . gave the best
and most concise Instructions for Performance, and the surest to
inform the Judgment of all who lov'd this noble Art. That they
who before were rather fond of it, than knowingly admir'd it,
might defend their Inclination by their Reason; that they might
understand those Excellencies which they blindly valu'd, so as not
to be farther impos'd on by bad Pieces, and to know when Nature
was well imitated by the most able Masters." Dryden laments
that the best pieces " are not very frequent in *France* or *England,*"
though besides examples of many Dutch and Flemish masters,
(" not inconsiderable, but for Design, not equal to the Italians ")

"we are not unfurnish'd with some Pieces of *Raphael, Titian, Correggio, Michael Angelo* and others." The general idea — and ideal — as preferable to the particular is recommended: "a learned *Painter* shou'd form to himself an *Idea* of perfect Nature"; though from this precept portraits are hastily excepted. "That *Picture* and that *Poem* which comes nearest to the resemblance of Nature is the best. But it follows not, that what pleases most in either kind is therefore good; but what ought to please"; — a precept important to remember as helping to account for the admiration bestowed on the highly idealized pictures of Claude, Poussin, and their imitators.

The popularity of Du Fresnoy's treatise throughout the century is one of the innumerable curiosities of taste. There were three other translations; one by J. Wright in 1728, one by a painter, James Wills, in 1754, and one by William Mason, to which the notes by Reynolds give value, in 1781. The frequent repetitions of *Ut pictura poesis* which occur seem to be derived as much from the opening line of Du Fresnoy as from Horace's

> Ut pictura, poesis; erit quae, si propius stes,
> Te capiat magis, et quaedam, si longius abstes;

and the elaboration of it,

> . . . muta Poesis
> Dicitur haec, Pictura loquens solet illa vocari,

was a commonplace unceasingly relished.

Some hints of the taste of the age are given by Addison in the *Spectator* for June 5, 1711, which has the pleasant conceit of Time creeping about the gallery and retouching the pictures with his beautiful brown varnish. The admiration for dark pictures held from the time of Dryden's lines to Kneller, which prophesy that Time's ready pencil shall

> Mellow the Colours and imbrown the Teint,

to the days of Constable, who rebelled when advised by Sir George Beaumont to adopt the colour of an old Cremona violin for the prevailing tone of his pictures.[2]   This solitary paper on painting, set over against the numerous papers on opera, suggests

---

[2] Leslie, *Life of Constable,* ed. 1896, p. 140. He replied by laying the violin down on the green turf. Beaumont himself painted with a picture of Gaspar Poussin's alongside his easel, to give the correct tone.

that painting was as yet too slight an interest to evoke Addison's satire, in spite of the numerous advertisements of picture-sales which appear on the back pages of the *Spectator.*

Shaftesbury, writing to Lord Somers in 1712, observes to that leading connoisseur that "though we have as yet nothing of our native growth in this kind worthy of being mentioned; yet since the Publick has of late begun to express a relish for engravings . . . and for the original paintings of the chief Italian schools (so contrary to the modern French), I doubt not, that in a very few years, we shall make an equal progress in this other science " with the progress which had been made in music since the English displaced French by Italian models.[3] In his *Characsticks* (1711) he refers to " the *Virtuoso*-Passion, the Love of *Painting,* and the Designing Arts of every kind." His *Second Characters* have much more to do with painting, especially the fragmentary *Plastics.* He realized the need of a critical vocabulary, and gave the rudiments of one, including such terms as Picturesque, Grotesque, Romantic. From this essay we learn explicitly that he warmly admired landscape painting, and owned two " perspectives " by Salvator, and one by Claude.[4] Though in his dying years at Naples, with means below his soaring ideals, he felt it not fitting to buy pictures for his own delight, he longed to increase the collections of his friends.[5] To one he says that since the great masters of history-painting, " the Carachs, the Guidos," have become very costly, " the next degree of painting (which is that of nature in perspective or landskip) will be that which best suits you, and which, I think, you have most taken to of late "; a significant remark, pointing toward a fast-growing taste.

Hints of Shaftesbury's love of painting are scattered throughout his essays. Is not a Claude (perhaps his own) behind the "pompous rural scene " in *The Moralists?* " It was a Mountain not far from the Sea, the Brow adorn'd with antient Wood, and at its foot a River and well-inhabited Plain; beyond which the Sea appearing, clos'd the Prospect "; and later, a sunrise scene: " The Sun, now ready to rise, draws off the Curtain of Night,

[3] *A Letter concerning the Art or Science of Design.* In *Republic of Letters,* I, 93–106, February, 1728.
[4] *Second Characters,* ed. Benjamin Rand, Cambridge, 1914, pp. 139, 157.
[5] *Life,* etc., ed. Rand, 1900, pp. 448–449, 484–485, 516.

and shews us the open Scene of Nature, in the Plains below."
Hints of Salvator occur in the sketch of wilder country,

> . . . where huge embody'd Rocks lie pil'd one on another, and seem to
> prop the high Arch of Heaven. — See! with what trembling Steps poor
> Mankind tread the narrow Brink of the deep Precipice! From whence
> with giddy Horrour they look down, mistrusting even the Ground which
> bears 'em; whilst they hear the hollow Sound of Torrents underneath,
> and see the Ruin of the impending Rock; with falling Trees which
> hang with their Roots upward, and seem to draw more Ruin after 'em.

And in the "deep shades of the vast Wood,"

> . . . which closing thick above, spreads Darkness and eternal Night below.
> The faint and gloomy Light looks horrid as the Shade it-self. . . .
> Here Space astonishes, *Sense* it-self seems pregnant; whilst an unknown
> Force works on the Mind, and dubious Objects move the wakeful Sense.
> Mysterious Voices are either heard or fancy'd; and various Forms of
> *Deity* seem to present them-selves, and appear more manifest in these
> sylvan Scenes; such as of old gave rise to Temples, and favour'd the
> Religion of the antient World.

The encouragement which Shaftesbury gave to the connoisseur
— he is probably responsible for the swift popularity of the word
Taste — was soon reinforced by that of Jonathan Richardson.
Richardson, the most important portrait painter of the period following Kneller's death, and a notable collector of drawings and
prints, published the first of his essays on painting and " connoissance " (his friend Prior suggested the word) in 1715; the second
in 1719; the notes on works of art in Italy in 1722; and the collected *Essays* in 1725. There were several editions of these
last; they were published, collected, in 1792 at the Strawberry
Hill Press. Richardson is best remembered now as the author
whose book moved the boy Reynolds to wish to be a painter;
but he must have influenced many others, by precept and example, to desire to be connoisseurs. In spite of the formal and
pompous style ridiculed by his contemporaries — there is a
legend that Fielding would run a furlong to escape him, and
called him " Dr. Fidget "[6] — his ardour and devotion are impressive even today.

[6] W. H. Pyne, *Wine and Walnuts*, I, 108–109. According to that gossipy
work, Richardson used to drop in at the coffee-houses to read his essays
aloud, — at Slaughter's, Will's, Button's, and Dick's; but not at The Devil,
which he would not enter, thinking the sign profane.

His first essay, *The Theory of Painting* (1715), a plea for the recognition of painting as a liberal art, suggests dense stupidity or indifference to be combated in his public. How unsympathetic an intelligent man might be we may guess from Theobald, who slurs works of art as " at best but poor Bunglings and imperfect Representations of Nature; but the Pride is that they were made by his *Fellow-Creature Man*. How often shall we see a rational Soul hung as it were by the Eyes, and fox'd with Admiration, upon *a fine Piece of Painting?* " [7] Judging from Richardson's plea, there was even need of arguing that a painter was not an artisan, that his art was noble, and that a gentleman did not too greatly stoop in knowing a good picture from a bad one, or even in painting pictures himself. He seems to try to shock his audience into attention by extreme statements: " To be an accomplished painter, a man must possess more than one liberal art . . . he must also be a curious artificer, whereby he becomes superior to one who possesses the other talents, but wants that. A Rafaelle, therefore, is not only equal, but superior to a Virgil, or a Livy, a Thucydides or a Homer."

The notion of rivalry or of fraternity between the two arts was especially common in the eighteenth century. *Ut pictura poesis* recurs often. Both Horace — " pictoribus atque poetis " — and Du Fresnoy were partly responsible, as has been said; also the *Critical Reflections on Poetry, Painting and Music* of the Abbé du Bos, translated into English in 1748. Shaftesbury treated conventionally of the relation between the arts in his first *Characteristicks*, but by the time he was composing the *Plastics* he had come to see the absurdities of this attempt to parallel things unlike, and inclined to ridicule Du Fresnoy and Dryden. " Scarce at any time in our modern poets or authors one single metaphor, allusion, simile grounded on the art and formed on the painter's business but what makes the painter blush . . . Comparisons and parallel ran [*sic*] between painting and poetry . . . almost ever absurd and at best constrained, lame and defective."

An example of such a parallel appears in *The Lay-Monastery* (1713), Nos. 31 and 32, prefaced, of course, by the text *Ut pictura poesis*. The art of the landscape painter, by which a country is contracted to grace the walls of a city palace, and " Groves

[7] *The Censor*, 1717, II, 51.

spread their Branches, Rivers flow, Fountains weep, and Shepherds tend their Flocks, in Rooms of State, and sometimes the Spectators are entertain'd with the Views of solitary Desarts," is compared, as it so often is, to that of the pastoral poet.

Walter Harte, friend of Pope and tutor (with dubious success) to young Stanhope, wrote as a youth in college his verse *Essay on Painting* about this time.

> Whatever yet in *Poetry* held true,
> If truly weigh'd, holds just in *Painting* too;
> Alike to profit, and delight they tend;
> The means may vary, but the same the end,

he begins. He shows considerable interest in landscape, which Du Fresnoy (whose work Harte had not then read) leaves out; and his Italian models for it are evident:

> But most of all, the *Landscape* seems to please
> With calm repose, and rural images. . . .
> See, absent rocks hang trembling in the sky,
> See, distant mountains vanish from the eye;
> A darker verdure stains the dusky woods;
> Floats the green shadow in the silver floods;
> Fair visionary worlds surprise the view,
> And fancy forms the golden age anew.[8]

"What is Poetry but the Painting an Object to the Mind in natural and lively Colours?" asks another contemporary minor poet, the unfortunate Henry Needler. "The nearer the *Poet* approaches to the *Painter*, the more perfect he is; and the more perfect the *Painter*, the more he imitates the *Poet*," says Hildebrand Jacobs in his essay *Of the Sister Arts*.[9]

The confusion of poetry and painting is important for better understanding the popularity of Claude, Salvator and the Poussins, whose landscapes were so easily related to literary conceptions. This was especially true of the pastoral landscapes of Claude, so naturally reminiscent of Theocritus and Virgil. The likeness between pastoral poets and landscape artists was soon noticed. "Each of these gives you Prospects of the Country,

---

[8] *Poems on Several Occasions*, 1727, pp. 3, 25–26.
[9] *Works*, 1735, p. 380. Another of the various essays is by Robert Hill, *On the Harmony between Poetry and Painting*, Poems, 1775, pp. 284–288.

with Variety of Rural Scenes."[10] "The Perfection of a Master
Painter is, to be able to perform the same Wonders by Colours,
which the Poet commands by Language. His ideas pass from his
Mind into his Pencil, and rise upon the Canvass in their full
Vigour and Proportion. His every Touch is a Creation; the
Canvass is no longer a level, lifeless Surface, but a Scene, diversify'd with Buildings, Mountains, Forests, or perhaps, a Sea
deform'd with Tempests."[11] "Poetry is said to be the sister art
of Painting," says another writer, "in nothing more nearly resembling it, than Description."[12]

Parallels of the names of painters and poets are frequent. So
John Nourse, in *Ut Pictura Poesis*, brings together Raphael and
Homer, the Caracci and Virgil, Titian and Ovid, Veronese and
Horace, Poussin and Theocritus:

> Lo! where *Poussin* his magic colours spreads,
> Rise tower'd towns, rough rocks, and flow'ry meads;
> What leagues between those azure mountains lie,
> (Whose less'ning tops invade the purple sky)
> And this old oak, that shades this hollow way,
> Amidst whose windings sheep and oxen stray,
> 'Tis thus *Theocritus* his landskip gives,
> 'Tis thus the speaking picture moves and lives.[13]

"Had Theocritus and Virgil seen the landscapes of Gaspar
Poussin, even those celebrated poets might have profited, from
the rural and pastoral scenery of those exquisite pieces of art,"
says John Stedman.[14] Names come only too readily to the pen
of any person of Taste, in the second half of the century. Miss
Seward, with wonted indiscrimination, terms Mason "the sweet
Claude of our science." An unknown versifier of Liverpool turns
off with dreadful facility a list like this, worth quoting as an instance of the commonplaces of the time:

> Majestic, nervous, bold and strong,
> Let ANGELO and MILTON vie;
> Oppos'd to WALLER's amorous song,
> His art let wanton TITIAN try;

---

[10] *Gentleman's Magazine*, 1734, IV, 42–143.
[11] *The Free-Thinker*, 1718. No. 63.
[12] *St. James's Journal*, April 20, 1723.
[13] Dodsley, V, 94. He doubtless means Gaspar Poussin.
[14] *Laelius and Hortensius*, 1782, p. 251.

> Let great ROMANO's free design,
> Contend with DRYDEN's pompous line;
> And chaste COREGGIO's graceful air,
> With POPE's unblemished page compare;
> LORAINE may equal THOMSON's name,
> And HOGARTH's equal BUTLER's fame.[15]

The Reverend Martin Sherlock considers Correggio the La Fontaine of painting, Albano its Anacreon, Rubens its Homer, Raphael its Virgil.[16]   Mrs. Piozzi compares " the sweetly playful pencil of Albano " with Waller, Domenichino with Gray, Guido with Rowe, " if such liberties might be permitted on the old notion of *ut pictura poesis*. But there is an idea about the world that one ought in delicacy to declare one's utter incapacity of understanding pictures, unless immediately of the profession." [17]

Poetry and painting were not only compared; they mingled. George Smith of Chichester, a landscape artist of great vogue, (he prospered far beyond Wilson), published in 1770 *Six Pastorals*. " His profession as a lanschape [18] painter," says he in the Advertisement, " induced him to study nature very attentively; and the beautiful scenes he often examined, furnished him with a great variety of ideas many of which, he flatters himself, are new; . . . But as he never made the art of writing his particular study, he has not always been able to convey his ideas to the Reader with the same force as he received them from the Book of Nature." His pastorals offer few descriptions of scenery, but are not without a pleasant homely freshness. George Keate, man of letters and also artist, attempted to improve on Nicolas Poussin by a dramatic poem entitled *The Monument in Arcadia* (1775). " PAINTING," he says, " can but half tell her story. . . . To unveil external appearances, and to paint that precious Disposition of the Mind, which fixed them . . . is an elder Sister's Province, and the peculiar Property of the Muse." Another combiner of the arts was George Cumberland. " It is delightful

---

[15] *Mount Pleasant:* a Descriptive Poem. To which is added . . . an Ode . . . Warrington, 1777. The ode is " on the Institution of a Society in Liverpool, for the encouragement of Designing, Drawing, Painting, &c."
[16] *Lectures*, 1781, I, 16.
[17] *Observations*, 1789, I, 250.
[18] The spelling of this word remains uncertain until late. Mickle in his Spenserian *Sir Martyn*, has *lawnskepe*.

to behold the harmony subsisting between the Sister Arts," observes a reviewer of Hayley's *Epistle to Romney* (1778). The English Prize Oration at Oxford in 1779 treated of the affinity between painting and writing, and is worth attention because of its very commonplaceness in representing accepted opinions. Landscape painting and pastoral poetry, the orator observes, both require a turn of mind for the romantic and picturesque. "Claude Lorrain and Titian are in the one what Theocritus and Virgil are in the other; and the same grotesque wildness equally characterizes the scenes of Thomson and Salvator Rosa; both become more interesting by the introduction of human figures." [19]

The eighteenth century liked art to be instructive. Artists themselves accepted the requirement, which had often as corollary the notion that the greater the idea or action portrayed, the greater the picture or poem. From this belief there resulted such dead weights of versification as *The Epigoniad* and *Leonidas,* such pictures as Hogarth's *Sigismunda,* and those appalling acres of grandiosity by Barry and West. Jonathan Richardson helped to propagate this idea. " A picture," he says, " is useful to instruct and improve our mind, and to excite proper sentiments and reflections, as a history, a poem, a book of ethics, or divinity: the truth is, they mutually assist each other." So history painting occupied the extreme top in the hierarchy of painting; portraits, as concerned with character, came next; and landscape took a lower station, along with fruit and flower pieces and " drolls." Perhaps the use of landscape for purely decorative purposes, over chimney-pieces and doors, helped to suggest the idea of inferior rank. " We PAINTERS are upon the level with writers, as being poets, historians, philosophers, and divines; we entertain, and instruct equally with them," says Richardson. From such a view of art, it follows that " a history is preferable to a landscape, sea-piece, animals, fruit, flower, or any other still-life, pieces of drollery &c. the reason is, the latter kinds may please, and in proportion as they do they are estimable . . . but they cannot improve the mind, they excite no noble sentiments; at least not as the other naturally does."

" LANDSKIPS, or Still Life, work much less upon us than

---

[19] *New Ladies Magazine,* 1786, p. 458. The many poets who played with painting, and Dyer, who attempted both arts, belong in later chapters.

Representations of the Postures and Positions of Living Creatures," says Steele.[20] " The finest Landskip, tho' drawn by Titian or Carrache, would not strike us so much, as the real Prospect of a beautiful or gloomy and dreadful Tract of Ground; such a Picture does not afford us the least Entertainment," says another literary critic of painting; and adds that judicious painters heighten their landscapes with figures " in order to give us Opportunity of employing our Reflections."[21] But there were those who took naïve pleasure in imitation. So *The Prompter* (1735): " To have Nature, as it were, forc'd from itself, and transplanted upon a Canvass, under the Representation of some delightful Landscape, enrich'd with the grateful Variety of *Sun-shine, Water, Greens, distant Views,* and interspersed with Figures, that seem animated, and in *Motion.*"[22]

Greater familiarity with the best examples of landscape painting, reinforced by the poetry of Thomson, raised landscape in esteem; yet the desire for figures held on. " Do you really think that a regular composition in the Landskip way should ever be filled with history, or any figures but such as fill a place — I won't say, stop a gap — or create a little business for the eye to be drawn from the trees in order to return to them with more glee? " wrote Gainsborough. But he was exceptional. Even Reynolds, who admired Claude and owned some fine examples of his work, placed landscape on a lower level than history or portrait. " Teniers, Borgognone, Watteau, Claude, " had in general the same right, in different degree, to the name of painter, that a satirist, an epigrammatist, a sonneteer, a writer of pastorals, has to that of a poet." " History painting is certainly the most elevated species," says William Gilpin, " a mode of epic; and tho the literary world abounds with admirable productions in the lower walks of poetry, an Epic is the wonder of an age."

2

Three appellations most frequent in polite English literature of the eighteenth century are *Virtuoso, Connoisseur,* and *Man of*

[20] *The Guardian,* 1713, No. 86.
[21] *London Journal,* August 26, 1727. *Cf.* Santayana, *The Sense of Beauty,* 1896, pp. 133–136.
[22] No. 49.

Taste. These titles we must examine, since the fashion which made them sought after was influential in diffusing Italian models of landscape in painting and gardening. The Virtuoso appeared earliest; at first in association with the Royal Society. Shaftesbury was a virtuoso in the arts; for him painting was " the true virtuoso science," and he noticed with reprobation the other sort of virtuoso, who collected anything at all, stones, shells, beetles, fossils, oddments of all three kingdoms.

The term *Connoisseur* was established by Jonathan Richardson. " I believe this is the only book extant upon the subject," he says, in his *Essay on the Science of Being a Connoisseur.* His advice shows how ignorant he supposed his audience to be.

> There are certain arguments, which a connoisseur is utterly to reject. . . . That a picture or drawing has been, or is much esteemed by those who are believed to be good judges; or is, or was, part of a famous collection, cost so much, has a rich frame, or the like. Whoever makes use of such arguments as these, besides that they are very fallacious, takes the thing upon trust, which is what a good connoisseur should never condescend to do. That it is old Italian, rough, smooth, &c. These are circumstances hardly worth mentioning, which belong to good and bad.

He tried " to persuade our nobility and gentry, to become lovers of Painting, and connoisseurs," to the end that " a much greater treasure of pictures, drawings, and antiques would be brought in."

The *Observations* of Edward Wright, made in the years 1720, 1721, and 1722, but not published till 1730, bear evidence to the great increase of connoisseurs in that decade:

> There are a considerable Number of Paintings, that I had taken Notice of, and set down, which I have still omitted, for Fear of being tedious on that Head; Tho' perhaps the general, and I had almost said, the fashionable Taste for those Things, which now prevails, and seems too in a Way of prevailing still more, rather than of declining amongst us, might well have justified my inserting more than I have done. We may well look upon this Taste as prevailing, when we see such Additions yearly made to the fine Collections of the Nobility. . . . And of this the Italian Virtuosi, who make a Traffick of such Things, are very sensible, as they constantly find the Sweets of it, with regard to themselves; and the Romans in particular, who have such a Notion of the English Ardour, in the Acquisition of Curiosities of every Sort, that they have this Expression frequent among them, Were our Amphitheatre portable, the ENGLISH would carry it off.

Wright shows the increased taste for the " fine landskapes " of Claude Lorrain, Gaspar Poussin, Salvator and others; and enjoys prospects with artistic pleasure.

" No Art is more affected to be understood, than Painting, nor any in Reality is so little understood," says Thomas Cooke in 1732. " Most People judge of it more by their Ears than their Eyes; for they seldom determine a Picture, or Painter, till they have taken the Opinion of a Person whom they take to be a Judge, and who perhaps gained that Character only by cunningly finding Faults in Pictures, when he could not find the Beautys, were there never so many." [23]   " Nothing is more talk'd of, or less understood, than *Painting*," says another writer of that year; adding that even painters themselves are not always the best judges, but " the Gentleman Critic, tho' ignorant of *Painting* as an Art," is the properest judge, because of his more liberal culture.[24]

The establishment of the Dilettanti Club in 1734 doubtless helped to seal connoisseurship as of the fashion, though the club had at first no end but social pleasure.   The word *Dilettanti* figures in John Breval's *Remarks on Several Parts of Europe* (1738): " To lessen the Trouble which young *Dilettanti* often meet with Abroad in their *Virtuoso* Persuits, has been one of my principal Aims in this Undertaking," says his preface, which enlarges on the stripping of Italian galleries by the English. " How far should we surpass all our Neighbours in *Virtuoso* Treasures of every kind, as much as we do in Pictures (which are out of the question) but for our Losses in the Rebellion? "

Acceptance of connoisseurship as part of the apparatus for a man of fashion was by 1740 definite.   A more general and gradually more intelligent interest in painting and prints is reflected in the magazines.   In place of, or at times alongside discussions of the art of the ancients, and vague, literary, pseudo-Platonic discourses on the text *Ut pictura poesis,* appear more and more accounts of the arts, brief and superficial, to be sure, but mildly technical.   The sixties and seventies bring great increase in both number and definiteness of such articles.   Technical terms are explained, rules given for judging the beauties of painting, lists

[23] *The Comedian*, 1732, p. 24.
[24] *Gentleman's Magazine*, 1732, II, 678-679.   The idea is taken from Coypel.

of collections are printed, with the prices fetched at auction; and accounts of the schools of painting and of individual artists, copious extracts from Walpole's *Anecdotes of Painting* (1762–1771), Gilpin's *Essay on Prints* (1768), and Pilkington's *Dictionary* (1770); and notes on exhibitions by the Society of Arts and the Royal Academy.

The term *Connoisseur* was very loosely used, as is shown by the title of the periodical paper published by Colman and Thornton, and by *The Connoisseur* (c. 1740), " a Satire on the Modern View of Taste." In fact, *Connoisseur* was used as synonym for the still vaguer *Man of Taste*. But however vague that latter epithet, and however often the mark of satire, few men of fashion would have liked its being withheld from them.

The word *Taste* seems sometimes to be the most used English word in the whole vocabulary of the eighteenth century. One complacent critic observes that the age of George III may well be known as " the age of taste," because of its great advance in connoisseurship and in the practice of the arts. For the entrance of the word *taste* into elegant society, Shaftesbury is certainly in part responsible; though he uses it in the *Characteristicks* interchangeably with *relish*, and *choice*. The progress of the term is analyzed by Henry Baker, son-in-law of Defoe, in his periodical, *The Universal Spectator*:

A poem of TASTE, written by a favourite Author, seemed first to bring it into Taste. Another Poet, fired by the Success of that Piece, writ one which he called *The Man of Taste*, and still brought the word more into use. When it became general, and an entire favourite Expression in the Town, a *Dramatick Author* embraced the lucky Opportunity and brought it on the Stage, and not injudiciously gave his Play the Name of *The Man of Taste*. It has now introduced so much Politeness among us, that we have scarce a grave Matron at *Covent* Garden, or a jolly Dame at *Stocks-Market*, but what is elegant enough to have a *Taste* for Things.[25]

Another satire of this decade refers to " This Thing call'd TASTE, this new-fam'd ALAMODE,"

This Term for something that was never found,
Which leaves our Sense and Reason lost in Sound,

[25] *The Universal Spectator*, by Henry Stonecastle of Northumberland, Esq., 1746, III, 46. (Written some twelve years before.) The references are to Pope's *Epistle to Burlington* (1731), J. Bramston's *Man of Taste* (1733), and James Miller's *Man of Taste* (1733).

as " the reigning Foible of the Times." [26]   To Baker's list should be added the print, *The Man of Taste*, by Hogarth, attacking Pope, and, nearly two decades later, Samuel Foote's comedy, *Taste* (1752).

" Taste is now the fashionable word for the fashionable world," writes Chesterfield in 1738; and discourses pleasantly on those who sacrifice their natural taste for an imaginary one.[27]   " I hear the word *Taste* introduced in speaking of Pictures, of Gardens, of Architecture, of Dress, of Furniture, of Music, of Dancing," — so Dodsley's *Museum*, in 1746. Never did a piece of fashionable jargon cause comment through so long a period. For years the essayists find their meat in it. In *The World* (1753) William Whitehead suggests that for *Taste* might be substituted *Whim*. *The Connoisseur* (1755) calls Taste " the darling idol of the polite world . . . the quintessence of almost all the arts and sciences." *The Spendthrift* (1766) knows of no topic that has given " more trouble to less purpose."

Robert Lloyd, in *The Cit's Country Box*, a satire on the pretentious tradesman aping his betters, discourses thus:

> Blest age! when all men may procure
> The title of a connoisseur;
> When noble and ignoble herd
> Are govern'd by a single word;
> Though, like the royal German dames,
> It bears an hundred Christian names;
> As Genius, Fancy, Judgment, Gout,
> Whim, Caprice, Je-ne-sçai-quoi, Virtù;
> Which appellations all describe
> TASTE, and the modern tasteful tribe.

The man of taste was concerned with improvements, like Burlington, if he had an acre of land; but certainly with pictures. Bramston describes him:

> In curious paintings I'm exceeding nice,
> And know their several beauties by their *Price*.
> *Auctions* and sales I constantly attend,
> But chuse my pictures by *a skilful Friend*.
> Originals and copies much the same,
> The picture's value is the *painter's name*.

[26] *The Modern Englishman* (173–?).   [27] *Fog's Journal*, February 11.

So *The Manners of the Age* intimates,

> All his nice pieces, furnish'd by the hand
> Of *Angelo's,* who studied in the Strand.[28]

" He is just returned from travel," says young Joseph Warton in a character-sketch, " and sets up for a great virtuoso. He imagines he has an excellent taste in painting, statuary, and medals; and is inviting his friend to come and see a genuine Otho, which I assure you, was coined at Rome about two years ago." [29]

The popularity of landscape painting with collectors appears in several satires. Charles Johnston in *The Reverie* (1763) has Mr. Connoisseur tell a noble patron: " Some of the landscapes came high; but they are very fine, very fine indeed." [30] *The Ladies Miscellany* (1770) shows a rich city knight, Sir Samuel Sapskull, and Mr. Pallet, a connoisseur-agent:

Sir Samuel. Well, Mr. Pallet, what curious little picture have you got in your hand?

Mr. Pallet. A curiosity, indeed, Sir Samuel. It is a landscape by Verdipratti; an original, and very scarce. There is not above three of them in England. . . .

Sir S. And pray, sir, what is the purchase of it?

Mr. P. An hundred guineas, Sir Samuel. . . .

Sir S. Why, 'tis as black as ink.

Mr. P. That's a proof of its age, Sir Samuel. 'Tis a prodigious advantage of pictures, they are mellow'd by time, Sir Samuel.

Sir S. I don't know what you mean by mellowed, not I, but I am sure I never saw trees of such a colour; you won't tell me, I hope, that those are green trees? . . . There's Tom Brusher will touch up a picture for a quarter of the money, as bright as noonday, that will dazzle your eyes to look at it. I hate these black trees.

Mr. P. I am sorry to hear you say so, because your taste will be universally condemn'd. Your neighbour, Sir Solomon, gave more money for another, by the same hand, not half so black. A Verdipratti, Sir Samuel, is not to be met with every day.

Sir S. Ha, ha, — say you so, why then . . . you may leave your Verdopratto. . . . 'Tis a little upon the gloomy order, to be sure; however, I'll hang Mr. Verdopratto up in the sun, and then we shall see what he would be at.

This reverence for age and darkness, along with neglect of native genius, is a frequent subject of ridicule. *The Prater* (1756) tells of being led by curiosity to visit the rooms of Lang-

[28] 1733, p. 71.   [29] Ed. Wooll, 1806, p. 181.   [30] 1763, I, 171–172.

ford, most fashionable auctioneer of the mid-century. As he surveys with admiration a fine Claude, he is addressed by a wretched artist:

If I had recourse to the dealers's arts, made use of the Spaltum-pot, and gave it out that [my pictures] were executed by *Signor Canvassini,* all the *Connoisseurs* in town would flock about them, examine them attentively with their glasses, and cry out in rapture, — *What striking attitudes! — What warm colouring! — What masses of light and shade! — What a rich fore-ground! — Did you ever see anything more riant!* . . . Once, indeed, I painted a landscape for a *dealer,* who gave me two guineas for it, and sold it for fifty, by telling every body 'twas *Poussin.*[31]

James Barry, in *An Inquiry into the Real and Imaginary Obstructions to the Acquisition of the Arts in England* (1774), ridicules the prevalent cant. In the English pursuit of art " the celebrated names of Michael Angelo, Da Vinci, Raffael," he says, " came to be lisped even by the children in picture knowledge, and men are zealous admirers of works they have never seen, who with all their enthusiasm, are likely enough to mistake these objects of their predilection for any thing else, and any thing else for them, when they encounter them by accident." The connoisseur is thus described by Francis Grose:

The first requisite, nay, I may say the *sine qua non* . . . is money, . . . purchasing, at great prices, the almost invisible pictures of the ancient masters. The next . . . is to have made the grand tour, and to have visited the city of Rome. . . . Some little study is indeed necessary . . . but this is a mere matter of memory — I mean names and terms, such as Michael Angelo, Raphael, the Carraches, Guido, Correggio, Titian, and Paul Veronese — the colouring of the Venetian school — clairo obscuro — keeping . . . grand gusto . . . with a fortnight's study of De Piles and Florent le Compte. . . . The candidate must on all occasions remember to decry the works of English artists, particularly those who have never travelled; it being absolutely necessary, in order to paint the portrait of an Englishman, . . . or to represent an English landscape, that the artist should have studied the men . . . and views of Italy.[32]

The spectacle which the ignorant and pretentious young Englishman made of himself on his travels was painful to his

[31] Second ed., 1757, pp. 78–83.
[32] *The Olio,* 1792, pp. 54–57.

countrymen of finer sensibilities. In 1740 Lady Hertford complained, writing from Florence to her friend Lady Pomfret:

> Mr. Coke . . . is one of the few that I have met with who *ought*
> to have been sent abroad. For most of our travelling youth neither
> improve themselves, nor credit their country. . . . Travelling is certainly
> carried a great deal too far amongst the English. . . . Could you see
> the inundation of poor creatures from all the three kingdoms, that,
> at the regular seasons, overrun the different parts of France and Italy,
> you would, with me, lament the approaching month of July, in which
> I am destined to receive them here.[33]

Such barbarians we have a glimpse of, two decades or so later,
in an anecdote of James Boswell's:

> If those who have no taste for the fine arts would fairly own it, perhaps
> it would be better. Mr. Damer and Captain Howe, two trueborn
> Englishmen, were in the great gallery at Florence. They submitted
> quietly to be shewn a few of the pictures. But seeing the gallery so
> immensely long, their impatience burst forth, and they tried for a
> bett who should hop first to the end of it.[34]

To offset such impressions, we recall that not only Mr. Coke,
heir of the Earl of Leicester and later famous in England and
America as Coke of Norfolk, but also Mr. Pitt, not to mention Mr. Gray and Mr. Walpole, and (on a different social plane)
Mr. Dyer and Mr. Thomson, are examples of the visitor who
carried home valuable stores of art. John Russell, a young
painter in Rome in the same year that Lady Hertford makes
her strictures, gives a pleasant account of young Pitt, who " does
not squander away his time and money, . . . but studies very
much, and diverts himself with music and drawing; in which
last he had made such proficiency that were he in our Academy,
I should soon grow jealous of him." And the next year he
writes:

> It is no small satisfaction to me to find, that most young gentlemen,
> who come hither, shew so great a regard for the art which I study,

[33] *Cf*. Soame Jenyns.
> " Just broke from school, pert, ignorant, and raw,
> Expert in Latin, more expert in taw,
> His honour posts to Italy and France,
> Measures St. Peter's Dome, and learns to dance."
> *The Modern Fine Gentleman, Poems*, 1750, I, 58.

[34] *Boswelliana.*

as not only to admire and endeavour to understand it in theory, but even to amuse and divert themselves in the exercise and practice of it. On holy days and at other times, when a recess from my business will permit, I take every opportunity of accompanying gentlemen to see the palaces, &c. for as those grand doors flie open only to the rich, I am glad to follow them as their shadow, and to crowd in as one of their attendants.[35]

Even the Mr. Squanders, such as Dr. John Moore presents in *Zeluco,* buying pictures because they were praised by the vendors, showed some sense of duty to be performed.

Probably there never was a time when impositions in painting were more shamelessly practiced; because the combination of zeal for acquiring pictures bearing famous names never went more uniformly with ignorance of painting. The copyist was, early in the century, a regularly employed means of securing favourite pictures. The references to Mr. Klosterman and his journeymen, in Shaftesbury's correspondence, show this. The *Monthly Review* in 1756 makes the melancholy reflection that the days of good copying are past; " Buckshorn was one of the last good copiers we have had in England." [36] If the impossibly numerous pictures of English ownership attributed to the greatest masters were not in themselves evidence of abundant copies and forgeries, there is testimony in plenty besides. " There was some Years since a Painter (now dead) who had a dexterous Hand at making a *Titian,* a *Guido,* or an *Angelo,*" says the *Weekly Oracle* in 1737, " by roasting them in a Chimney over a proper fire; this Painter, for want of a Name, could scarce get three guineas for an original of his own; but has had almost as many hundred for a copy from a Man of Quality, who imagined himself one of the greater Connoisseurs of the Age." In the *London Magazine* of the same year, an admirer of Sir James Thornhill and native talent denounces " your *Picture jobbings from abroad,*" who decry English artists as hurtful to their trade " of continually importing ship loads of dead *Christ's, Holy Families, Medusa's,* and other dismal, dark subjects neither entertaining nor ornamental, on which they scrawl the terrible cramp name of some *Italian* master, and fix on us poor *Englishmen* the character

---

[35] *Letters from a Young Painter* (Second ed.), 1750, I, 58, 75-76.
[36] XV, 285.

of Universal Dupes." John Northall, in *Travels through Italy*
(1766), warns his countrymen against "a set of people in Rome
distinguished by the appellation of Antiquarians, who offer themselves to strangers of quality, to serve them as guides. . . . Too
many of our young English noblemen have been deceived and
imposed upon by these persons, especially if not competent
judges in paintings and antiquities. These Antiquarians will
make such novices believe a copy to be an original of Raphael,
Angelo, Titian or some other great master." Smollett too
cautions against "a set of sharpers (some of them of our own
country) who deal in pictures and antiques, and very often impose upon the uninformed stranger by selling him trash. . . .
The English are more than any other foreigners exposed to
this imposition. They are supposed to have more money to
throw away. . . . The moment they set foot in Italy they are
seized with the ambition of becoming connoisseurs . . . and the
adventurers of this country do not fail to flatter this weakness for their own advantage." The Hon. William Ponsonby,
in the next century, speaks of a painter at Rome "who paints
Claudes and Salvators for the use of the *forestieri* in a most
extraordinary manner, and has taken in numbers of us." [37]

The very experts were strangely credulous and uncertain. In
1787 two of the chief dealers, Desenfans and Vandergucht, were
involved in a suit over the authenticity of a Poussin, and leading
artists were summoned to testify, — Gainsborough, West, Copley,
Cosway. It must have been a queer exhibition; after listening
to their testimony, one of the counsel quoted Sterne, " Of all the
cants in this canting world the cant of criticism is the most tormenting." Gainsborough was apparently as easily deceived as
any gentleman amateur, as the values set on the pictures in his
collection indicate.[38]

The tricky dealer and ignorant amateur are not unknown in
other centuries. But the eighteenth century differed from the
present, for instance, first in the far greater proportion of amateurs to the whole literate population; second — partly for this
reason — in the far greater importance given to pictures; and

[37] Lady Morgan's *Memoirs,* II, 164. James Edward Smith, in 1786,
tells of a landlord at Pisa offering miserable daubs cheap as choice originals
of Salvator and others. *Sketch of a Tour,* 1793, I, 273.
[38] Whitley, *Thomas Gainsborough,* 1915, pp. 275-281, 321.

finally, perhaps, in spite of such consummate collectors as Jacky Barnard, in the lack of discrimination which raised Guido Reni to a place only just below the highest, and admired Vernet and Zuccarelli almost as greatly as Claude and Gaspar Poussin. The importance of all this for the subject in hand is in the need for understanding the diffusion of art, the state of the public mind toward it, the exaltation of Italian landscape art as an ideal and model for English artists and English landscape, the literary manner in which landscape art was regarded, and the confusion of standards and weakness of taste which classed the feeble imitation with the great original, and partly accounts for the monstrosities which developed in the landscape gardening, and the general monotony of the conceptions of landscape beauty.

III

ENGLISH KNOWLEDGE AND OPINION OF CLAUDE AND SALVATOR

THE very ignorance of the English in matters of art, their tendency to judge of pictures by literature, or by names, as well as to follow artistic fashions sheeplike, helped to develop the taste for Italian landscape art. In the first place, that art represented the land which has always laid a spell over the English spirit; and in the second, these artists had, what the Dutch and Flemish had not — except those who, like the English favourites, Both and Swanevelt, had come under Italian influence — the classic tinge, the ruined fragments of that antique world which to the English was reverend. Moreover, the highly elaborated compositions pleased; a picture by Claude or by Gaspar Poussin had a great deal in it. Connection with literature was easy, too, and made more easy by the ostensible subjects of the pictures, which made of them not mere landscapes, but history pieces. The very names of Claude Lorrain and Salvator Rosa had poetry in them, an exotic quality which undoubtedly made them more delightful. As Hartley Coleridge exclaimed much later, " Salvator Rosa — never was man so blest in a name! " There was a legend, firmly believed by Mrs. Nollekens, who particularly admired Claude, that Claude, Salvator, and the Poussins all lived as neighbours in Rome. The general styles of Claude and Salvator were easily discernible; especially if their pictures hung side by side, one informed upon the other. The veriest dullard in art could soon distinguish a piece in the manner of Salvator, or of Claude; and though imitations and copies might to his untrained eye rank equal with the genuine, even the imitations and copies conveyed, however crudely and extravagantly, those things for which he most admired the genuine: that classic, remote and thrilling scenery, which removed him from the less exciting world he knew, or, later, interpreted the more picturesque parts of that world to him; and the spacious and grandiose designs. For of technical knowledge he was guiltless; even if he was himself an artist, he was often strangely impervious to technical excellencies of his art. Finally, the personalities of the two men were interesting in their different ways; like characters out of some romance, especially the bizarre Salvator.[1] The eighteenth century, even at its close, was still so near that oral tradition of them was current. For instance, Sir George Beaumont, when a young man in Italy, met an old painter, who in his youth had known an old painter who used to see Claude setting forth of a morning, with Gaspar, their sketching materials loaded on mules, to go for a long day of loving labour in the Campagna.[2] And Shaftesbury, at the opening of the century, tells from hearsay a tale of how Salvator dashed together one of his grand landscapes.

I

Claude's quiet life and personality appealed less than did those of " savage Rosa." The one thing which stood out was that he had been apprenticed to a pastry-cook, and had run away to become an artist, " nobly disdaining" the low employment to which he was originally bred, as Northcote said in his *Dream,* " with all its advantages of competence and ease." It was agreed that, though Claude could scarcely write his name when he went to Italy, he was well read in the rules of nature. That he studied " in the open fields," as his friend Sandrart recounted, seems to have impressed the eighteenth century mind, and with reason; in fact, the impact made by both him and Salvator, the freshness and strength of their very different representations, came from just this resort to nature, and sketching directly from it, though their great compositions were built up in the studio.

Of his personal quality, the " schöne Seele " which Goethe divined,[3] which Sandrart and Baldinucci imply — " beneficus

---

[1] So Count Algarotti calls him. *Saggio sopra la Pittura,* Venezia, 1784, p. 162.

[2] Rogers' *Table Talk,* ed. Dyce, 1887, pp. 190–191.

[3] " Da sehen Sie einmal einen vollkommenen Mensch . . . der schön gedacht und empfindet hat, und in dessen Gemüt eine Welt lag, wie man sie nicht irgendwo draussen antrifft. . . . Claude Lorrain kannte die reale Welt bis ins kleinste Detail auswendig, und er gebrauchte sie als Mittel, uns die Welt seiner schönen Seele auszdrücken." *Gespräche,* Gesamtausg., Leipzig, 1909, IV, 101.

CLAUDE LE LORRAIN.

Published March 25th 1777 by John Boydell Engraver in Cheapside London.

Josiah Boydell feci?

CLAUDE LE LORRAIN.

Mezzotint by Josiah Boydell for the *Liber Veritatis*, 1777.
(From the copy owned by Horace Walpole.)

tamen et candidus, gaudiumque nullum quaerebat aliud, quam quod e sua pronasceretur vocatione," " fu amico di ognuno e desideroso di aver pace con qualsifosse " — his friendliness to young artists, his reverent devotion to nature and his art, there seems to have been little appreciation. Northcote comes nearest to it in his imaginary portrait:

It was the early hour of the morn, when the sun had not risen above the horizon. . . . At a little distance a young shepherd played on his flageolet as he walked before his herd. . . . The atmosphere was clear and perfectly calm: and now the rising sun gradually illumined the fine landscape, and began to discover to our view the distant country of immense extent. . . . The only object which appeared to fill this natural, grand, and simple scene, was a rustic who . . . led a poor little ass, which was loaded with all the implements required of a painter for his work. After advancing a few paces, he stood still, and with an air of rapture seemed to contemplate the rising sun; he next fell on his knees, directed his eyes toward Heaven, crossed himself, and then went on with eager looks.

Hints from Baldinucci and other Italian writers as to Claude's merits were adopted generally: his skill in depicting light, and the sun, especially at rising and setting; and also seas, rivers, splendid buildings, and " distances." The charm of his trees was less noticed. His weakness in figures was notorious. Baldinucci gives a saying which was later misundertood: "Era solito dire che vendeva il paese, e le figure ne donava." Claude's practice of having other artists paint the figures probably contributed to the notion, mistaken, so Constable asserted, that he could not draw them. Shaftesbury remarks upon the grotesque disproportion of the figures, by Giordano, in the example of Claude which he owned. The *Critical* ridicules Grainger for praising the figures of Claude, " who is remarkable for his having left his figures tame and unfinished, that they might not conflict with the general effect of his landscape.[4] " A palpably apocryphal tale told by William Gilpin shows how far he was from understanding Claude's humility:

I have heard, that Claude had a higher opinion of his own excellence in figures than in any part of his profession. Sir Peter Lely, we are told, wished for one of Claude's best landscapes; but delicately hinted to him, that he should rather chuse it without figures. Claude felt

[4] February, 1759. III, 157.

himself hurt at Sir Peter's depreciating that excellence which he himself valued. He filled his landscape with more figures, than he commonly introduced; and desired Sir Peter, if he did not like it, to leave it for those that understood the composition of landscape better. His picture is at present, I am told, in the hands of Mr. Agar in London.[5]

Perhaps a distortion of the same story is responsible for what " Recluse " relates in the *General Magazine* in 1791. After a list of Claude's merits, he adds: " His figures are without life. [Yet] he piqued himself more . . . upon his historical than rural representations."

Claude's rank as a landscape painter was taken for granted by Richardson, as, with Gaspar Poussin and Salvator, on the highest plane; with the proviso that mere landscape was a lower form of art than history. Claude was " delicate," says Richardson, as Salvator was " great." " Of all the Landskip-Painters *Claude Lorrain* has the most Beautiful and Pleasing Ideas; the most Rural, and of our own Times." [6] The Richardsons would choose Claude for painting the landscape of Milton.[7] Graham repeats from his continental authorities a note on " the *Delicacy* of his *Colouring*," but also, what a later critic would have ridiculed, " his wonderful *Conduct* in disposing his *Figures*." [8] Sir William Freeman in 1718 refers to " Claud Lorain," (whom his note explains as " one of the finest landscape painters that ever lived, and remarkable for his happy imitation of sunshine ") :

> Ah! were that touch the living pencil mine,
> That artful nature, which Lorain, was thine
> Some glowing canvass where the noon-tide ray
> Shone forth effulgent in the blaze of day.[9]

Gray's brief characterization, in the list of painters compiled when he went on the grand tour with Walpole, says: " Excelled in rural and pleasing scenes, with various accidents of Nature, as gleams of sunshine, the rising moon, etc." Horace Walpole speaks of his " tranquil sunshine," which, in comparison with the sunshine of Rubens, he finds too uniform, but Claude to him is " the Raphael of landscape painting." Arthur Young, a vir-

---

[5] *Catalogue of Drawings*, 1802.
[6] *Account of the Pictures in Italy* (Second ed.), 1754, p. 186.
[7] *Explanatory Notes and Remarks on Milton's Paradise Lost*, 1734, p. 378.
[8] *De Art Graphica*, 1695, p. 335.
[9] *Letters on Several Occasions* (New ed.), 1765, pp. 14–15.

tuoso in landscape both real and painted, is always sure to mention canvases by Claude or attributed to Claude; such attributions he never questions, — indeed, it was not a doubting age in that respect; if he finds a gallery of unlabelled pictures, he does not attempt to assign them to their probable artists. Claude's genius he pronounces " elegant," his general brilliancy and harmony admirable. But though he never fails to write " Fine," or " Very Fine " as comment alongside the title of a Claude, he disqualifies himself as regular connoisseur by his honesty. " I had rather praise what the critics call an execrable piece, than be guided merely by the dictates of a common fame: Many a *Vernet* may please me as well as a *Claude.*" This is too headstrong to suit the *Critical Review;* " this free-thinking sometimes grows into infidelity, and a too temerarious contempt of great masters."

" A temperate hand, and colours dipt in Heav'n," are attributed to Claude by the Della Cruscan, William Parsons;

> He watch'd the progress of the struggling dawn,
> Or mark'd at eve, how light's departing beam
> On the broad wave display'd its golden gleam.[10]

The Reverend William Gilpin, himself something of an artist in landscape, with very pronounced theories about it, is inclined to be captious. He grants Claude colour and light, but constantly finds fault with other things, as one of those critics who show their skill by their dissatisfaction. It was his method in dealing with Nature, too, as we shall see later.

> — Think how *Claude*
> Oft crowded scenes, which Nature's self might own,
> With forms ill-drawn, ill-chosen, ill-arranged,
> Of man and beast, o'erloading with false taste.[11]

We must remember that his unfavourable comments may be based on pictures not genuine or in bad condition. He never questions attributions. Claude's want of " composition " is his chief complaint. " If the most vivid effusions of light, and the most harmonious touches of nature can make a good landscape, this undoubtedly is one. But here is no country described; no

---

[10] *A Poetical Tour,* 1787, pp. 151–152.
[11] *Three Essays. . . . With a Poem on Landscape Beauty* (Third ed.), 1808, p. 119.

beautiful objects; no shapes; no composition." " A pleasing country; but for want of good composition, all its beauteous tints, and hues of nature can scarce bring the eye to it with pleasure. On account of the great deficiency in composition, obvious in so many of the works of Claude, I have thought few masters are less indebted to the engraver than he. The print gives us the *composition* chiefly of the master, which is what we least value in Claude, but it can give us no idea of that lovely colouring, in which alone his works excel all others." [12] We suspect that Gilpin had read De Piles, whose *Principles of Painting*, translated " by a painter," was published in London in 1745. De Piles seems to hold Claude in contempt for " insipid choice in most of his situations," and fear of innovation. What Gilpin meant by " composition " seems to have been arrangement of objects, especially figures. He shows no gleam of recognizing those more important matters of composition in which Claude excels, his treatment of tones and masses, his vast noble design.

The other two prophets of the picturesque, Uvedale Price and Richard Payne Knight, regard Claude with an admiration scarcely this side idolatry. "We find in Nature or in Claude," Price is given to saying.[13] " Every person of observation must have remarked, how *broad* the lights and shadows are on a fine evening in nature, or (what is almost the same thing) in a picture of Claude." The mood conveyed by the picture is to him the main concern. " *Il riposo di Claudio* is his peculiar excellence." The thesis itself of his essays on the picturesque shows his regard for Claude and the other landscape painters of the Italian school: that the landscape gardener should take the paintings as his model in planning and adorning grounds. Richard Payne Knight has much the same opinions, but goes farther, in finding Claude's very blemishes merits. Claude to him is

> Nature's own pupil, fav'rite child of taste!
> Whose pencil, like Lycippus' chisel, trac'd
> Vision's nice errors, and with feign'd neglect,
> Sunk partial form in general effect,

and he adds this note:

[12] *Cambridge*, 1809, p. 65.
[13] *Essays on the Picturesque*, 1810 (First ed. 1794), I, 148; see also 156, 161.

Claude has furnished his landscape more elaborately than any other artist, even among the Dutch, ever did; but by continually working from nature, and artfully throwing in touches of apparent ease and negligence, has effectually avoided every peculiarity of manner, and all that liny formality and smoothness, which usually results from excessive finishing. In particular forms he is often inaccurate, and sometimes studiously indistinct; but his general effects are always perfect.

Claude was greatly admired by artists, who were often, however, as obtuse as the general public in judging his virtues and faults. Sir Joshua felt, like Richardson, that landscape was a less noble form of painting than history; but he granted that perfection in an inferior style may be preferred to mediocrity in the highest walks of art, and so a landscape by Claude be preferred to a history by Luca Giordano. Claude's practice of composing ideal landscapes rather than copying real ones Reynolds (who owned several Claudes) approved as against the Dutch literalness; for " its Truth is founded upon the same principle as that by which the Historical Painters acquire perfect form." The artist who selects his materials and elevates his style " like Claude Lorrain, . . . conducts us to the tranquillity of Arcadian scenes and fairy-land." Hazlitt is the authority (did he hear it from Northcote?) for a remark by Sir Joshua, that there would be another Raphael before there was another Claude.[14]

Gainsborough, too, though by his practice he seems to prefer Ruysdael or Wynants, was evidently an admirer of Italian landscape. Accounts of his early landscape suggest the Italianate Both and Berghem, and he left a book of " fifty-eight Italian Scenes of architecture and landscape," [15] though he never visited Italy. To Lord Hardwicke, who had evidently asked him to paint a particular scene in the neighbourhood of his seat, he wrote: " With respect to Nature in this country, he has never seen any place that affords a Subject equal to the poorest imitations of Gaspar or Claude." The pretentious Barry finds that

[14] To Sir Abraham Hume Sir Joshua left " the choice of his Claudes." A story is told in Whitley's *Life of Gainsborough* of Sir Joshua's selling to the dealer Desenfans, whose pretences he despised, a copy of Claude as a genuine one, and, after receiving the cheque, returning it with a sarcastic note.

[15] Whitley, p. 351.

the treatment of clouds by his fellow-countryman Barret (who painted Mr. Lock's landscape room at Norbury, of which more later) makes him " discover a lack in the aerial part of my favourite Claude's performances "; and he considers that Claude's deficiencies in clouds are due to his uninventive genius, " not the only mark of timidity which may be discovered in that sweet artist." Another compatriot of Barry's, named unhappily Butts, has " a cast of genius much like Claude's "; he has " a tenderness, vivacity and art of nature which Claude only shares with him." But Barry imputes to Butts incontestable superiority in figures, cattle, buildings, and herbage.[16] Farington reports Hoppner as admiring a sea view in the Bridgewater collection; and adds, oddly, " He thinks it more probable we shall see another Cuyp than a Claude." [17] Sir George Beaumont was one of the most extravagant worshippers of both Claude and Gaspar. He owned a number of Claudes, and used to take one of the small ones — the picture now in the National Gallery, called *The Annunciation* — about with him in his coach on journeys. This picture the boy Constable saw when Sir George was visiting the dowager Lady Beaumont, and the sight of it, as he afterwards said, marked an epoch in his life. To the list of artists whose admiration for Claude is expressed, we might add Turner, whose imitation was so marked, and whose queer illiterate will directing that two of his best pictures should be given to the National Gallery, provided " the said pictures or paintings shall be hung kept and placed that is to say Always between the two pictures painted by Claude the Seaport and Mill " shows his sense that Claude was his chief rival; also his failure to perceive the risk to himself.

Constable's devotion to Claude was the most ardent and at the same time intelligent. He spent valuable time in copying

<hr/>

[16] Peter Pindar doubtless had such critics in mind in his *Lyric Odes:*

> Claude's distances are too confused —
> One floating scene, — nothing made out, —
> For which he ought to be abused
> Whose works have been so cried about.
>
> *Lyric Odes,* 1783.

[17] *Diary,* I, 343. — Farington gives also a conversation between himself, Mitford (author of the History of Greece), and Beaumont, in which Mitford thought that Claude's main character was grandeur, and the other two argued that it was beauty.

Claude's pictures. " The very doing it will almost bring me into communion with Claude himself," he said. When he was visiting at Sir George Beaumont's he wrote to his wife: " I do not wonder at your being jealous of Claude. If anything could come between our love it is him." The fragmentary notes which Leslie gives of his lectures at the Academy show much space devoted to his beloved artist. " Brightness was the characteristic excellence of Claude . . . the calm sunshine of the heart." " The most perfect landscape painter the world ever saw . . . serene beauty . . . sweetness and amenity, uniting splendour and repose, warmth and freshness."

The literary views upon Claude are better shown in the descriptions of scenery which copy his pictures, than in comments. These are often feeble in the extreme, and vague, like Miss Seward's constantly recurring " Claude and Salvatorial pencil." She has so faint a glimmering of Claude's real quality that she bursts into ardent eulogy of " the British Claude," Glover, whose name was anathema to Constable. Mrs. Piozzi, like Uvedale Price, associates " Nature and Claude." The author of a *Hymn to the Dryads* (1776) shows typical generalities and superficialities :

> Thus CLAUDE united majesty and ease,
> The grand and beautiful, with matchless art.
> Warm glow his tinted skies, with Heaven's own fire;
> Smooth stands his wide expanse, or waters fall
> Precipitately down, as Nature's hand
> The lake had spread, or pour'd the quick cascade.
> His woods rise graceful, or they seem to wave,
> As calm the sky, or gently blows the gale.

Hazlitt's admiration for Claude is fervent. With Constable, of course, he belongs in date to the nineteenth century; but they both represent so fittingly the climax of the worship which Ruskin's infatuated attack was before long to turn (so far as the literary world went) into coolness, that we cannot spare them. Hazlitt combats the heresy that either Wilson or Turner is on the same level as Claude. Claude is above and apart. "Truth with beauty suggests the feeling of inevitability. No Dutch picture ever suggested this feeling. . . . No one ever felt a longing, a sickness of the heart, to see a Dutch landscape twice; but those of Claude, after an absence of years, have this effect. The name of Claude has alone something in it that softens and harmonizes the mind. It touches a magic chord. Oh! matchless scenes, oh! orient skies, bright with purple and gold; ye opening glades and distant sunny vales, glittering with fleecy flocks, pour all your enchantment into my soul; let it reflect your chastened image, and forget all meaner things!"

2.

For a public which took painting largely as a form of literature, Claude was not so satisfactory as Salvator Rosa. Claude's personality was to them rather nebulous; Salvator's vivid and stirring. It is a question whether the glamour of that romantic personality, the tales of his consorting with banditti and with revolutionaries, did not greatly help to make his reputation as artist with the English. Certainly, what was known or thought to be known of his life delightfully reinforced his pictures. He is the sort of person about whom stories cluster, as he steps out of the pages of Passeri and Baldinucci, a vigorous, impetuous, bold, and arrogant presence: " Era allora graziosa cosa il videre il pittore passeggiare le strade di Roma in posto di gravità, con uno bene addobbato servitore per accompagnatura di sua persona; ed esso con ispado al fianco, con guardia di sodo argento, e con altre si fatte boriose dimostranze, che tutt' altro facevanlo parere da qual' ch'egli eravi stato conusciuto per avantir." [18]   Many are the tales which display both his wit, and his pride; like that of his cutting short the loquacious amateur who presumed to praise a painting in the master's presence: " Think what you would see there if you were Salvator Rosa! "

How many English visitors besides Shaftesbury, in the early years of the century, must have picked up such scraps of studio gossip as are noted in the *Plastics?* — For example, Shaftesbury, has named Nicolas Poussin as almost the only French artist worthy of criticism, and goes on: " Being invited back to France, and caballed against fled to Rome with detestation of his country, which made him and Salvator Rosa (as I have been assured by the old virtuosos and painters there) so good friends:

[18] Baldinucci, xix, 8.

the latter being a malcontent Neapolitan, dissatisfied with his countrymen as his satires show. Both these by the way were honest moral men, the latter over-soured and mortal enemy of the priests, who had nothing to take advantage of against him, besides the supposed familiarity had with his woman servant, on which account he married her." So late as 1770 Dr. Burney was able to find the artist's great-granddaughter, and obtain from her the manuscript volume of music and poetry which he used for his *History of Music;* and Lady Morgan, in the next century, reported members of the family as living, though uncommunicative to her. Salvator's house was long pointed out, along with those of his contemporaries and associates, Claude and the Poussins. Hazlitt lodged in it, but found it, to his disappointment, no help to the imagination.

Though Salvator's relations with "all the Men of Rank and Quality," who "courted and admired" him, were noticed by Graham, Hayley found surprising the revelations of Salvator's letters that he was a sociable being, and remarked that " he was one of the few characters who have possessed a large portion of pleasant vivacity and delightful humour, with a sublime imagination." They preferred to imagine him as a solitary figure, against a background of wilderness. So Northcote in his naïve *Dream* depicts him, in armour and with sabre and lance, rather than pencil and palette: " He trod about in the wild scenery as if he defied the elements. I took him to be one of a banditti, till my conductor informed me it was no other than Salvator Rosa."

His fame as satirist and poet gave the more reason for viewing his paintings as literature. How much his satires in verse were read, we may question. Two Italian editions were published in England, in 1787 and 1791. They seem not to have been translated, which suggests that they were not very popular, in spite of the assertion made by a writer in the *European* for 1792, that they are in everyone's hands.[19] Hayley quotes from them in his note on Salvator as if they were not readily

[19] XXII, 104 (*Drossiana*). An instance of Salvator's repute as satirist is found in a satirical poem: *The Group* . . . painted in an Elegy on the Saddest Subjects, the Living, Dead, and Damned; such as Hogarth . . . Inscribed to John Wilkes . . . and Charles Churchill. By Salvator Rosa . . . Poema est Pictura loquens. *Hor.* London, 1763.

accessible. He felt, no doubt, that Salvator's endowment by the sister muses (it is hard not to use Hayley's own idiom) established him more surely as a kindred spirit, even though unrefined by Taste. Hayley's view is representative not merely of himself, but of his numerous tribe:

> Untrodden paths of art SALVATOR tried,
> And daring fancy was his favourite guide.
> O'er his wild rocks, at her command, he throws
> A savage grandeur, a sublime repose. . . .
> His bold ideas, unrefin'd by taste,
> Express'd with vigour, tho' conceiv'd in haste,
> Before slow judgment their defects can find,
> With awful pleasure fill the passive mind.
> Nor could one art, with various beauty fraught,
> Engross the labour of his active thought;
> His pencil pausing, with satiric fire
> He struck the chords of the congenial lyre.

The picture-loving botanist, James Edward Smith, does not admire the satires. He quotes the inscription on Salvator's tomb and on the words "pictoribus sui temporis nulli secundum, poetarum omnium temporum principibus parem" comments: " Surely the praise ought rather to have been reversed, and still his poetry would have been over-rated."

Poetic enthusiasm is generally imputed to him. So Mason, in *The English Garden:*

> SALVATOR! if where, far as eye can pierce,
> Rock pil'd on rock, thy Alpine heights retire,
> [Art] flung her random foliage, and disturb'd
> The deep repose of the majestic scene.
> This deed were impious. Ah, forgive the thought,
> Thou more than Painter, more than Poet! HE,
> Alone thy equal, who was " Fancy's child."

The association of his name with Shakespeare's is not infrequent, though not always so fervid. Price remarks, as a commonplace, that they are like in being self-taught. Walpole compares one of his monsters to Caliban. Shaftesbury thought that in treatment of the comic grotesque Salvator surpassed Shakespeare; " Remember . . . our Shakespeare's Jack Falstaff; a character . . . But overdone and spoilt both by poet and players. The painter (a Salvator Rosa and tolerable good satirist in poetry) would not hyperbole so; but moderate the hyperbole and strike the imagination far better."

Residence in Naples naturally heightened Shaftesbury's admiration of Salvator, whose works seem to have been more abundant in his native city at that time than they were later on. When Shaftesbury commends landscapes to his friend Sir John Cropley, as the most desirable pieces for his collection, he thinks especially of Salvator:

As I remember, you have, besides the copies of Poussin, a copy of Salvator Rosa also by Mr. Closterman, which you told me you could not bring to Reigate, because of its bigness. Now I could at this instance for little more than double what you paid for such poor prentice copying, procure an original piece or two of the same Salvator Rosa (a townsman of this very place) equal and even beyond those very fine originals which Mr. Closterman by help of his journeymen, took copies of, and sold to you.

This is valuable testimony to the English admiration of Salvator in the first decade of the century.

Salvator's choice of subjects was generally admired. " He understood his subject as a painter, and as a man," says one critic. " His enthusiasm . . . was the child of knowledge; his ideas were rude and majestic, because he drew them from a romantic source. He was faithful to what he saw; — he was an enthusiast to what he felt; . . . could account for, as a poet, what as a painter he could describe." [20]   When in his *Lectures* on the English poets, Percival Stockdale wishes to praise Milton's picture of Sin and Death, he says that by comparison with it " the expression of Salvator Rosa, and of Michael Angelo, is deadened; and their colouring is eclipsed." Such an association of names would not have surprised Sir Joshua Reynolds.

To the verb *dash,* which, thanks to Thomson, almost inevitably accompanies the name of " savage Rosa," Shaftesbury gives amusing warrant in a circumstantial story of the painting of one of those large perspectives which he owned. Having sketched out on a great canvas trees and rocks of stupendous proportions, the artist began to put in the figures:

And being pushed on still by that vanity to make these also in great perfection . . . he designed and painted them on a forward ground,

[20] *General Magazine,* 1791, pp. 543-545.

in full size, or rather larger than naturally the perspective would allow at so near a distance. He had no sooner done this than he perceived what injury he had done at the same time to his first design, and that after doing all in his power to magnify his rock, and raise the majesty and grandeur of that form . . . he had pulled it back again . . . rendered it diminutive, which in that peculiar form and shape of horrour and dismay would prove a sort of burlesque. . . like a little elephant. . . . But what does Salvator upon this. In an instant, ere the paint was well laid, he strikes out with a dash or two of his pencil, destroys his giants niched in his hollow cave. . . . Upon yet nearer ground places just such another figure or two at least three sizes less, by which his hyperbole once again came right, the grandeur of parts in perspective restored, and his rock majestic, terribly impending, vast, enormous; as it should be, and as he first designed it.

Such fine carelessness, if it did not raise his reputation with artists, made part of his charm for the public; for, as Mr. Fitz-william Darcy once pointed out, the mere doing things quickly is felt to be meritorious. An account of Salvator in the *Weekly Miscellany* makes much of this " freedom of pencil " and fire. " His genius was most irregular. Without ever consulting nature he did all from practice. . . . He was the creator of his own style of painting, which is like no other." [21]

One of his best qualifications as hero, even better than his being a poet, or dashing, was his having been, as Northcote puts it, " one of a banditti." " A roving disposition," says the Rev-erend Mr. Gilpin, " seems to have added a wildness to all his thoughts. We are told, he spent the early part of his life in a troop of banditti; and that the rocky and desolate scenes, in which he was accustomed to take refuge, furnished him with those romantic ideas in landskip, of which he is so exceedingly fond. . . . His *Robbers* . . . are supposed also to have been taken from the life." To how many law-abiding and amiable gentlemen and ladies, like the Reverend Mr. Gilpin, who thus speaks, or Anna Seward, William Mason or Mrs. Montagu, must not the consideration that these wild scenes and personages which they beheld with pleasure, were taken from the life, have imparted an extra thrill? And for the liberty-intoxicated spirits at the close of the century, his supposed association with the rebellion of Masaniello was an even greater merit. We sus-

[21] IV, 755–761.   (c. 1760) — A list is given of paintings by him still to be seen in Italy, and of engravings after him.

pect that much of Hazlitt's affection for Salvator is due to this; he regrets that he cannot always admire the pictures, when he so loves the man. To Lady Morgan, judging by her preface, it is a dominant consideration in the writing of her romantic biography. Was it that biography, or Salvator's own satires which furnished Ruskin with his tragic conception of Salvator as a sort of fallen angel, a dark and tortured spirit holding in himself " the last traces of spiritual life in the art of Europe . . . the last man to whom the thought of a spiritual existence presented itself as a conceivable reality," his life passed " in horror, disdain and despair "?

Graham's account of Salvator's merits as painter, prepared before " sublimity " was in vogue, yet stresses that quality in his art which was later so labelled. " He was fam'd for his *copious* and *florid Invention,* for his *solid Judgment* in the *Ordering* of his *Pieces,* for the *gentile* and *uncommon Management* of his *Figures,* and his general *Knowledge* in all the parts of Painting: But that which gave a more particular *Stamp* to his Compositions, was his *inimitable Liberty* of *Pencil,* and the *noble Spirit* with which he animated all his *Works.*" " Salvator Rosa has generally chosen to represent a sort of wild and Savage Nature," say the Richardsons; " his Style is Great and Noble." The Expression in his *Witch of Endor* of " Horror and Witchery is in Perfection." Gray summarizes: " Excelled in savage uncouth places, very great and noble style; stories that have something of horror and cruelty." Though he was esteemed popularly as history-painter, we notice that Buckridge, in 1754, pronounces him greater in landscape.[22] Walpole says, " His thoughts, his expression, his landscapes, his knowledge of the force of shade, and his masterly arrangement of horror and distress, have placed him in the first class of painters." Sir Joshua Reynolds, while denying him this rank, yet honours him highly: " He gives us a peculiar cast of Nature, which . . . though it has nothing of that elevation and dignity which belongs to the grand style, yet has that sort of dignity which belongs to savage and uncultivated nature; but what is most to be admired in him, is the perfect correspondence which he observed between the subjects which he chose, and

[22] *Lives of the Most Eminent Modern Painters,* 1754, p. 15.

his manner of treating them. Everything is of a piece: his Rocks, Trees, Sky, even to his handling, have the same rude and wild character which animated his figures." *Jacob's Dream,* one of Salvator's finest landscapes, Reynolds names as one of the examples of " the poetry, as it may be called, of the art; and they are few indeed." The story as set forth on canvas has " the same power of inspiring sentiments of grandeur and sublimity " as in the language of Scripture.

Sir Robert Strange (who had some pictures by Salvator in the collection which he brought from Italy for sale in 1769) speaks of his spirited figures, and the " truth and freedom " of the whole, as well as the intelligence.

> Why do Salvator's daring strokes delight,
> While Mieris' care and labour Tire the sight?

Thus an anonymous versifier expresses the common distinction between Italian and Dutch art. He explains in a note, " Salvator Rosa; a famous Italian painter, remarkable for the fire and spirit in all his compositions." [23] Rosa was primarily " the painter of force, — force Romantically charming," [24] or such as was able " to pierce, to rouse, to terrify the soul." [25]

> How drear the scenes that Rosa chose!
> Naught but the dark and dreary pine,
> Or rocks immense of height sublime,
> Co-aeval they with hoary Time,
> The marks of Pow'r Divine.[26]

The effect of art on the average cultivated person of the time is well seen in Arthur Young. To him Salvator appears more generally pleasing than Claude. " A rock, with the broken branches of trees hanging from its clifts; (I apprehend by *Salvator*) the expression very noble, and romantic wildness of the scene most excellently caught." " The famous picture of *Belisarius* . . . has more expression in it, than any painting I think I ever saw." " *Prodigal son* . . . Prodigious expression . . . amazingly fine." " A landscape with rocks, wild as the

---

[23] *Polite Companion,* 1751, p. 100.
[24] Thomas Dermody, *The Harp of Erin,* 1807, II, 237.
[25] *Poetical Tour, op. cit.,* p. 151.
[26] George Monck Berkeley, *Poems,* pp. 84–85.

winds, but fine." " Rocks and trees jumbled together in the wildness of that romantic genius, which seemed formed by nature to catch her sublimest hints; with a little group of figures dropped from a whirlwind." The tourist Sulivan describes Salvator as having an " enlarged and comprehensive genius; a lively, fertile and poetic imagination . . . great freedom of pencil, and infinite fire in his compositions." Price and Knight, more skillful admirers, are even more enthusiastic, without a jot of dispraise. Price especially admires the " noble and animated wildness of Salvator's stems and branches." Though " the savage grandeur of that sublime, though eccentric genius " is less lavishly praised by him than the beauty of Claude, his "picturesque effects " serve constantly as examples, to illustrate Price's theory. " In no other master are seen such abrupt and rugged forms, such sudden deviations both in his figures and his landscapes; and the roughness and broken touches of his pencilling, admirably accord with the objects they characterize." Knight especially praises his trees. " Scenery . . . to be really sublime, should be, not only wild and broken, but rich and fertile; such as that of Salvator Rosa, whose ruined stems of gigantic trees proclaim at once the vigour of the vegetation . . . and of the tempests that have shivered and broken them." He exalts Salvator's sublimity in the *Witch of Endor* above Michelangelo's Sistine frescoes. " Salvator indeed scarcely ever attempts grandeur of form, in the outlines of his figures; but he seldom misses . . . grandeur of effect in the general composition of his pictures. In the wildest flights of his wild imagination, he always exhibits just and natural action and expression."

Gilpin apparently admires Salvator more than he does Claude; Salvator is easier to admire for one with literary point of view, and such Gilpin's was, more than the artist's, in spite of his own artistic performances. Salvator's figures, and his blasted trees — the most obvious elements — are especially commended; and the brown or " sober " tint, to which Gilpin often refers lovingly. " For the use and beauty of the *withered top* and *curtailed trunk,* we need only appeal to the works of Salvator Rosa." " The chesnut in maturity . . . is a noble tree, . . . This is the tree which graces the landscapes of Salvator

Rosa. . . . That it is naturally brittle . . . might be one reason for Salvator's attachment to it." "The chesnut of Calabria is consecrated by adorning the foregrounds of Salvator Rosa." He criticizes unfavourably however, the expression and the realism of some of the histories, and becomes less enthusiastic over Salvator as time wears on. He has often judged falsely at first sight, he says, which implies a fault in the picture, since it should impress favourably at once, if good. An amusing bit of evidence of his waning appreciation appears in the changes made by him in a paragraph of his *Essay on Prints*. In 1768 Salvator is "very great" in composition, draws his "nobly expressive" figures in "exquisite taste," groups them "beautifully," and has a manner "wonderfully pleasing." The later edition softens these respectively to: "often happy," "expressive," "good taste," "well," and "pleasing."

Perhaps this retrenching is due to Gilpin's discovery that artists did not altogether approve of Salvator. Northcote, for instance, follows the imaginary portrait quoted above with: "He raised no sensations in my mind which created any interest." Fuseli, who admired his landscapes, finds that in histories "his line is vulgar; his magic visions . . . are, to the probable combinations of nature, what the paroxysms of a fever are to the flights of vigorous fancy." (This from the painter of *The Nightmare!*) His banditti are "a medley made up of starveling models, shreds and bits of armour from his lumber room, brushed into notice by a daring pencil." Barry, who admires him, speaks of his being "condemned, as frantic, by some cold spiritless artists" who have not viewed the alpine scenery which he depicts. Strutt, in 1785, notes his landscapes as "very wonderful performances!" "He had savages for his masters in painting, and he painted savage subjects," says Constable; "Salvator Rosa is a great favourite with novel writers, particularly the ladies . . . but there is a meanness in all his compositions of history which must ever exclude him from its first ranks." But he too, grants him power in landscape, though not on a level with Claude or Gaspar.

The "ladies" to whom Constable referred probably meant Lady Morgan, though he may have had Mrs. Radcliffe in mind as well. Lady Morgan gives admirably the literary view

of Salvator. " The least of his landscapes were pregnant with
moral interest, and calculated to awaken human sympathies.
His deep and gloomy forests . . . is [*sic*] only given as the
shelter of the formidable bandit. . . . The long line of stony
pathway cut through masses of impending rock, is but the de-
file in which the gallant cavalier . . . is overtaken by the
pitiless outlaw — or, by the rush of storms. . . . The way-
worn traveller, the benighted pilgrim, the shipwrecked mari-
ner . . . become images that engage the heart as well as the
eye, and give to the inanimate character of landscape a moral
action and an historical interest." Feeble as is Lady Morgan in
critical acumen, she represents the public of her time, and the
time before hers. Such feelings as hers made Salvator popular.

Among the admirers of Salvator, and enjoyers of " the terrible
sublime," Gray and Walpole are significant examples. The
few pictures on which Gray's notes are extant include a disproportionate number of what Gray took for Salvators.
" Aeneas and the Sybil, sacrificing to Pluto by torch light in
the wood, the assistants in a fright. . . . Sigismunda, with the
heart of Guiscardo before her. . . . Hannibal passing the Alps;
the mountains rolling down rocks upon his army; elephants
tumbling down the precipices." These paintings of " Horrour
. . . and thrilling. Fears " are reflected in the one scenic picture in *The Bard*:

> On a rock, whose haughty brow
> Frowns o'er old Conway's foaming flood,
> Rob'd in the sable garb of woe,
> With haggard eyes, the Poet stood. . . .

Walpole's suggestion that only Salvator could paint " up to
the horror " of it is not surprising. Walpole thinks of Salvator, too, as the only one to make endurable the picture of
Theodore and Honoria ordered by his nephew; or fitly to illustrate *Macbeth* for Alderman Boydell's Gallery. He dims his
tribute, to be sure, by using Salvator's name for a compliment
to Bentley, and to Lady Di Beauclerk for her drawings, " in
sut water," for *The Mysterious Mother,* which have " all Salvator's boldness in landscape."

Smollett suggests Salvator as the artist who might have represented poor Lismahago's escape from the imagined fire; and

mentally repaints an unsatisfactory Carlo Maratti: " I imagine
Salvator Rosa would . . . amidst the darkness of a tempest
. . . have illuminated the blasphemer with the flash of lightning by which he was destroyed; this would have thrown a dismal gleam of light upon his countenance, distorted by the
horror of his situation, as well as by the effects of the fire; and
rendered the whole scene dreadfully picturesque." Mrs. Piozzi
is of course thrilled by Salvator: " A sight of the Santa Croce
Palace, with its disgusting Job, and the man in armour so
visibly horror-stricken, puts all painters but Salvator Rosa for
a while out of one's head." The effect lasts over well into the
nineteenth century. Shelley thought that the only things at
Rome which sustained comparison with antiquity were Raphael,
Guido and Salvator Rosa.[27] Hazlitt describes one picture thus:
" Rough, grotesque, wild — Pan has struck it with his hoof —
the trees, the rocks, the foreground, are of a piece, and the
figures are subservient to the landscape. The same dull sky
lowers upon the scene, and the bleak air chills the crisp surface
of the water." [28]

3

Constantly the names of Claude and Salvator are linked;
·occasionally the praise of one is at the cost of the other, as
when Gilpin takes Claude to task for failing to see the sublime.
" Claude and Salvator received, or might have received, their
ideas from the same archetypes. . . . While one . . . admired
the tamer beauties of Nature, the other caught fire and rose
to the sublime." Oftener they are presented in contrast, especially after the appearance of Burke's *Essay,* one representing
the beautiful and rural, the other the sublime and wild. So
Percival Stockdale finds in Spenser " pictures drawn by the
hand of a master endowed with contrasted talents; the mild
and beaming skies of Claude Lorrain; and the rude and tangled
precipices of Salvator Rosa." But as early as 1737 Lord Chester-

[27] *Letters,* ed. Ingpen, II, 682.
[28] One more reference to Salvator may be given, from the *Hymn to the
Dryads, op. cit.,* as an example of ineptitude:
" Sedate SALVATOR, by his genius led
To contemplate the grand and the sublime,
View'd Nature in disorder, not in smiles.
Calmly he sat, and view'd her when in storms " . . .

field, writing to Lyttelton, makes use of the contrast with a political application, as if it was familiar: " We have a prospect of
the Claud Lorraine kind before us, while Sir Robert [Walpole]'s
has all the horrors of Salvator Rosa. If the Prince would play
the Rising Sun, he would gild it finely." [29]

Uvedale Price, one of the chief spokesmen of the Picturesque
School, presents them thus. He loves the beauty of Claude,
but admires Salvator as an example *par excellence* of the picturesque. In the *Dialogue* written as a reply to his friend
Knight, who identified the beautiful and the picturesque, he
uses Claude and Salvator to prove his point. Two connoisseurs,
Mr. Hamilton, standing for himself, and Mr. Howard, for
Knight, argue the question in the presence of their friend Mr.
Seymour, appropriately named, for his eyes are opened to see
more of the picturesque. They begin with real scenery; a gypsies'
hut, with Salvatorial adjuncts of gloom and ruined oak, at which
the two connoisseurs wax ecstatic, and the unpicturesque Mr.
Seymour is disgusted; then " an extensive view over a rich
country," with Claudian distances, river, bridge, which Mr.
Seymour enjoys in itself, and his friends enjoy because it is like
Claude. They enter a gallery, and an excellent display of the
average eighteenth century Englishman in a gallery follows. Mr.
Seymour, observing with pleasure that the names of the painters
are written on the frames, begins the round, " not stopping
long at any of them till he came to one of Claude Lorraine."

He at once recognizes the likeness to the fine prospect lately
observed. " It is seen in the same manner, between trees; and
the river, the bridge, the distant buildings and hills are nearly
in a similar situation. I have great pleasure in seeing the same
soft lights, the same general glow which we admired in the real
landscape represented with such skill, that, now the true
splendour of, the sun is no longer before us, the picture seems
nature itself." And he adds a comment which, we suspect, be-
trays one strong reason for the English admiration of Claude:
" What a picture would this be to have in one's sitting-room!
to have always before one such an image of fine weather, such
a happy mixture of warmth and freshness! "

Soon he is placed before a Salvator, and admires it with due

[29] Hon. Mrs. Wyndham, *Chronicles of the Eighteenth Century*, 1924, I, 60.

sense of contrast. " There is a sublimity in this scene of rocks and mountains, savage and desolate as they are, that is very striking; and the whole, as you say, is a perfect contrast to the Claude; and it is really curious to look from one to the other. In that every thing seemed formed to delight the eye, and the mind of man — in this, to alarm and terrify the imagination; in the Claude, the inhabitants inspire us with the ideas of peace, security, and happiness — in this of Salvator (for now I recollect and feel the full force of those lines I only admired before) —

> Appears in burnish'd arms some savage band. . . .[30]

In that sweet scene, the recesses amidst fresh woods and streams, seem bowers made for repose and love; in this, they are caves of death, the haunts of wild beasts, —

> Or savage men, more dreadful far than they.

What a stormy, portentous appearance in those clouds, that roll over the dark mountains, and threaten, further on, still greater desolation! while that mild evening sky, and soft tinge upon the distant hills, seem to promise still more charming scenes beyond them! " " Why, Seymour," observes Mr. Howard, " you talk with more enthusiasm than either Hamilton or myself! " And Seymour utters the great explanation of the popularity of Claude and Salvator. " Where there is so much poetry in pictures, it is not necessary to have a painter's eye to enjoy them; although I am well persuaded that a knowledge of the art would greatly enhance the pleasure." [31]

[30] From Knight's poem, *The Landscape*.

[31] An explanation given by Walter Friedlaender of the popularity of Claude among the English applies also to Salvator; the irrational and unlimited in picture; infinite space, in contrast to the defined boundaries of Nicholas Poussin, for example. *Claude Lorrain*, Berlin, 1921, p. 216.

IV

" ITALIAN LIGHT ON ENGLISH WALLS "

— I admire
None more admires — the painter's magic skill,
Who shows me that which I shall never see,
Conveys a distant country into mine,
And throws Italian light on English walls.

The Task, Bk. I, ll. 421–425.

I

SINCE, rich as English galleries were, or came to be, in the work of Claude, Salvator Rosa, and Gaspar Poussin, the actual number of canvases was inevitably limited, and they could be visited by but a limited number of persons, how did a conception of landscape largely derived from them spread so very widely?

English visitors to Italy, increasingly numerous as time went on, had much influence in extending the fashion, through what they themselves saw, through the paintings and prints they brought back, and through the books they published. A vast increase of travel on the continent took place between 1698, when Richard Lassels was almost apologetic in regard to travel, and 1740, when Lady Hertford found summer in Italy dreadful, because of the hordes of English visitors. With the increase of travel developed the taste for scenery and the taste for pictures, and for picture galleries. When John Evelyn, a virtuoso if ever there was one, visited Rome, his comments on pictures were surprisingly slight, and of landscape, then greatly in favour in Rome — all four of the great painters of Italian landscape were at the height of their reputation at the time of his visit — he had nothing to say except one reference to " an ample landscape " by Paul Bril. In 1689 he commends to Pepys prints of " Ruines, Landskips, if from real subjects, not fancies, which are innumer-able & not necessary." For Lassels, the picture gallery is a minor interest. Jewels, water-works, mechanical toys, and, above all, antiquities, especially buildings, were more important to him, and to the average traveller of his day. Addison was most interested in antiquities. William Bromley, in Italy at the same time, was interested in contemporary art, but mentioned landscapes only briefly, nor did he know how to talk about pictures, or even to use adjectives, — later how easy!

Shaftesbury is the first in whom I have discovered anything like a modern taste in painting. To him, in his last years at Naples, painting was a leading interest; and in his earlier visit to Italy, from 1686 to 1689, he clearly, as his son says, " acquired a great knowledge of the polite arts." His most famous piece of writing on the subject has nothing to do with this discussion; but it is worth recalling that his *Notion of the Historical Draught of the Judgment of Hercules* holds a place of some importance in the history of aesthetics. In 1709 he wrote a letter to " a Young Man at the University," giving advice as to visiting galleries intelligently, with a view to systematic training of taste, especially for one who aspired to be himself a painter. " If you fix your Eye on that which most strikes and pleases you at the first Sight; you will most certainly never come to have *a good Eye* at all. . . . A FLEMISH, or a FRENCH *Manner* will more prevail with you, than the true ITALIAN. . . . If you find no Grace or Charm at the first Looking; look on, and continue to observe all, that you possibly can: And when you have got one *Glimpse;* improve it; copy it; cultivate the *Idea;* and labour, till you have work'd your self into a *right* TASTE."

Though Shaftesbury's instructions were evidently followed by few, a conscientious treatment of galleries began to develop. By 1722 Jonathan Richardson, who had not himself visited Italy (" O Rome! thou happy repository of so many stupendous works of art, which my longing eyes have never seen, nor shall see . . . ") compiled from his son's notes, *An Account of the Statues, Bas-Reliefs, Drawings, and Pictures in Italy, France, &c.* and published it in 1722, explaining in his preface that it is the first account of the works of art in Italy, though there were some catalogues. Before beginning to recount the landscape pictures in the Roman palaces, he thought a brief explanation needful; which implies the still insecure position of landscape:

Landskips are in Imitation of Rural Nature, of which therefore there may be as many Kinds, as there are Appearances, of This sort of

Nature; and the Scenes may be laid in Any Country, or Age, With
Figures, or Without; but if there are Any, as 'tis necessary there should
be, Generally speaking, they must be Suitable, and only Subservient
to the Landskip, to Enrich, or Animate it; Otherwise the Picture loses
its Denomination, it becomes a History, a Battel-piece, &c. or at least
'tis of an Equivocal kind. This sort of painting is like Pastoral in
Poetry; and of all the Landskip-Painters *Claude Lorrain* has the most
Beautiful and Pleasing Ideas; the most Rural, and of our own Times.
Titian has a Style more noble. So has *Nicolas Poussin,* and the Land-
skips of the Latter are usually Antique, as is seen by the Buildings, and
Figures. *Gaspar's* Figures are Such, otherwise he has a Mixture of
Nicolas and *Claude. Salvator Rosa* has generally chosen to represent
a sort of wild, and savage Nature; his Style is Great, and Noble;
Rubens is pleasant, and loves to enrich his Landskip with certain
Accidents of Nature, as Winds, a Rain-Bow, Lightning, &c. All these
Masters are Excellent in their Several kinds, but I think *Poussin* has
sometimes Err'd in the Figures he has put into his Landskips.

About the same time that this work, which long remained a
standard guide-book, was in preparation, Edward Wright was
making the notes which he published in 1730 in two large
quartos. He liked " Landskapes," and notes several " fine and
large " Claudes, though the most he has to say is, " The setting
sun, a most lively repose," and frescoes by Gaspar in the Colonna
Palace and San Martino. Salvator Rosa he refers to as one of
the " great Masters " in the Altieri Palace. His work, an elaborate affair with many plates, was republished in 1764.

Lady Hertford, in 1740, is interested in the " extremely fine
and beautiful landscapes, by Claude Lorrain, Nicolo Poussin,
Salvator Rosa, and others," in the Colonna Palace; and picks
up at the Pamphilio Palace the information that Gaspar Poussin,
of whose work there were many examples in that collection,
" was a menial servant in the family, and worked for eighteen
pence a day." She visits the tomb of Salvator, " very deservedly esteemed . . . for landscapes." The collections at
Rome, she reports, " are quite spoiled, or are spoiling as fast as
possible," and she is glad to find at Bologna collections so fine
and so widely distributed. Horace Walpole, in Rome the same
year, tells of the dispersal of many of the finest collections, and
the enriching of the English collections in consequence. The
young painter, John Russell, also in Rome at this time, mentions
visiting the galleries in the train of young gentlemen of fortune,

and a little later, says there are sixteen British artists in Rome, studying painting or sculpture.

The names of Claude and Salvator appear more frequently in later accounts. Smollett, in 1765, enjoys the Claude and the Salvator landscapes at the Colonna Palace. John Northall notes those in the Altieri, Barberini, Chigi, Colonna, Pamphilio and Palavicini Palaces, and others elsewhere. Lady Miller of Bath-Easton is profuse of adjectives in her *Letters from Italy* (which the magazines quote largely). She admires Salvator, it seems, more than she does Claude, whose trees are too trim, and of too fine a green; she prefers the contrast of " withered branches and fantastic old rocks and trunks of trees." But she grants that his pictures are highly finished, and the glowing warmth of his skies is inimitable. She thinks it strange that the Royal Gallery in Turin has no Salvator or Correggio; and finds among the pictures most to her taste, Salvator's St. Anthony " at handy cuffs with the Devil," at the Pitti Palace; the martyrdom of St. Stephen, and that of the Innocents, at Bologna; a magician making a pact with infernal spirits; and the Prometheus: " The vulture dragging out and feeding on his bowels. All the horrors attendant on such a scene are represented to the life." Not that she does not admire Salvator's landscapes at the Altieri and the Chigi Palaces, along with the fine Claudes. James Edward Smith, the botanist, on his tour of 1786 and 1787, greatly admires the landscape painters, especially Claude: " The more we saw of Italian landscape, the more reason we found to admire this excellent painter. The glowing refulgence of his evenings, and the clear brightness of his midday skies, which one is sometimes apt to think exaggerations and improvements on nature, are the very tints of nature herself in this delightful climate, and all his variations of effect are strictly and exactly her own." Mariana Starke, who frankly designed as a guide-book her *Letters from Italy*, between 1792 and 1798, goes through the galleries with care. Exclamation points with her are like stars in Baedeker: " Job on the Dunghill, by Salvator Rosa!! . . . A battle, by Salvator Rosa!!! " " A beautiful landscape by Claude Lorain!!!! On the other side, an almost equally beautiful one, by Poussin!! above the cabinet a landscape, by Poussin!!! . . . Two capital landscapes by Salvator Rosa!!! "

"Cain and Abel, by Salvator Rosa! . . . a Claude!!! a Claude!!! . . . a Claude!!!! . . . Two landscapes by Claude! "

2

Some of the great collections of pictures in England had their beginning in the eighteenth century, a few in the late seventeenth. The three great collections of the early seventeenth, those of Charles I, the Duke of Buckingham, and the Earl of Arundel, were dispersed, and many of the pictures went back to the Continent. Charles II, though his love for art was not profound, loyally bought back all of his father's pictures that could be found, and in spite of the fire at Whitehall in 1697, the royal collection was at the end of the century again the finest in England. The growing interest in pictures is reflected in Evelyn's *Diary*. In 1649 he spends a day visiting various " virtuoso's," including a merchant and an artist. Among the gentlemen whom he names as amateurs between 1658 and 1696 are the Earl of Northumberland, the Duke of Norfolk, Lord Newport, Lord Sunderland, Lord Melford, Lord Mulgrave, and Lord Pembroke. He rarely mentions landscapes, and never any of importance.[1] Sir Peter Lely (who owned a Claude) had the most distinguished private collection of that time; his methods of acquiring it, especially the drawings, were under suspicion. Daniel Defoe attributes to King William the increased interest in painting. He " brought into England the Love for Paintings as well as for Gardens," says Defoe in his *Tour* of Great Britain, but with doubtful accuracy; and continues: " The love for fine Paintings so universally spread itself among the Nobility and Persons of Figure all over the Kingdom, that it is incredible what Collections have been made by *English* Gentlemen since that Time; and how all *Europe* has been rumag'd, as we may say, for pictures to bring over hither, where, for Twenty Years they brought immense Profit to such as collected them for Sale. But the Rates are abated since that, and we begin to be glutted with the Copies and Frauds of the *Dutch* and *Flemish* Painters, who have imposed greatly upon us." Defoe gives the Earl of

[1] July 20, 1654, " Hunting landskips by Pierce," at Wilton; July 9, 1661, " some incomparable *paisages* done in distemper," at Sir Fr. Prujean's; January 24, 1685, a figure piece by Poussin.

Exeter as the most distinguished private owner. Richardson names the Duke of Devonshire, Lord Somers, the Earl of Pembroke and Dr. Mead as the chief private collectors of his time.

In the frenzy for improving and building which began early in the century to sweep through Britain, each new or newly adorned great house had a picture gallery showing great names — " Originals and Copies much the same " — just as it had grounds improved by the latest fashionable gardener, Switzer, Bridgeman, Kent, Brown, or Repton. There was Holkham, seat of the Earl of Leicester; Wilton, the Earl of Pembroke's; Burleigh House, the Earl of Exeter's; Woburn Abbey, the Duke of Bedford's; Belvoir Castle, the Duke of Rutland's; Luton House, the Marquis of Bute's; Longford Castle, Earl Radnor's; Panshanger, Earl Cowper's; Althorp, Earl Spencer's; Knole, the Duke of Dorset's; Longleat, the Marquis of Bath's; and above all, for pictures, Houghton, Sir Robert Walpole's. And there were Stow, Radnor Castle, Petworth, Lowther Castle, Blaise Castle, Norbury Park, Temple Newsham, Stourhead, Fonthill Abbey, Leigh Court, Belvedere, Ditchley, Hagley, Kedleston, and many another. Mrs. Powys, indefatigable visitor of great houses and picture galleries, observes in 1760 of Lord Melcombe's seat that it had few pictures, " a thing surprising, at a time when it seems to be the peculiar taste of the gentlemen of this age to make collections, whether judges of paintings or ambitious to be thought so." [2]   There were collections in London: John Barnard's — the Jacky Barnard whose mark today enhances the value of a print or drawing; Paul Methuen's, for a time in London; the Devonshire collection; Caleb Whitefoord's; Charles Jenness' of Holborn; and many others. Generally the artists were collectors; Sir Joshua Reynolds one of the most discriminating. Prince Frederick and his son George III were both patrons (less discriminating) of painting. The dealer Desenfans got his start by selling a Claude to the King for a thousand guineas. " Since the arts have found protection and encouragement from the throne," says the *Fugitive Miscellany* (1775), " the taste for virtù has become universal; persons of all ranks and degrees set up for connoisseurs, and even the lowest people tell familiarly of Hannibal Scratchi, Paul Varnish, and Raphael Angelo."

[2] *Passages from the Diary of Mrs. Philip Powys*, ed. Climenson, 1899, p. 63.

In nearly all the great collections, and in many a small one, the pictures by Claude Lorrain, Salvator Rosa, and Gaspar Poussin were conspicuous. Waagen notes in the introduction to his *Treasures of Art in Great Britain* that owing to the English predilection for Claude and Gaspar, their pictures were frequently the brightest gems of the private galleries. The collection of Jacky Barnard is typical: a landscape by Claude, one by Salvator and three by Gaspar.[3] Dr. Mead owned two Claudes — they fetched the highest prices in his sale, in 1754; two Salvators — *Ravens Bringing Food to Elijah,* and a *Landscape with High Rocks*; three Gaspar Poussins; and landscapes by Elsheimer, Paul Bril, and Wootton. In Sir Luke Schaub's collection were four Salvators, three Claudes, five Gaspars, three Brils, and an Elsheimer. The Duchess of Portland paid £102 for one of the Claudes, — one of the highest prices paid at the sale, at which, incidentally, she spent altogether over £2000. The prints from British collections published by Arthur Pond in 1744 shed some light on the number of these landscapes owned in England at that time, and on their distribution.

The *English Connoisseur,* " containing an Account of whatever is curious in Painting, Sculpture, &c. in the Palaces and Seats of the Nobility and Gentry of England, both in Town and Country," a small handbook in two volumes, published in 1776, shows the great popularity of the landscape, and the domination of the Italian model, though it makes only a beginning at recounting the collections. Early in the nineteenth century Lady Morgan enumerates one hundred and eighteen pictures by Salvator Rosa in England, as against sixty-five on the continent. Her figures, unreliable as they are, give correctly the proportion of admiration. Sir Samuel Romilly, visiting Paris early in the nineteenth century, is amazed to find no picture by Salvator Rosa or by Gaspar Poussin in the Museum at that time. As to Claude, Smith's *Catalogue Raisonné* shows one hundred and four of the pictures represented in the *Liber Veritatis* owned in England; this includes replicas, and presumably unauthentic works. Lady Dilke in her more careful survey names eighty-three Claudes, distributed among thirty-four collections. Some of these did not reach England till the close of the century,

[3] *English Connoisseur,* I, 4, 6, 8.

and the scattering of the great French and Italian collections caused by the Revolution and the Napoleonic Wars; but the *English Connoisseur* shows how many there were by 1776.

Attendance at sales and exhibitions was fashionable. Many sales are advertised on the back pages of the *Spectator* in 1711 and 1712. In several appear names of the Italian landscape painters, but often the announcement is only of " A curious Collection of Original Paintings, lately brought from beyond Sea, by a Gentleman who collected them in his Travels," or the like. They are sold at various places, though " Mr. Pelitier " finally seems to have established something like a regular auction room in " a new house near the Wheat-sheaf." The hour for sales of paintings was usually ten in the morning; prints and drawings were sold in the evening. In 1715 Mr. James Graham announces in Steele's *The Lover* the establishment of his large gallery, " new garnisht, from top to bottom, with the finest paintings *Italy* has ever produced; I dare promise myself you will find such Variety, and such beautiful Objects, of both History and Landschape, Profane and Sacred, that it will not only be sufficient to please and recreate the Sight, but also to yield Satisfaction and Pleasure to your Mind, and instructive enough to inform and improve every Bodies else." In the middle of the century Langford was the chief auctioneer of pictures, succeeding Christopher Cock in 1748. The famous Christie's was founded in 1766. The author of *The Female Spectator* (1745) is sceptical about visitors at sales: "It is true that most of our Nobility and Gentry profess themselves great Admirers of this Art, and when Notice is given of any capital Pictures to be disposed of by way of Auction, the Rooms . . . are sufficiently crowded; but . . . three Parts in front of those numerous Assemblies are drawn thither more by the Desire of seeing one another than any other Motive." Samuel Foote in *The Minor* (1760) ridicules the fashionable auctioneer; and his own entertainment, about 1748, was in the form of an auction of pictures.

According to Edward Wright, collecting was established as " a fashionable Taste " by 1730. In 1738 John Breval consoles himself that the losses of Italy are the gain of England. " We have not for many Years past a Traveller of Quality or Fortune, that has not enrich'd his Country with *Connoissance* of one sort or another. . . . The *Farnesian* Gallery is already stripp'd, and 'tis to be fear'd, the *Medicean* is *Proximus Ucalegon*." Walpole gives a longer list of galleries that were breaking up between 1740 and 1743. " Commerce . . . daily brings us something from Italy. How many valuable collections of pictures are there established in England on the frequent ruins and dispersion of the finest galleries in Rome and other cities! "

We have to remember that a good deal of this imported art was not first-rate. " Les Anglois enlèvent tout d'Italie," says Montesquieu, " cependant les Anglois enlèvent rarement du bon. Les Italiens s'en défont le moins qu'ils peuvent et ce sont les connoisseurs qui vendent à des gens qui ne le sont pas." [4]

The preference for Italian art was shown by the Houghton collection (which Horace Walpole thought better worth seeing than most of those left in Italy) as by most others; though some Flemish and Dutch painters were highly valued, to Walpole's disgust. " As for the Dutch painters, those drudging mimicks of nature's most uncomely coarsenesses, do not their earthen pots and brass kettles carry away prices only due to the sweet neatness of Albano, and to the attractive delicacy of Carlo Maratti? " And he exhibits the taste of his age: " It was not so much want of genius in the Flemish masters, as want of having searched for something better . . . Rottenhamer and Paul Bril, who travelled in Italy, contracted as pleasing a style as any of the Italian masters. Lord Orford's landscapes of the latter are very near as fine, as pure, and as genteel, as Claude's and Titian's." One of the most vaunted glories of the Houghton collection was the *Prodigal Son,* by Salvator Rosa. There were three others by Salvator, two by Claude, and five by Gaspar Poussin. In 1779 Lord Orford sold the collection, which had cost Sir Robert Walpole over £100,000, to the Empress Catherine for £30,000,[5] to Horace's despair (though if it had not been sold, it would have been destroyed by the fire, soon after); but Horace owned a few pieces from it, and had also at Strawberry Hill landscapes by Gaspar, and Paul Bril, and a Salvator which Sir Horace Mann had given to him.

In drawings the English took extreme delight, and owned some

[4] *Voyages,* Bordeaux, 1894, I, 170.
[5] The Claudes were valued at £1200, the *Prodigal Son* at £700,

of the finest collections in Europe, notably Richardson's at one end of the century and Lawrence's at the other. Richardson's was sold in 1747, with his paintings, the sale lasting eighteen days, the amount received being £2760; which with all the difference in money values seems small beside Lawrence's expenditure of £40,-000. Another great collector of drawings in the first half of the century was Arthur Pond, the engraver, whose collection was bought by Sir Thomas Astley. The Duke of Devonshire, Dr. Mead, Sir Joshua Reynolds, Benjamin West, Lord Eldon, Charles James Fox, the Reverend Clayton Cracherode, and Richard Payne Knight were among the many important collectors of drawings later on. Knight was especially proud of his collection of Claudes, now in the British Museum.

A reflection of the fashion for private galleries is seen in *Sir Charles Grandison,* who possesses the tastes for improving grounds and collecting pictures suitable for a gentleman of the mid-century. He has, vaguely, some of " the best masters of the Italian and Flemish schools." Mrs. Delany's letters, and Arthur Young's travels testify to the abundant private collections, the ease with which a person of decent breeding might see them, and the importance, in the life of a polite person, of an interest in seeing them. The picturesque tourists, Gilpin, Hutchinson, Shaw, Bray, visit galleries assiduously. Mrs. Powys goes to Longford Castle particularly to see " the two celebrated pictures of Claude Lorraine, of the rising and setting sun, amazing fine landscapes indeed."

The question of originals began to exercise the mind of the amateur after the middle of the century, though even then attributions seemed to be taken generally with childlike trust. But Mrs. Delany reports one anxious soul: " Mr. Floyd is a virtuoso and collector of pictures; he was almost in fits when he saw the copy of the little Coreggio I gave the Duchess, and asked in a trembling voice, if the original was the same size as the copy, and if I had omitted any particular in the background? When I assured him, the size and *every speck* was as nearly the same as I could make them, he recovered himself, and said, ' *Then mine is still an original, for it is some inches bigger, and has a palm tree in it.*' I never saw such symptoms of virtuosoship, I could hardly keep my countenance." The quality

of Mr. Floyd's virtuosoship makes reasonable the announcement by Mr. William Jones at Bath in 1766 of a collection
including Rubens, Murillo, Holbein, and Poussin; and though
ridiculed by the press, he came back two years later with
Rembrandt, Vandyke, and Claude.[6] Lord Chesterfield at the
close of his life bought a Claude for four hundred guineas and
a portrait of Madame de la Vallière for four. " Well! if I am
laughed at for giving so much for a landscape, at least it must
be allowed that I have my woman cheap! " said he. And the
recounter, of course Horace Walpole, adds, " Is it not charming
to be so agreeable quite at the door of one's coffin? " A few
days later Horace calls it a landscape " which somebody was so
good as to paint a few months ago for Claude Lorrain." Beckford was the stock example of the amateur who lacked discrimination; though he did possess for a time the Altieri Claudes,
for which he paid about £7000 and which he sold to Hart Davis
for £12,000.[7]

What the picture gallery could do for literature is best shown
in that shining example, pointed out by Sir Sidney Colvin, of
what happened to young Keats, whose friend Severn made him
a frequenter of the British Museum and British Institution. If
Claude's *Sacrifice to Apollo* could be transmuted into certain
lines of the *Grecian Urn,* and the *Enchanted Castle* evoke

> magic casements opening on the foam
> Of perilous seas,

to how many less finely strung and less qualified to express the
emotions awakened by the pictures did the golden light of
Claude's unreal Arcadian scenes or the terrors of Salvator's

[6] Whitley, *Thomas Gainsborough,* p. 92.

[7] Smith, *Cat. Rais.* VIII, 278–279. They finally went to John Miles of
Leigh Court. Some notes on prices may be interesting. At Dr. Mead's sale
one Claude brought the best price in the sale, £113, and its companion £110.
Walsh Porter paid 1000 guineas for the beautiful *Enchanted Castle,* now at
Lockinge House, Berkshire, which had sold not long before for £520. A sea-
port of Salvator's brought £446 in 1798; the Colonna landscape, in 1802,
£1550. Mr. Sloan asked £5000 for a Salvator in 1802. Claude's *Dido and
Aeneas,* a Colonna picture, brought £800 in 1802. On the Chigi Claude Mr.
Buchanan's agent set a value of 1500 guineas, and 1200 for the Colonna.
The *St. Ursula* from the Barberini Palace fluctuated from £5000 to £1200 and
back to £1500 in a short space of time.

rocks and forests bring vague delight and dreamy unrest which prepared an audience for Coleridge, for Scott, for Shelley, for Keats himself?

3

Pictures (and copies) of Claude, Salvator, and Gaspar, numerous though they were, would not by themselves have sufficed to spread the forms of Italian landscape through England, nor to account for the debased and insipid manifestations of those forms which appear in painting, gardening, and literature. The enormous popularity which made these artists, especially Claude, even in their own lifetime, victims of counterfeiters and imitators, worked on afterwards into imitations of imitations, until at the close of the eighteenth century all three arts concerned with landscape moved back into closer relation with nature. Though the names of the imitators never rose quite to the level of the great originals, it may be assumed that Arthur Young was not alone in honestly preferring at times a Vernet to a Claude. Diluted and debased, and wholly artificial as many of the imitations were, they yet held the charm of the unfamiliar in landscape and figures; and if they helped to propagate the notion that landscape was beautiful only as it resembled Italian landscape, they also had part in making untrained eyes find beauties hitherto unnoticed in the Lakes, the Highlands, the mountains of Wales, even the nearer Derbyshire, because in these regions some resemblance to the pictures could be traced.

Almost the unique instance recorded of Claude's anger is his outburst against the young Sebastian Bourdon, who, having watched the master at work, himself went forth and with his chameleon gift of imitation painted the same landscape, and exhibited the counterfeit to the public as Claude's own. To this and similar frauds has been attributed the *Liber Veritatis,* the book of drawings in which Claude represented the pictures which he wished to establish as his own; though the book may well have been, as has been suggested, memoranda for his own pleasure and recollection. Bourdon, " visionary, romantic, abstracted," as Constable described him, was very popular in England. Other imitators were Pierre Patel, and Claude's pupil, Giovanni Domenico. Hermann Swanevelt, " the Hermit of

Italy," said to have been admitted to Claude's studio, and certainly a most faithful copyist of his designs, was a prolific artist, and the teacher in turn of other artists, — of Jacques Rousseau, for instance, who came to England and was employed by the Duke of Montagu to decorate his house in Bloomsbury Square, later to be the British Museum. Jacques Courtois, known as "il Borgognone," imitated Salvator Rosa, but chiefly his battle-pictures. Jan Both borrowed somewhat widely; he shows traces of Claude, of Gaspar, perhaps of Salvator, and probably of Bril and Elsheimer. Hans van Bloem, called "Orizonte" for his delicate distances, was also more Italian than Dutch. Berghem did not visit Italy, but his work shows signs of Italian, or of Dutch-Italian influence, in its rocky scenery. All these men, and the earlier Paul Bril and Elsheimer, were great favourites with the English, and frequent in their galleries.

Various later continental artists in the manners of Salvator and of the Claudians were popular in England. One was Claude-Joseph Vernet, who favoured sea-views and rocky harbours, much in the manner of Salvator, whom he admired intensely. There is a story of Vernet's having himself lashed to the rigging of a ship in a wild storm, and exclaiming in rapture, while the lightning and thunder terrified his companions, "What a noble scene!" Vernet's contemporary and friend Zuccarelli was so honoured as to have his pictures the special passion of Frederick, Prince of Wales. François Paul Ferg, a Viennese artist, who established himself in London and died in 1740, painted scenes of ruins and cattle in the approved manner; Strutt says that they were much sought after by the virtuosi; though Ferg had a bad habit of accepting an advance payment and pawning the picture on its completion.

The popularity of many of these imitators and minor artists may be seen in glancing through the lists in the *English Connoisseur,* or by the lists given in Arthur Young's tours.

> But chiefly here regales your eyes
> Whate'er the Flemish school supplies,
> Of landscapes rare, with labour'd skill,
> By Barchem, Brughel, or Paul Bril,
> Names which the Connoisseur reveres,
> Tho' harsh to nice poetic ears,

says Richard Graves, writing *On Mrs. C ——'s Villa at Hampstead* in 1766. Thanks to the number of imitators and followers of the greater painters, it was indeed a poor pretender to fashion and taste who could not show some examples of the art of landscape hanging on his private walls.

Constable classed several of these derivative artists together, along with Loutherbourg, as men of talent and even power, who " lost sight of nature, and strayed into the vacant fields of idealism." Berghem and Both, he says, " by an incongruous mixture of Dutch and Italian taste, produced a bastard style of landscape, destitute of the real excellence of either." At one of his lectures he exhibited a print from Vernet, with trees in the manner of Salvator and rocks in that of Berghem, and " an emaciated French dancing-master in a dress something like one of Salvator's banditti, intended by Vernet for a fisherman," and went on to observe that imitators always render the defects of the model more conspicuous. " Sir George Beaumont, on seeing a large picture by a modern artist, intended to be in the style of Claude, said, ' I never could have believed that Claude Lorraine had so many faults, if I had not seen them all collected together on this canvas.' "

Sir George Beaumont was himself an offender ; luckily he could not persuade Constable to follow his example. " Sir George Beaumont called. He liked what I was about, but wanted me to imitate pictures," writes Constable in a letter.[8] One day Constable found Sir George at work, with a picture of Gaspar Poussin's beside his easel. " Now if I can match these tints I am sure to be right," said he. " But suppose Gaspar could rise from his grave," replied Constable, " do you think he would know his own picture in its present state? or if he did, should we not find it difficult to persuade him that somebody had not smeared tar or cart-grease over its surface, and then wiped it imperfectly off? " The process by which the average landscape painter did his work went further than Beaumont's, as Solomon Gessner reveals :

I determined to draw after nature. But I soon found that my precision in copying from this master led me astray. . . . I found that I must form myself upon the works of the best masters. . . .

[8] Leslie, p. 180.

Trees were the first things I essayed, and I chose for my model Waterloo. . . . I accustomed myself at the same time to work after Swanefeld and Berghem. . . . For rocks, I chose the bold masses of Berghem and Salvator Rosa, as my models. . . . Lorrain instructed me in the disposition and harmony of foreground, and in the representing of soft fading distances. And I had recourse to Wouvermans, for those gently flowing slopes. . . . Sandy and rocky heights, overgrown with shrubs and underwood, I copied from Berghem. . . . The bold genius of Salvator Rosa astonished and delighted me. . . . But the two Poussins and Claud Lorrain at last possessed me entirely.[9]

If we could see specimens of the work of all the landscape painters enumerated by Walpole in the *Anecdotes of Painting,* we should probably find most of them showing the influence of Italian or Dutch-Italian forms. The connection with Salvator of Cooke, Coloni, John Griffier, and Philip Boul, painters of landscape in England early in the century, has been already noticed. Joseph Goupy (d. 1763), whom Strutt pronounced "a man of genius," painter, engraver, and fashionable drawing master, excelled in imitations of Salvator. John Mortimer (1743-1779), himself given to reckless living,[10] "charmed with the wild spirit of Salvator Rosa, made the exploits of lawless banditti the chief subject of his pencil." For this his horror-relishing contemporaries admired him.

> The rapid MORTIMER, in fancy strong,
> Marks the just horrours that to Vice belong,

says Hayley, in commendation. Walpole did not admire him; "Barry," he writes to Mason in 1783, "calls Mortimer superior

[9] *Works,* Liverpool, 1802, I, 177 ff. Mr. William Whitley quotes a critic of the Royal Academy in the *Gazetteer* for 1790, as follows: "Many of our landscape painters have made their pictures by a receipt. Never having lived out of the metropolis, or seen any green thing except a pickled cucumber in an oil shop, they form their ideas upon the style of the old Flemish masters, copy their trees from Hobbema, their water from Ruysdael. . . ." *Thomas Gainsborough,* p. 300.

[10] "Heaven-favoured, yet unhappy Mortimer! who could penetrate with gloomy enthusiasm the darkest recesses of horror, and irradiating the phantom'd dome with the awful beams of thy genius, couldst appal the gazer's soul with scenes beyond the reach of human thought! — Oh! would not thy energetic mind have soared to still sublimer heights, had not thy daring wing been clogg'd by the fetters of vulgar dissipation?" *Universal Magazine,* vol. 88, p. 323.

to Salvator Rosa, though his best merit was in being Salvator's imitator." Like Salvator, Mortimer was considered to excel in his spirited figures, and often supplied the figures in the landscapes or sea-pieces of his contemporaries. Another somewhat Salvatori-ally-inspired painter was Philip Loutherbourg (c. 1740–1812), who was, like Goupy and some other artists of reputation, a scene painter, being employed by Garrick at Drury-Lane soon after he arrived in England, about 1771. Loutherbourg was one of the many painters of the Lakes. His contemporaries found in his work grandeur of design and vigour of execution; Barry pronounced his manner to be " somewhat between Berghem and Salvator Rosa." The Eiduphusikon, an entertainment which he devised about 1782, showing scenes on bits of canvas, with painted cork for foreground, and changing lights thrown on the whole, was largely a landscape show-box; the program began with sunrise over an Italian seaport, and included Niagara, Dover Castle at sunset, moonrise on a rocky coast, and a lurid portrayal of Milton's Hell. To the British Salvators should perhaps be added Joseph Wright, "Wright of Derby" (1734–1797), whose grottoes, rocky coasts, and Italian seaports were numerous; he also painted Italian ruins, and other classic scenes more in the Claudian manner.

The British Claudes were still more plentiful. John Griffier, son of the first John, was " a good copyist of Claude." So was James van Huysum, brother of the popular painter of fruit and flower pieces. James lived a year or two with Sir Robert Walpole at Chelsea, says Walpole, " and copied many pictures of Michael Angelo Caravaggio, Claude Lorrain, Gaspar, and other masters, which are now over the doors and chimneys in the attic story at Houghton." The most prosperous imitators of Claude blended their model with Gaspar, and with the Dutch-Italians. The popularity of John Wootton (1678?–1765) arose primarily from his pictures of horses and dogs; he got forty guineas for a single horse, life-size. " He afterwards applied to landscape, approached towards Gaspar Poussin, and sometimes imitated happily the glow of Claud Lorrain," says Walpole; " at a long distance," Redgrave qualifies. Constable cites as a crowning ex-ample of absurd imitation " the English Wootton, who painted country gentlemen in their wigs and jockey-caps, and top-boots,

LANDSCAPE BY JOHN SMITH OF CHICHESTER.

Second Premium, Society of Arts, 1760. Engraved by William Woollett.
Museum of Fine Arts, Boston, Massachusetts.

with packs of hounds, and placed them in Italian landscapes resembling those of Gaspar Poussin." Wootton's pictures were
much used for decoration over chimney-pieces and doors, at other
houses than Houghton; for example, at Ditchley, where were
also "striking pieces of Ruins, Rocks, and Cascades" brought
from Italy.

The scene painters, Goupy and George Lambert, were also
imitators of Claude. Goupy was better known for imitating
Salvator, but worked in both manners. Lambert (1710–1765)
was a pupil of Wootton's, and like him a decorator of doors and
chimneys, positions regularly assigned to landscape. He was
also a painter of stage scenes, at Lincoln's Inn Fields and Covent
Garden, and originator of the famous Beef-steak Club. Not the
least important influence on public taste was stage scenery.
Lambert "followed the manner of Gaspar, but with more richness in his compositions," says Walpole. "His trees were in a
great taste." Hogarth makes flattering reference to him in *The
Analysis of Beauty* (1753): "The imitation of [the rising and
setting sun] was Claude's Lorain's peculiar excellence, and is
now Mr. Lambert's." Haydon reports old Wilson as pronouncing
Lambert's foliage to be eggs and spinach; "yet Lambert got hundreds, where Wilson could hardly get shillings."

A third British Claude was George Smith of Chichester, very
warmly admired in his own day. "Thy pencil was The very
wand of nature," a reverend admirer addresses him, and contrasts
unfavourably with his "pure undissembled truth" Claude's
"proud palaces" and Loutherbourg's "Red skies and metal-
colour'd trees." John Smith, younger brother of George, was
another Claudian. Though the Irish George Barret (1728?–
1784) father of the water-colour painter, was famous for his dewy
verdure and truly English colouring, he often followed Claude
and the Italians in the forms of his compositions. Barret, it is
said, might have been rich if he had lived more sensibly; he was
certainly popular, and had several noble patrons, especially the
Dukes of Portland and of Buccleugh. It was Barret who painted
that famous landscape room (of which more presently) for Mr.
Lock at Norbury Park.

In the year 1760 George Smith won first premium of the Society of Arts for a large composition in the manner of Claude.

That same year the earliest (if Gainsborough is not so accounted) of the great British landscape painters, Richard Wilson, finished his *Niobe*. But though Wilson found some patrons, he failed to attain the prosperity of Smith and Lambert, or the popularity of Barret. It is said that he often lacked money to buy canvas for a new picture, and would part with one of his paintings for a pot of beer and the heel of a cheese. " When somebody is dead, somebody's pictures will sell better," he used to say to Beaumont ; and it proved true. Whatever the other influences upon him — Both and Vernet, Guardi, or the Dutch — that of Claude is evident not only in frequent choice of classic subject and in aerial perspective, but in the " strong diagonal or criss-cross of diagonals, emphasized usually by a tree in one corner of the picture, and sometimes by a ruin in the other," as Mr. Frank Rutter describes the popular pattern ; insisting, however, that Wilson uses the pattern not of preference, but for pot-boiling. Wilson was truly of his time in making nature the handmaid of art. " He looked on cattle, as made only to form groups for his pictures, and on men as they *composed* harmoniously. One day, looking on the fine scene from Richmond Terrace, and wishing to point out a spot of particular beauty to the friend who accompanied him, ' There,' said he, holding out his finger, ' see near those houses, — there, where the figures are.' He stood for some time by the waterfall of Terni in speechless admiration, and at length exclaimed, ' Well done ; water, by God ! ' "

Wilson was the strongest influence on Turner in his early work, but soon gave place to Claude, long Turner's chief model, and finally his rival. When Turner used to go as a youth to copy the portraits at Sir Joshua's, he worked in the room with the Velasquez and the Claudes ; and his patron, Dr. Munro, owned a number of Claude's etchings.[11] The terms of his will certainly imply a sense of rivalry, if not jealousy.

The English water-colour school assisted in spreading Italian forms. It derived from the taste for antiquities and the taste for improvements, which together created demand for topographical draughtsmen. From the wash drawing to the water-colour sketch was a short step, and many of the draughtsmen

[11] Thornbury, *Life of Turner*, pp. 36, 55–58. Dr. Munro had also a landscape of Salvator's.

took it, with good effect; for example, Paul Sandby, Webber, Hearn, and Girtin. Several of them were reminiscent of Italian painting, — George Barret the younger, Glover, Mortimer, Ibbetson. The water-colour painter was the companion of travellers and antiquaries, as Alexander went with Lord Macartney to China, Webber with Captain Cook on his last voyage, Hearn to the Leeward Islands, John Smith with the Earl of Warwick to Italy, Girtin with James Moore, the antiquarian, and Cozens as part of the princely retinue of young Beckford on the grand tour. The water-colour artist was often a teacher, as Paul Sandby was to the royal children, and Girtin to Lady Gower and other noble patrons.

One instance of imitation is worthy of separate mention, as showing not only the interest in landscape but also the peculiarly artificial treatment of it. It is told of Claude by his friend Sandrart that he painted on four walls of a room in a Roman palace a set of landscapes which united in one whole.[12] An Englishman of taste, Mr. Lock of Norbury Park, had George Barret (whose skies Barry thought an improvement on Claude's) paint such a room for him. The result was a curiosity much admired by tourists. James Woodhouse, Shenstone's cobbler protégé, devotes to it a poem, *Norbury Park* (1789), and Mr. Gilpin admiringly describes it thus, in part:

The whole room represents a bower, or arbour, admitting a fictitious sky through a large oval at the top, and covered at the angles with trelliswork, interwoven with honeysuckles, vines, clustering grapes. . . . The sides of the room are divided by slight painted pilasters, appearing to support the trellis roof; and open to four views. That toward the *south* is real, consisting of the vale inclosed by Fox-hill, and the hills of Norbury and Dorking. . . . The scene represented on the west wall, is taken from the lakes of Cumberland. It is an exact portrait of none of them; but a landscape formed of some of the happiest circumstances which belong to all. No real view could present so beautiful and complete a picture. . . . Woods are scattered about every part, which give these scenes a greater richness than nature hath given to any of the lakes of Cumberland. . . . All this scenery is contained in various removes of distance. . . . The other grand landscape . . . is sylvan. . . . In the distance it sinks into a rich flat country, through which a sluggish stream, winding its course, discharges itself into the sea. The

[12] Lady Dilke thought traces of it were discoverable in a palace of the Muti-Papazurri family. *Claude Lorrain*, pp. 33–34.

north side . . . offers two landscapes; divided by the breast of the chimney; which is adorned by a pier-glass, let into the wall, and covered thick with a frame-work of honey-suckles, vines, wild roses. . . . These two pictures are a continuation of the scene exhibited on the western wall, which they unite with the landscape on the *east*. . . . The time of day is about an hour before the sun sets, which after a rainy afternoon is breaking from the watery clouds. . . . In the *north-east* angle, a ray of sunshine, breaking through the gloom, gilds a castled cliff. . . . All the landscapes, both within and without the room, appears illumined by the same sun. The union too between natural and artificial landscape is still further assisted by a few straggling trees, which are planted before the windows.[13]

The Claudian touches here are obvious; though Gilpin says that the room is in imitation of one done at a villa near Rome by Gaspar Poussin. Why such rooms did not spring up all over the country is hard to understand. Only one other is recorded, that of Sir Nigel Gresley's, which Miss Seward found entrancing. It had the additional beauties of a grotto of spars, ores, and shells in the chimney-piece, and a real green paling with little wicket-gates ajar, set a few inches from the walls. " The perspective is so well preserved," she concludes, " as to present a landscape deception little inferior to the watery panorama."[14]

4

For training the eye, the invention of prints was, as Shaftesbury said, " answerable to printing in the commonwealth of letters." The print made the masters of landscape intimately familiar to thousands, whereas the paintings could be known, and that for the most part only by brief encounters, to but hundreds. " By prints the pictures of the most celebrated artists

---

[13] *Western Parts,* pp. 14–19. The astonishing thing is that Gilpin in the next breath condemns as inartistic a carved head from Otaheite, which had real hair. " The mixture indeed of reality and imitation is very disgusting." The room at Norbury was still in existence when John Thomas Smith was living, but now is vanished with the house. *Nollekens,* ed. W. Whitten, 1920, II, 100.

[14] *Letters,* III, 380 (1794). The panorama deserves at least a note. Girtin painted one of London. (*Century of Painters,* I, 399.) There was one called " The Fashionable Tour Along the Banks of the Clyde," shown in New Bond Street, " Tickets for the season, not transferable, 5s." It had an explanatory poem by James Arbuckle, M. A., called *Glotta* (London, 1810). See Wordsworth, *The Prelude,* Bk. 7.

are infinitely multiplied," says the Abbé du Bos; and compares prints to prose romances, paintings to poems.

Print collecting was fashionable in the seventeenth century, among the initiate; near the close of the eighteenth, it was general. " Almost every man of taste is in some degree a collector of prints," — so Strutt opens the preface to his *Dictionary of Engravers* (1785). The very process of mezzotint was attributed, thanks to Evelyn's *Sculptura,* to Prince Rupert, a leader of taste in his time. If Evelyn's work is a gauge of the " connoissance " of that period, we must conclude that discrimination was then but faint. Evelyn seems to consider sharp relief the highest quality in a picture. He shows little interest in landscapes. When he pleads for " more *Landskips,*" he means " views of the Environs, Approaches, and Prospects of our nobly situated Metropolis." Presumably he had in mind such prints as Hollar's topographical views, which anticipated the numerous topographical drawings of the next century. Pepys had, we know, two great books filled with prints illustrating the history of London. The collection of Prince Eugene, said by Gilpin to have included all the works of all the chief engravers, and to have cost £80,000, is significant of the desire for mere amassing which characterized many a collector of repute in the eighteenth century. English residence on the continent during the Protectorate helped to increase interest in prints. The brilliant work of Faithorne in portrait must have enhanced an appreciation initiated by the productions of Nanteuil. Faithorne, devoted royalist, as he had proved in battle and prison, opened a shop near Temple Bar after the Restoration, where he sold not only his own and other English work, but also prints from continental hands. His work on engraving appeared in 1662, a sign — along with several other English publications on the subject — that the virtuoso in this field was recognized. The prints which Sir John Somers used to carry about in his coach seat on journeys were portraits. But prints of history-pictures and landscapes, by engravers like the great Marc Antonio, by the Sadelers and Perelle, were also very popular, and very numerous. The English visitor to Italy brought back prints as modern travellers bring photographs. Evelyn tells of his efforts to secure them. But Richardson, though he often refers to the prints of paintings, says that he is

" Not very conversant with These; those that Are will find that those References are not so frequent as they might have been." His remarks about prints, by the way, show how uneducated in elementary matters was the public he addressed. Wright speaks frequently and familiarly of prints of the pictures he mentions.

Etchings by Claude, Salvator, and Gaspar were too few in number to be of great influence; and in spite of the admiration for his painting, there was obtuseness to those merits of Claude's etching which seem to have waited till modern times to reach the warmest appreciation, such as Seymour Haden and Hamerton bestow. He was rather an etcher for artists than for the public; as Hamerton says, " No etcher was ever less anxious to produce an impression of cleverness." Those who would value his special qualities were even rarer in the eighteenth century than they are now. Moreover, his plates were few in number, wretched impressions were (and are) many; the best very few. It is not surprising that Gilpin, who admits that he has not seen *Le Bouvier*, pronounces them often " the dirty shapes of something, which he could not express." Salvator's work also was not abundant; and his popularity made unscrupulous dealers retouch worn plates till the number of bad impressions was discouraging. We suspect that Salvator's merits of vigour and originality — " dash " — received fuller recognition than the quieter charms of Claude. The few plates by the Poussins were sought after, in a way which makes us doubt whether the special qualities of the etching were much recognized by the average collector of that time. Far more numerous and more popular were the etchings by Both, Berghem, Swanevelt, and Waterlo, — often better work as etching than their painting as painting. Swanevelt was especially prolific, and provided the ruin-lovers with much entertainment for their eyes, in the hundred or more plates he produced. It is significant of the taste of the age that Gilpin speaks slightingly of Rembrandt's landscape prints as having " little to recommend them besides their effect." Even Strutt, who praises Rembrandt highly, names of his landscapes only the *Three Trees* and the *Mill*. The etchings by British artists were chiefly inferior, and not numerous. Chatelain, John Griffier, George Lambert, Ferg,

LANDSCAPE BY CHATELAIN.

(Soft ground etching.)

and de Lerpinière all executed landscapes, on the approved model.

Diffusion of the Italian ideal of landscape came chiefly through the engravers. A few continental engravers contributed. Sadeler, of whose prints Walpole speaks with some affection, engraved after Bril, as did van Nieulant, also of the seventeenth century. Dominique Barrière made some contemporary prints after Claude. Gabriel Perelle, much respected, produced not only engravings from Gaspar Poussin but also compositions of his own often decidedly in the Italian manner. In the eighteenth century Volpato engraved after Salvator, Isaac Moucheron from Gaspar, and the gentleman-amateur, Claude-Henri Watelet, from Jan Both.

The British school of landscape engraving, which came into being in the course of the last three quarters of the eighteenth century, was both the result and in turn a leading cause of admiration for the Italianate mode of landscape. In the development of this school Arthur Pond (1705–1758) and his partner, George Knapton, were influential. Their most famous production, the large volume of prints in the chalk manner in imitation of drawings of the great masters, contains many examples of Italian landscape, chiefly of the familiar form. Among the prints by Pond which make up some two-thirds of the collection, are specimens from Claude, Salvator, the Poussins, Jan Both, and Grimaldi. Two large oval landscapes with figures are probably the prints " after Salvator " with which Pond is credited by Walpole. Pond was important as a collector of prints and drawings — he was one of the chief connoisseurs of his day — and as a publisher, the most important of the time preceding Boydell. In 1744 he published a set of prints after pictures in British collections, which gives evidence as to the number and the contents of these collections, the taste for Italian landscape, and also, in many instances, the low standard of landscape-engraving.

Among those who worked for Pond was the eccentric Jean Baptiste Claude Chatelain (1710–1771), engraver, etcher, painter — he was one of the first to copy the scenery of the Lakes — drawing-master, and teacher of engraving. He was an amusing person. Living in an old house in Chelsea, which he took because of a dream that it held treasure, he spent days lying face down on the floor, listening for the betraying chink of coins which might be shaken by the jar of passing coaches, or pulled at the wainscoting until his hands were too bruised to do his work. " Had this man been possessed of prudence and assiduity, equal to his great abilities," sighs Strutt, " what might not have been expected at his hand? " Examples of his original etching show his respectful following of the conventional pattern. He engraved after Gaspar Poussin. One of his pupils in engraving, John Wood (c. 1720–c. 1780) reflects no great credit upon his teacher; among Wood's mediocre productions is an engraving after a small painting by Salvator which was in the collection of William Kent. Another of Chatelain's pupils, much more creditable, was Francis Vivares (1709–1780), also of French birth, who is especially known for his engravings after Claude, some of them done in association with Woollett, whom he partly instructed in the art of engraving. As predecessor and teacher of Woollett, Vivares may be called the founder of the British school of landscape engraving.

William Woollett (1735–1785) was the greatest of the school, in technical excellence. " His print of *Roman Edifices in Ruins*," says Frederick Keppel, " is probably the finest landscape in engraving." " Kupferstiche die eine Kraft, Wärme, und Harmonie darbieten, wie sie, vor ihm, im Landschaftsfache kein Künstler hervorgebracht hat," says Adam von Bartsch. Modern taste has grown away from these magnificent great plates with their infinitely laborious rendering of detail and of light and shade; but to one who goes to them prepared by re-reading of Thomson, Dyer, Collins, Gray, or many of the letter-writers of the eighteenth century, they have a charm which interprets their enormous popularity in their own time. Woollett developed the use of preliminary etching of the main lines as it had never before been employed. Sometimes he would expose a plate to four or five preliminary bitings. Often he etched the plates for other men to finish with the burin. It would have been impossible for one man to do all the work on those enormous reproductions. Even granted assistance, it is not surprising that Woollett celebrated the completion of a picture by firing off a cannon from the roof of his house in Rathbone Place, Charlotte Street. To

Woollett partly, but also to Hogarth and Sir William Strange, may be attributed the shift which, by 1788, made the value of British prints exported to France greater than that of French prints imported into Britain. Woollett engraved not only from Claude — his most famous work was after Claude, including such pictures as *The Sacrifice to Apollo* (1764), and *The Enchanted Castle,* which he completed when Vivares left it unfinished at his death — but also from Wilson, George Smith, Zuccarelli, Vernet, and Swanevelt.

Another engraver of masterly technique was Richard Earlom (1742–1822), who combined etching with mezzotint. Earlom's masterpiece was the reproduction in etching and mezzotint of Claude's drawings in the *Liber Veritatis,* in the Devonshire collection. This elaborate work of two hundred plates on which Earlom was engaged for several years was first published in 1777. In 1819 Earlom added a third volume, made up after other drawings by Claude. So popular was the *Liber* that Earlom retouched the plates several times for reprinting. Its influence on the public was very great; for the amateur artist it was a resource, a book of patterns; and for the landscape gardener it was rich in suggestions, as Knight's poem, *The Landscape,* indicates. Though the drawings in the *Liber,* being made after instead of before the finished picture, lack the peculiar values of Claude's drawings in general, and though Earlom may, as Lady Dilke accuses him of doing, have done violence to the designs he copied, still his work has much beauty and much technical interest. As is familiarly known, it gave the inspiration for Turner's *Liber Studiorum;* and for Earlom's *Liber,* as for Turner's, we have examples of the delicate pure line preliminary etching. Earlom was by no means confined to landscape in his engraving; but among the pictures which he copied for Boydell are several from Salvator Rosa, including *Jacob and the Angel,* and some from the Houghton Collection.

A long line of minor engravers may be briefly noticed, too important in the spread of these pictures to be omitted, though their work is of varying excellence. For Salvator there is the early Hamlet Winstanley (1698–1756), son of the famous and unfortunate builder of the Eddystone light, who was, by the way, also an engraver of original landscape. Hamlet Winstanley was a pupil of Kneller in painting, and went to Italy to study; but on his return to England confined himself to engraving. He produced several plates after Salvator, including *Hagar and Ishmael, Glaucus and Scylla,* and a picture of robbers; some of this work as early as 1730. Another, and an important engraver of Salvator, whom he also imitated in painting, was Joseph Goupy (c. 1700-1763), drawing-master to royalty and gentility, and foe of Handel. Goupy's set of seven pictures after Salvator, from British collections, though but tame reproductions, were widely known. Simon François Ravenet (1721?-1774), who lived and died at Mother Red Cap's, executed Salvator's *Prodigal Son,* and Poussin's *Monument in Arcadia;* not primarily landscapes, to be sure. John Brown (1719-1790), fellow-apprentice and later on assistant to Woollett, won reputation with his *St. John* and also engraved *Apollo and the Sibyl.* Though not landscapes, the *Belisarius* (1757) and the *Laomedon* (1775) of Sir Robert Strange, the great classical engraver, may be noticed. Of the former the *Critical,* not altogether from Scottish prejudice, remarked that it was " by far the most elegant and best finished print that any artist of this nation ever produced " up to that time. At the Society of Artists, R. Pranker exhibited a *View* from Salvator in 1761; and Lady Augusta Louisa Greville won medals for various prints after Salvator; one of these is of 1759, one of 1762. From their style, we surmise that Lady Greville was a pupil of Goupy. Later representations of Salvator are by James Heath (b. 1757), a study of soldiers, and by William Sharp (b. 1749), *Diogenes;* and two coloured landscapes in 1799 by John Murphy (1748-1820).

Claude was far more frequently engraved, and indeed lent himself better to engraving. James Mason (1710-1783) worked after Gaspar Poussin and Claude for Pond and for Boydell; he did prints after Claude in 1744, 1769, and 1774. Mason was a collaborator with Vivares, and his early work is very closely in the manner of Vivares. Thomas Major (1720-1799), who, unlike most of the British school, studied in Paris — he was imprisoned in reprisal after Culloden — was the first engraver elected to the Royal Academy. He worked after several of the landscape artists, and from Claude took a seaport and a pastoral landscape, the latter in 1753. John Brown's *Cephalus*

LANDSCAPE WITH RUINS.

Colour print by John Baptist Jackson.

Museum of Fine Arts, Boston, Massachusetts.

and Procris was published in 1779. James Peak (1730?–1782) was one of the more excellent minor engravers, and also an etcher of some merit. He engraved a *Morning* from Claude in 1767. Of the lesser engravers, Pierre Charles Canot (1710–1777), better known for sea-pieces, also worked after Claude and Gaspar. John Sebastian Miller (fl. 1760) did one landscape from Claude. William Byrne (1743–1805) was a prolific workman, of technical skill, who worked after Bril, Both, Zuccarelli, Vernet, Wilson, and Smith; he copied one of the Methuen Claudes. Joseph Strutt (c. 1749–1802) engraved two of Claude's landscapes in the chalk manner; James Fittler (1758–1835), chiefly a marine engraver, the *Ursula*, and the *Arch of Constantine*; James Newton (b. 1748), various pictures after Claude and Zuccarelli; and Wilson Lowry (b. 1762) after Claude and Poussin. Some of the colour prints of John Baptist Jackson, designer of wall-papers, were in the Italian style, with ruins and distances.

Illustrations in books often showed traces of Italian influence. Some early examples (they become too numerous to list, later on) are the frontispiece by Kirkall to *Miscellaneous Poems,* published by Lintot in 1712; Kirkall's plate in Elijah Fenton's *Poems on Several Occasions,* in 1717; the plates by Kent in Gay's *Poems on Several Occasions,* 1720; those by Wootton in Gay's *Fables,* 1727. William Kent is particularly given to weak imitation of Italian models, with original complications. He is said to have gained his inspiration for landscape gardening from working on the illustrations to the *Faery Queene*; his designs for the four seasons in the first complete edition of *The Seasons,* 1730, are full of Italian landscape reminiscences. An amusing late example is the frank parody of Claude, in the first volume of Richard Graves' *Columella* (1779) a satire on landscape gardening; the plate shows the hero's grounds, stream, wooded hill, Sibyl's temple, and low-placed sun. Even Hogarth shows a few hints of Italian influence, — a Salvatorial tree in *The Good Samaritan,* and the little cherub gazing at a Sibyl's temple, in one of his smaller plates. That temple was omnipresent; it is always cropping up in the fanciful designs which adorn the magazines.

The growth of print collecting may be read in many references. It was a passion already strong in 1687. Describing the sale of

Sir Peter Lely's prints and drawings in that year, Roger North says: " It was wonderful to see with what earnestness people attended this sale. One would have thought bread was exposed in a famine. Those that bought laid down their guineas, which a receiver immediately fingered, ten, twenty, thirty, &c., and gat their papers up, well covered with a sort of soft paper we had in plenty for them, and put them either in their bosoms, or very close and near to them."[15] Advertisements in the *Spectator* reflect considerable interest in prints. But greater interest developed toward 1750, when other artistic tastes were strong. Advertisements of prints in the papers increase; there are five in the *Evening Advertiser* for March 7, 1754. Gilpin's *Essay on Prints,* first published in 1768, was composed, he says, some fifteen years earlier. It was evidently popular, for there were five editions, the second that same year, the last in 1802. If Gilpin was representative of polite taste in matters of art, as Walpole's praise, and the frequent excerpts in magazines indicate, then it had not gone far since Richardson. Important for us to notice is his pronounced predilection for the Italian style of landscape. Not only does he slight Rembrandt, but comparing Waterlo with Swanevelt, he says that Waterlo " saw nature through a Dutchman's eye," whereas Swanevelt had " warmed his imagination with the grandeur and variety of Italian views."

No person of taste could be without a collection of prints. From Thomson to John Wilkes, from duke to lace-merchant, the collectors seem to include almost every person of even moderate intelligence and fortune. Few collections reached the size of Dr. Mead's, the sale of which took fourteen nights, in 1755. At the other end of the century, Turner's patron, Dr. Munro, was such a devotee that he had a special rack built in his travelling carriage, to carry a portfolio for his pleasure as he journeyed. Thomson, as his praise of engraving in *Liberty* would lead us to expect, had a large collection which he left to his friend Gray. We hear from John Thomas Smith of Nollekens and his wife, one collecting prints after Poussin, the other after Claude; and as the engravers could be cajoled into presenting them with copies, the collection cost them nothing.

15 *Autobiography,* ed. Jessopp, 1887, p. 199.

Looking over prints was a polite form of entertainment. They were usually kept pasted in great scrapbooks, with the list of the contents carefully written in front. Such a scrapbook, from Wilton House, is to be seen at the print room of the Metropolitan Museum, with a list of contents showing that it was given over to Italian landscape, the names including Claude, the Poussins, Salvator, Paul Bril, Grimaldi. "In the afternoon," says Mrs. Delany in 1736, describing the employment of time where she is staying, "there are billiards, looking over prints, coffee, tea, cribbage." Next year, "When you see Sir Robert Throck, pray make him my compliments; I hope to be in town time enough to restore him his book of prints." Of Rouseham, Sir Clement Cotterel's, "A new library was added to it not many years ago, a most magnificent room, and finished with the highest expense. There are . . . nearly five thousand volumes, and prints that cost between two and three thousand pounds, — I mean the prints only" (1743). "This day se'nnight we are to spend at the Bishop of Derry's, a day of *virtu,* in the morning prints, drawings, pictures; in the evening, music." "Where I have not pictures *I must* have prints; otherwise, I think prints best in books," she observes. Miss Talbot, apologizing to Mrs. Carter for remissness in writing, gives as one of her activities, "Somebody has sent us a fine set of prints that must be looked over directly" (1751). We remember Sir Joshua Reynolds' *Portraits of Two Gentlemen,* looking over prints, painted in 1777.

The development of the landscape print brought new interest. Lady Luxborough writes Shenstone in 1750 of her pleasure in seeing the prints brought to her by Smith, the engraver. Shenstone refers frequently to his enjoyment of them. He and Lady Luxborough have show-boxes for them; Shenstone's cost fourteen shillings, and in it "Smith's Views (with a little colouring) appear ravishing." Sir John Hawkins conformed to the taste, as Johnson did not (though it is interesting to observe Johnson's not infrequent use of the language of painting).

One evening at the Club, [says Hawkins] I came in with a small roll of prints — I think they were by Perelle, — and laying them down with my hat Johnson's curiosity prompted him to take it up and unroll it; he viewed the prints severally with great attention, and asked me what sort of pleasure such things could afford me; I told him, that as representations of rural nature, containing an assemblage of such particulars as render rural scenes delightful, they presented to my mind the objects themselves, and that my imagination realised the prospect before me; he said, that was more than his would do, for that in his whole life he was never capable of discerning the least resemblance of any kind between a picture and the subject it was intended to represent.

The passage is often cited in proof of Johnson's limitations of vision; but a glance at Perelle's highly mannered compositions suggests that there is something to be said in Johnson's defence, so far as these particular pictures were concerned.

We may imagine the childhood experience of Sir Samuel Romilly duplicated in many another life:

[My father] was an admirer of the fine arts, but pictures being too costly for his purchase, he limited himself to prints. . . . I found a great deal of amusement in turning over the prints he was possessed of, became a great admirer of pictures, never omitted an opportunity of seeing a good collection, knew the peculiar style of almost every master. . . . I love to transport myself in idea into our little parlour, with its green paper, and the beautiful prints of Vivares, Bartolozzi, or Strange, from the pictures of Claude, Caracci, Raphael, and Corregio [sic] with which its walls were elegantly adorned.

The part which the prints in Leigh Hunt's room, where Keats used to stay the night, may have played in developing his imagery, is suggested by Sir Sydney Colvin. Hazlitt gives an instance from his own youth:

A print [of the *Arch of Constantine*] hung in a little room in the country, where we used to contemplate it by the hour together. It was the most graceful, the most perfect of all Claude's compositions. The Temple seemed to come forward into the middle of the picture, as in a dance, to show its unrivalled beauty, the Vashti of the scene! Young trees bent their branches over it with playful tenderness; and on the opposite side of a stream, at which cattle stooped to drink, there grew a stately grove, erect, with answering looks of beauty: the distance between retired into air and glittering shores. Never was there scene so fair, so absolute, that in itself summed all delight!

5

Prints were frequently the medium by which ladies and gentlemen arrived at the practice of painting. Sometimes they got no further than using the prints for interior decorating,

Perelle jm et fec.

Le Blond exe Cum Privil.

LANDSCAPE DESIGNED AND ENGRAVED BY GABRIEL PERELLE.

framing them by ingenious home-made devices, adorning chimney-boards and corner-cupboards, or making them into transparencies, such as were displayed in the attic room at Mansfield Park, " Tintern Abbey holding its station . . . between a cave in Italy and a moonlight lake in Cumberland." Print transparencies are as old as the seventeenth century. Edward Orme had a special varnish, to make the paper transparent, instead of scraping it off.[16] A process of colouring them to make them look like oil paintings was sold to ladies under a pledge of secrecy; Mr. Gilpin describes some of the results at Inverary Castle, in 1776:

> In one of the apartments we were struck with a number of small paintings in a fine old mellow style; but all of them evidently by the same hand. . . . We found them all copies from pictures we knew. . . . We were informed, they were all the work of the present duchess of Argyle; and were in fact mezzotinto prints, varnished with gum copal; and painted on the back, in a manner lately invented. I have seen no invention of the kind that has so much merit. Coloured prints are in general miserable daubings.

For learning to paint, the print was considered almost indispensable. Mrs. Delany writes in 1732: " I hope you draw sometimes. I fancy if you copied some landscapes, and did them in India ink, you would like it better than faces. I am sure, with very little application, you would do them very well; but copy only from the best prints." This use of prints by herself and the Countess of Hertford is shown in Mrs. Rowe's letters, and also the landscapes in India ink. Miss Talbot, who like Mrs. Delany was a pupil of Goupy, is better advised. She tells Mrs. Carter not to take landscapes from prints, but to draw in black and white for some years; " and in drawing, you must attend not so much to the finishing and shading as to the exactness and spirit of the outline. For this you must copy from the best prints of the best masters . . . and begin with figures rather than landscapes. . . . I don't mean to say any thing of taking sketches from nature, which is a different art, and a very pretty one to be sure."

Advertisements in the newspaper show how amateur artists were multiplying between 1730 and 1765. In the former year,

[16] Hind, *Short History of Engraving*, second ed., 1911, p. 13.

Alexander Emerton, Colour-man, announces to the Ladies that he sells "all sorts of Water-Colours and Varnishes, with every thing necessary for the new Japanning." Next year is published *The Art of Drawing and Painting in Water Colours*; "whereby a Stranger to those Arts may immediately be rendered capable of delineating any View or Prospect with the utmost Exactness; of colouring any print or Drawing in the most beautiful Manner." In the *Weekly Amusement* for 1735 appear instructions, given at a female correspondent's request, for painting in water-colours in either "the light Italian way," or "the dark way." The young lady is told to take a print or painting, lay over it a piece of oiled paper, trace the outline in black, turn over the oiled paper and trace again in red chalk, then lay it chalk side down on the paper she is to paint on, and go over the lines with a quill. It seems assumed that she will paint landscapes; as Mrs. Delany said, they were easier than faces. Numerous drawing books were advertised after 1750: *The Art of Drawing in Perspective* (1755); *The Complete Drawing Book,* containing "Landskips, Views and Ruins, with outlines to each plate. Made easier to the Comprehension of Beginners than any Book of this Kind hitherto made public" (1755); *The Complete Drawing-Master* (1764); *The Whole Art of Drawing. The Artist's Vade Mecum.* "Elegantly engraved in 100 Folio Copper Plates. . . . Collected from the Works of the greatest Masters" (1764); *The Practice of Perspective on the Principles of Dr. Brook Taylor* (1764); *The Ladies New and Polite Memorandum Book for the Year* 1764, containing among other things "the most plain Directions for the Art of Drawing" as well as "Twenty-four new Country Dances."

The drawing-masters were not very numerous until the last third of the century. Artists like Richardson and Jervas gave instruction on occasion. There were also Liotard, a portrait-painter (who used to walk the streets in Turkish dress and long beard), the eccentric Chatelain, and Joseph Goupy. A story much repeated in the magazines, after Goupy's death, of his appealing to George III for aid in his poverty and distress, on the ground that when the king was a small boy, under paternal displeasure, Goupy had begged his release from durance, suggests that the drawing-master's lot was not always prosperous.

Farington gives the testimony of "Mr. Melchair" of Oxford in 1800: "He mentioned how much the Arts had advanced in this country, and said that when He first taught musick & drawing in London there were only 5 or 6 drawing masters — viz. P. Sandby, — Bonneau, who had been brought from the Spa by some Ladies, — Chatelain — & some few others, — now said he there was hundreds. . . . He spoke of Sir George Beaumont, & Lord Aylesford with great pride as having been his former pupils." Paul Sandby taught the royal children; Girtin had many noble pupils. Gainsborough lived for a time at Holkham, and gave instruction to the two older daughters of the art-loving Thomas Coke of Norfolk. Crome — but that was near the edge of the next century — taught Richenda Gurney, the sister of Elizabeth Fry. Mr. Percy Lubbock, in *Earlham,* gives a delightful account of her productions, which were just what hundreds of other young ladies produced: "Winding paths, and broken gates, and ivied walls in unlikely places; and the tree that coils, and the tree beside it that zigzags, and the third, just beyond, that is evenly scored with flowing curves." . . . "Pictures of Earlham . . . resolutely picturesque, as though the drawing-master had stood looking over the shoulder of the artist, pointing out the bough of a tree should always chance to arch over the foreground, and a figure in a red cloak pass across the middle distance in a woodland scene. The facts of the landscape gave way if they conflicted with the rules of the game, which the artist played conscientiously; but they were pretty pictures, not without an elegant distinction."

It is easy to sympathize with old Richard Wilson, who, being asked out of pity to dinner by Beechey, first inquired, though starving, "You have daughters, Mr. Beechey, do they draw?" and only on being assured that they were musical, accepted. The fashionable damsel depicted by Hannah More in *Coelebs* is of course exaggerated: "I have gone on with my French and Italian . . . and am beginning German. Then comes my drawing master; he teaches me to paint flowers and shells, and to draw ruins and buildings, and to take pictures, and half a dozen fire screens which I began for mama. . . . I learn varnishing, and gilding, and japanning, and next winter I shall learn modelling, and etching, and engraving in mezzotinto, and acquatinto,

for Lady Di Dash learns etching, and mama says as I shall
have a better fortune than Lady Di, she vows I shall learn every
thing she does." This goes beyond Miss Bingley's list of ac-
complishments for an elegant female. Though the Pompadour
and Queen Victoria both etched, that accomplishment among
ladies in general seems to have been rather rare; Strutt lists
Miss Blake, "a young lady of distinction," for her portraits,
and Lady Greville for her etchings after Salvator and others.
Lady Greville's younger brother, Lord Charles, it may be noted,
achieved some aquatints of topographical landscapes.

The young lady artist is a subject for writers of verse. The
paintings by Mrs. Anne Killigrew, described by Dryden, were
no doubt better than the works of Clarinda, who both painted
and did wax-work, in 1686:

> Sometimes you curious *Landskips* represent,
> And arch 'em o'er with gilded *Firmament:*
> Then in JAPAN some *rural Cottage* paint. . . .[17]

Mrs. Elizabeth Rowe "lov'd the pencil when she had hardly
strength and steadiness of hand sufficient to guide it . . . and it
never ceas'd to be her amusement, at times, till her death," —
the one exception among diversions; for she was sternly set
against all frivolous employment of time. But she doubtless
agreed with *The Female Spectator* (1745), that "Painting,
especially History, Landscape and Sea-pieces, is also an excellent Promoter of Reflection; — Such Prospects charm the Eye,
and thence gain an easy Passage into the Soul, exciting Curiosity
in the most Indolent."

Mrs. Delany, pupil of Goupy, was a celebrated female amateur;
though her paper flowers brought more fame than her painting.
She began her studies when past thirty, and chiefly copied from
pictures and prints, but also sketched from nature. The study
of drawing she preferred to that of music, for the young, as
leading into better company. Another famous amateur was
Lady Diana Beauclerk, whose pictures "in sut water" for his
Mysterious Mother won Horace Walpole's unqualified encomiums: "Guido's grace, Albano's children, Poussin's expression, Salvator's boldness in landscape," "such drawing that Sal-

---

[17] *Poetical Recreations,* 1688, p. 172.

vator Rosa and Guido could not surpass their execution and poetry." Georgianna, Duchess of Devonshire, travelling in the Alps with Elizabeth, the later Duchess, wrote poetry which Elizabeth illustrated with landscapes of her own composing. Arthur Young was cordially disposed toward the lady amateur. " In Mr. *Ramy's* house on Yarmouth-Quay, he has furnished a parlour with drawings of Mrs. Ramy's execution with a hot poker. These are several pieces of ruins after Panni . . . and some Landscapes. There is frequently a spirit in the strokes superior to the original prints." He considered copies of paintings in needlework, by Miss Morret, " the most curious things to be seen at York." They included landscapes by Zuccarelli, Gaspar Poussin, and Salvator; and if the rocks were not those of Salvator, the fault was not Miss Morret's, but that of the picture she was copying.

Jane Austen makes the sensible Eleanor an artist, while her emotional sister is merely an admirer of the picturesque. It is notable that Marianne finds Edward's lack of enthusiasm for pictures almost a damning fault. Ladies' sketch-books are gently ridiculed by Scott: " I could not help hinting that the cataracts delineated bore a singular resemblance to hay-cocks, and the rocks much correspondence to large old-fashioned cabinets with their folding-doors open." " I would have you cultivate your talents for drawing. It will be a constant source of amusement and delight; and who knows . . . but it may hereafter be a resource against the inconveniences of adversity," admonishes Charlotte Smith in *Rural Walks*. Charlotte was herself an artist, taught by George Smith of Chichester. " As for Charlotte Smith, her landscapes are perfect Claudes," writes Mrs. Hervey to Beckford, " and I was not at all surprised to hear that her pencil equalled her pen."

Painting was far from being set aside as an amusement only for the more light-minded sex. Pope's absorption in it, about 1713, is well known. " My eyes have so far got the better of my ears that I have at present no notion of any harmony besides that of colours," he writes to Caryll. The paintings he describes himself as doing are portraits or figure pieces; but he " stole some strokes," Spence says, in a landscape of Tilleman's. His *Epistle to Mr. Jervas* implies Italian landscape:

> Together o'er the Alps methinks we fly,
> Fir'd with ideas of fair Italy.
> With thee, on Raphael's Monument I mourn,
> Or wait inspiring Dreams on Maro's Urn:
> With thee repose, where Tully once was laid,
> Or seek some Ruin's formidable shade:

but its dying fall is of portrait,

> Alas! how little from the grave we claim!
> Thou but preserv'st a Face, and I a Name.

Bishop Berkeley encouraged his wife and children to paint, and sent a portrait of his wife's work to a friend, in 1746, remarking that two or three families in the neighbourhood are " bent on painting; and I wish it were more general among the ladies and idle people, as a thing that may divert the spleen, improve the manufactures, and increase the wealth of the nation." Mr. Robinson, father of Mrs. Montagu, was a landscape painter, " excelling most of the professed artists of his day."

Painting was attractive to men of letters. Shenstone left a manuscript note-book with many pages of water-colour painting, awkward little pictures of groves, streams, cascades, lakes, vistas of blue hills, and ruins.[18] Sterne, according to his friend Croft, had fits of enthusiasm for art. " He chiefly copied Portraits. He had a good idea of Drawing, but not the least of mixing his colours." Cradock in early life " took great pleasure in making hasty sketches of picturesque situations." Cowper set to work in 1780 with India ink and brushes (" as far as a few shillings. I do not think my talent in art worth more "). He was seized for a time by a passion for landscape. (" It is a most amusing art, and like every other art, requires much practice and attention "): " I draw mountains, valleys, woods and streams, and ducks and dab-chicks. I admire them myself, and Mrs. Unwin admires them." Arthur Young, economist, agriculturist, and lover of the picturesque, was himself something of an artist, and illustrated his *Tour of the North* with cascades and other scenes; he had, like most of his contemporaries, a special weakness for cascades, fostered manifestly by Gaspar Poussin. With George

---

[18] Now in the Alice Freeman Palmer Collection at Wellesley. It is described by Alice Hazeltine in her *Study of Shenstone*, 1918.

Keate, and William Hayley, painting was an interest at least almost equal with letters; and for Humphrey Repton, essayist and gardener, a part of his profession. Walter Scott felt apology necessary for his deficiencies in art. He took lessons in youth "from a little Jew animalcule — a smouch called Burrell — a clever sensible creature, though. But I could make no progress either in painting or drawing." "Even the humble ambition which I long cherished, of making sketches of those places which interested me, from a default of eye or hand, was totally ineffective. After long study and many efforts, I was unable to apply the elements of perspective or of shade to the scene before me, and was obliged to relinquish in despair an art which I was most anxious to practise."

Never was the amateur's lot happier than in the eighteenth century. His achievements were applauded by kind friends beyond the bounds of reason. There was Mr. Taylor of Bath, whose performances Matthew Bramble admires extravagantly. " I must own I am no judge of painting, though very fond of pictures," he prefaces his criticism upon Mr. T. " If I am not totally devoid of taste, . . . this young gentleman of Bath is the best landscape painter now living. . . . His trees not only have richness of foliage and warmth of colour, which delights the view; but also a certain magnificence in the disposition, and spirit in the expression, which I cannot describe. His management of the *chiaro oscuro*, or light and shadow, especially gleams of sunshine, is altogether wonderful, both in contrivance and execution; and he is so happy in his perspective, and marking his distances at sea, by a progressive series of ships, vessels, capes, and promontories, that I could not help thinking I had a distant view of thirty leagues up the background of the picture." This fervent admiration of the amateur brings to mind the Mr. Taverner, a proctor in the Commons, who painted landscapes for his amusement, and " was extolled above all professional artists," says Farington. " Taverner had much quaiking about shewing his pictures, which raised their reputation. It was very difficult to get a sight of his pictures." Walpole mentions two of them which " must be mistaken for, and are worthy of Gaspar Poussin." Another well-advertised amateur was C. W. Bampfield, also a famous improver of grounds and creator of cascades.

Richard Graves, his friend and admirer, pays him an Addisonian tribute:

> In B-mpf-d's pencil we delighted trace
> Salvator's wildness but with heighten'd grace:
> Hence rocks and waves a pleasing landskip form;
> We're charm'd with whirlwinds, and enjoy the storm.[19]

Gainsborough's friend, William Jackson of Exeter, notices, in *The Four Ages* (1798) the tendency of the amateur to copy Claude. " It is the first effort of every smatterer in landscape painting." W. H. Pyne in the *Somerset House Gazette* regrets that the *Liber Veritatis* is so often recommended to amateurs " by learned connoisseurs, as an example of light, shadow, and composition. It has moreover been resorted to, and that most erroneously, by certain teachers of drawing, as a store for subjects to lay before their pupils." Claude direct, and Claude through Thomson, were likely to be in the amateur's mind. " I was just going to read the *Seasons* . . . to give him hints for a landscape," says a father who is supervising his son's artistic employment.[20] A poem on *Landscape Painting* by the Reverend Samuel Bishop gives the formula:

> Let next in order due succeed
> The mingled hues of vale and mead;
> The road in devious windings wrought,
> Now lost, and now at distance caught;
> Whose broken track directs us still
> To some brisk streamlet's glassy rill;
> Whence lessening in progressive guise,
> Long levels stretch, abrupt rocks rise,
> 'Till Light's last lines the view complete,
> And woods, skies, plains and mountains meet.

[19] *Euphrosyne,* I, 129.
[20] *The Prater,* second ed., 1757, p. 150.

V

ITALIAN LANDSCAPE IN ENGLISH POETRY
OF THE EIGHTEENTH CENTURY

I

An extended rolling plain, or wide valley opening to the south, traversed by a winding stream, and encircled, amphitheatre-like, by wooded hills; a foreground of plants and trees, richly leaved; a middle distance of plain and hill, adorned with groves, villas, bridges, castles, temples of antique pattern, vine-hung ruins; a far distance of faint blue hills, and often the sea; all this overspread with golden light, preferably of sunrise or sunset: such was the familiar Claudian landscape. The Salvatorial showed precipices and great rock masses of fantastic form, cascades, torrents, desolate ruins, caves, trees dense of growth, or blasted trunks, and shattered boughs. The two kinds of landscape were combined by later artists, such as Vernet and Zuccarelli, or used in contrast, as by Mrs. Radcliffe. Throughout the century a literary landscape was formed, generally, on these models: extended prospect, variety of objects, amphitheatre form, sunset and sunrise light; or cliffs, cascades, hanging woods, torrents, " delightful horrors." Not until late was the beauty of quiet and gentle scenery generally recognized, or indeed, in literature, recognized at all.[1]

The word *prospect* seems at first to have been used to express some such wide and far-stretching scene, viewed from a height, and considered as forming a picture much like those of Claude. There came to be a differentiation between *prospect* and *landscape,* which apparently was not felt early in the century. Shenstone said: " I use the words landskip or prospect, the former as expressive of home scenes, the latter of distant images. Pros-

---

[1] From letters it is evident that such beauty *was* recognized; Goldsmith and Cowper are the most conspicuous early appreciators of such scenery. Gainsborough's landscapes are other examples; but even he resorts to theatric tricks, such as dead trees.
Certain poets and poetasters are discussed in the later chapter, on gardening.

pects should take in the blue distant hills; but never so remotely, that they are not distinguishable from clouds. . . .
Landskip should contain variety enough to form a picture upon
canvas." With more interest in the arts of landscape, in painting and gardening, a technical language developed, which Gilpin,
Arthur Young, Hutchinson, and others of the last half of the
century used fluently. With them *landscape* means about what
Shenstone meant by it, a more unified, less vast, paintable scene,
though often still extensive, and *prospect* a view from a height,
too vast for the canvas.

Dyer and Thomson were the first of the great landscape designers in poetry, in their century. A few intimations appear
before them, the clearest by John Hughes, who was, like many
another poet, himself a dabbler in graphic arts. His *Court of
Neptune* (1700) tells of

> Landscapes of rising Mountains, shaggy Woods,
> Green Valleys, smiling Meadows, silver Floods,
> And Plains with lowing Herds enrich'd around. . . .

and in his verses *To Mr. Constantine, on His Paintings,* he
describes painted landscape:

> Here tufted Groves rise boldly to the Sky,
> There spacious Lawns more distant charm the Eye,
> The Chrystal Lakes in borrow'd Tinctures shine,
> And misty Hills the far Horizon join,
> Lost in the azure Borders of the Day,
> Like Sounds remote that die in Air away.

He has a view of the ruins of Rome, " Old Temples, open to the
Day," which, with walls moss-grown, and broken columns,
" Rear up their Roof-less Heads to form the various Scene," [2] —
characteristic expression of an age which constantly regarded
nature as a stage set for man, or Nature personified as an artist
working with pencil and palette.

Tickell translates the native scenery into Italian, in a vague
generalizing to which the Claudian landscape easily led. Indeed, we may well believe that to this generalizing in eighteenth

---

[2] *Poems,* 1735, II, 300. Hughes compares the descriptions of morning in
the poets to " so many fine skies differently colour'd and interpers'd with
Clouds, by the best Masters in Landskip." I, 331.

century descriptions of landscape, as in Tickell's *Oxford* (1707), their favourite pictures were conducive:

> . . . Wheresoe'er I turn my wond'ring Eyes,
> Aspiring Tow'rs and verdant Groves arise,
> Immortal Greens the smiling Plains array,
> And mazy Rivers murmur all the way.

Pope comes close to Claude in *The Temple of Fame* (1711):

> Here sailing Ships delight the wondering eyes,
> There trees and intermingled temples rise:
> Now a clear sun the smiling scene displays,
> The transient landscape now in clouds decays,

and in *Windsor Forest* (1713), " Where order in variety we see ":

> Here waving groves a chequer'd scene display, . . .
> There, interspers'd in lawns and opening glades,
> Thin trees arise that shun each other's shades.
> Here in full light the russet plains extend,
> There, rapt in clouds, the blueish hills ascend.[3]

The elder Thomas Warton shows some signs of the taste for painting and for scenery which developed more fully in his sons. His *Poems on Several Occasions* (1748) hint of his seeing " Nature's Landscapes " with a picturesque eye: " Dark woods and pensive Waterfalls," " desert Prospects rough and rude," " a green Valley's wood-encircled Side." He admires more arts than one, as a gentleman of his time should do:

> Then *Harmony* and *Picture* came,
> Twin nymphs my Sense to entertain,
> By times my Eye, my Ear was caught
> With *Raphael's* Stroke and *Handel's* strain.

His *Ode to Taste* classically addresses that " beauteous Queen of Life-refining Art " ;

> Or in some ruin'd temple dost thou dwell,
> Of ancient Rome, deserted of the world,
> Where prostrate lies in Dust
> The shapely Column's height?

[3] Salvator is suggested in " The shapeless rock, or hanging precipice." *Essay on Criticism*, I, l. 158.

In 1726 Richard Savage published the *Miscellaneous Poems
and Translations* which included preliminary sketches of *Grongar
Hill,* and the poem in its final form appeared in D. Lewis's *Miscellaneous Poems,* that same year.   Dyer is so much more a
painter of landscape in these poems than is Thomson in *Winter,*
also published in 1726, that he may be taken as the pioneer of
descriptive poets of landscape.   He was a painter of both portraits and landscapes, a pupil of Richardson's, and in 1726 was
rambling about south Wales and the neighbouring counties,
painting not only with brush but with words " Rural Scenes in
simple Grandeur," as Savage says, in which " Vales, Hills, Lawns,
Lakes, and Vineyards feast our eyes." [4]   In *The Country Walk*
Dyer gives his own idea of landscape :

> Where am I, Nature? I descry
> Thy Magazine before me lie!
> Temples! — and Towns! — and Tow'rs! — and Woods!
> And Hills! — and Vales! — and Fields! — and Floods!
> Crowding before me, edg'd around
> With naked wilds, and barren Ground.

The earlier *Grongar Hill* is in couplets and quatrains of irregular length, and cumbrous style ; the landscapes less effectively
described than in the revision.[5]

Another poem in Savage's miscellany is Dyer's *Epistle to a
Famous Painter,* which gathers together the ideals of that age
for landscape painting :

[4] *Poems,* 1726, p. 28.   *To Mr. John Dyer, a Painter.*   " I have often
heard Sir George Beaumont express a curiosity about his pictures, and a
wish to see any specimen that might survive," says Wordsworth.

[5] Brief parallel passages show Dyer's improvement:

The quick'ning Sun a Show'ry Ra-	Half his beams Apollo sheds
diance sheds,	
And lights up all the Mountain's	On the yellow mountain-heads!
russet Heads.	
Gilds the fair Fleeces of the distant	Gilds the fleeces of the flocks:
Flocks,	
And, glittering, plays betwixt the	And glitters on the broken rocks!
broken Rocks.	

See *The Two Versions of Grongar Hill,* by Garland Greever, *Jour. Eng.
and Ger. Phil.,* xvi, 274-281.

The beauteous Shapes of Objects near!
Or distant Groves confused in Air!
The golden Eve, or blushing Dawn,
Smiling on the lovely Lawn!
And pleasing Views of chequer'd Glades!
And Rivers, winding thro' the Shades!
And Groups of merry Nymphs and Swains! . . .
Or some old Building, hid with Grass,
Rearing its sad ruin'd Face;

Whose Columns, Friezes, Statues lie,
The Grief, and Wonder of the Eye!
Or swift adown a Mountain tall,
A foamy Cataract's sounding Fall. . . .

Grongar Hill is not composed in one single picture,[6] but presents Claude's wide country outspread, river, woods, and hills. " Old castles from the cliffs arise," and above all there is abundance for the eye, and golden light:

Ever charming, ever new,
When will the landskip tire the view!
The fountain's fall, the river's flow,
The woody vallies, warm and low,
The windy summits, wild and high,
Roughly rushing on the sky!
The pleasant seat, the ruin'd tow'r,
The naked rock, the shady bow'r;
The town, the village, dome and farm . . .
   See on the mountain's southern side,
Where the prospect opens wide,
Where the evening gilds the tide. . . .

There is also, what Claude sometimes had, and this age felt desirable, moral; later we shall find moral brought into landscape gardening less gracefully than Dyer's reflection on the ruined tower:

A little rule, a little sway,
A sun beam in a winter's day,

---

[6] Gilpin, in his *Observations on the River Wye,* criticizes it adversely for failing to contrast foreground and distance. " His hill's extensive view would probably have afforded several completed landscapes, but it is not clear that he aimed at producing any." John Scott, *Critical Essays,* 1785, p. 112.

> Is all the proud and mighty have
> Between the cradle and the grave . . .
> And see the rivers, how they run,
> Thro' woods and meads, in shade and sun,
> Sometimes swift, sometimes slow,
> Wave succeeding wave, they go
> A various journey to the deep,
> Like human life to endless sleep.

The Ruins of Rome (1740) shows the same reflective and didactic turn, but also a fine sense of pictorial values in " Latium's wide champain, forlorn and waste." The images are present to the eye, not evoked from a printed page; but the memory of such pictures of Claude's as *Roman Edifices in Ruins* is evident:

> . . . the rising sun
> Flames on the ruins in the purer air
> Tow'ring aloft, upon the glitt'ring plain,
> Like broken rocks, a vast circumference,
> Rent palaces, crush'd columns, rifled moles,
> Fanes roll'd on fanes, and tombs on buried tombs. . . .

> . . . Globose and huge,
> Grey-mould'ring temples swell, and wide o'ercast
> The solitary landskip, hills and woods,
> And boundless wilds. . . .

> Hence over airy plains, by crystal founts,
> That weave their glitt'ring waves with tuneful lapse. . . .
> And dells, and mould'ring shrines, with old decay
> Rustick and green and wide embow'ring shades. . . .
> . . . From yon blue hills
> Dim in the clouds, the radiant aqueducts
> Turn their innumerable arches o'er
> The spacious desert, bright'ning in the sun . . .
> Proud and more proud in their august approach. . . .

The Fleece (1757), in which Wordsworth found " beauties of a high order," was written after Dyer had given up his dream of being a painter, and had settled down as a country rector in Lincolnshire. " 'Tis now precipitated to the press, with such faults, as must be imputed to the air of a fenny country," he writes to Duncombe, just before it was published. For such

passages of landscape as it contains, he goes back to Wales and
Shropshire, ignoring the " fenny " country, and recalls

> . . . Snowden, for its lofty terrace fam'd,
> Which from a mountain's ridge, elate o'er woods,
> And girt with all Siluria sees around
> Regions on regions blended in the clouds,
> Pleasant Siluria, land of various views,
> Hills, rivers, woods, and lawns, and purple groves. . . .

or Bredon with

> . . . various views unnumber'd spread beneath!
> Woods, tow'rs, vales, caves, dells, cliffs, & torrent floods;
> And here & there, between the spiry rocks,
> The broad flat sea . . .

or Salvatorial Usk,

> . . . that frequent, among hoary rocks,
> On her deep waters paints th' impending scenes,
> Wild torrents, craggs, & woods, & mountain snows. . . .[7]

Richard Savage, who, according to Dr. Johnson, " had no
knowledge but from pastorals and songs " of the country, may
have been influenced by Dyer. For a city poet he takes rather
marked interest in landscape. But *The Wanderer* leans toward
Salvator, with its cataracts, and " rocks in rough assemblage,"
in amphitheatre form; and there is a " distance " where the
ocean " Points a blue arm where sailing ships delight, In Prospect
lessen'd," and a sunset, and a ruined circular temple, through
whose arch the sun shines.

Thomson is, *par excellence,* the poet of pictorial landscape.
Yet his *Winter* (1726) shows slight use of it, in comparison with
the other *Seasons*. The subject gives fewer chances for landscape of the Italian kind; though there is one such:

> At last the Muddy Deluge pours along,
> Resistless, roaring; dreadful, down it comes
> From the chapt Mountain, and the mossy Wild,

---

[7] The *Critical* treats the poem as a picture: " In this agreeable landscape
we perceive that the objects are properly placed, the figures well grouped,
and the ordonnance of the piece just and natural. The colours are excellent,
the strokes masterly, and the whole picture highly finished." Criticism in
such terms could not have been conceived in 1726.

> Tumbling thro' Rocks abrupt. . . .
> Betwixt two meeting Hills, it bursts away,
> Where Rocks, and Woods o'er hang the turbid Stream,
> There gathering triple Force, rapid, and deep,
> It boils, and wheels, and foams, and thunders thro!

But the far more abundant later use of landscape implies that Thomson had both grown more interested in making pictures, and had better learned the technique of the art, after that first venture. Perhaps his friend Dyer's miscellany poems had helped to suggest it; more likely the sight of pictures in the houses of his friends and patrons. The Prince of Wales (himself a pupil of Goupy) was a collector of landscape paintings, and the gentlemen of his circle were largely men of taste. The Countess of Hertford, one of Thomson's important patrons, was not only a lover of pictures, but proficient in painting landscapes from prints, if we may believe her friend Mrs. Rowe. Thomson's friend, the painter, Aikman, had been in Italy three years a while before, and if he did not return with a sheaf of prints and drawings, was the exception among painters of his time.

In the second edition of *Winter* Thomson inserted another Salvatorial bit, —

> . . . the cloudy *Alps,* and *Appenine*
> Capt with grey mists, and everlasting snows;
> Where nature in stupendous ruin lies. . . .

But in *Summer* (1727) there is a gallery of paintings, — Claudian sunrises and sunsets, extended views, pastoral scenes:

> . . . Young *Day* pours in a-pace,
> And opens all the lawny Prospect wide.
> The dripping Rock, the Mountain's misty Top
> Swell on the Eye, and brighten with the Dawn. . . .

> But yonder comes the powerful *King* of Day,
> Rejoicing in the East. The lessening Cloud,
> The kindling Azure, and the Mountain's Brim,
> Tipt with aethereal Gold, his near Approach
> Betoken glad: and now apparent all,
> Aslant the Dew-bright Earth, and colour'd Air,
> He looks, in boundless Majesty, abroad;
> And sheds the shining *Day*, that, burnish'd, plays
> On Rocks, and Hills, and Towers, and wandering Streams,
> High-gleaming from afar . . .

A Design by William Kent for *The Seasons*, 1730.

And what a pleasing Prospect lies around!
Of Hills, and Vales, and Woods, and Lawns, and Spires
And Towns betwixt, and gilded Streams! till all
The stretching Landskip into Smoak decays. . . .

Low walks the Sun, and broadens by degrees,
Just o'er the Verge of Day. . . .
'Tis all one Blush from East to West! and now
Behind the dusky Earth, He dips his Orb,
Now half immers'd, and now a golden Curve,
Gives one faint Glimmer, and then disappears. . . .

While wavering Woods, and Villages, and Streams,
And Rocks, and Mountain-tops, that long retain'd,
Th' ascending Gleam, are all one swimming Scene,
Doubtful if seen. . . .

Others might be given; the group of cattle by the brook,
the waterfall, the sea that " in long Visto . . . Darts a green
Lustre, trembling, thro' the Trees," the mountain-pine " Black
from the Stroak . . . a leaning shatter'd Trunk," the precipice
" Projecting Horror on the blacken'd Flood." The wide prospect swells into views too vast for a canvas in some passages
added in 1744:

Majestic Woods of every vigorous Green
Stage above Stage, high waving o'er the Hills,
Or to the far Horizon wide diffus'd,
A boundless deep Immensity of Shade. . . .

. . . Plains immense
Lie stretch'd below, interminable Meads,
And vast Savannahs, where the wandering Eye
Unfixt, is in a verdant Ocean lost. . . .

In *Spring* (1728), dedicated to the Countess of Hertford, the
poet views himself as a painter, vainly attempting to seize living
beauty; " Daubing all Will be to what I gaze; for who can
paint Like NATURE?" But he attempts a sunset after rain:

Till, in the Western Sky, the downward Sun
Looks out illustrious from amid the Flush
Of broken Clouds, gay-shifting to his Beam.
The rapid Radiance instantaneous strikes
Th' illumin'd Mountain, thro' the Forest streams,

> Shakes on the Floods, and in a yellow Mist,
> Far-smoking o'er th' interminable Plain,
> In twinkling Myriads lights the dewy Gems.
> Moist, bright, and Green, the Landskip laughs around.
>
> . . . The hurried Eye . . .
> Now meets the bending Sky, the River now
> Dimpling along, the breezy ruffled Lake,
> The Forest-running road, the rising Spire,
> Th' aetherial Mountain, and the distant Main.

In the edition of 1744 — that is, after his visit to Italy and his collecting of prints — appears the most elaborately composed of all his landscapes, with real Claudian distances. It is the view from Hagley Park:

> Meantime you gain the Height, from whose fair Brow
> The bursting Prospect spreads immense around;
> And snatch'd o'er Hill and Dale, and Wood, and Lawn
> And verdant Field, and darkening Heath between,
> And Villages embosom'd soft in Trees,
> And spiry Towns by dusky Columns mark'd
> Of rising Smoak, your Eye excursive roams . . .
> To where the broken Landskip, by degrees,
> Ascending, roughens into ridgy Hills;
> O'er which the *Cambrian* Mountains, like far Clouds
> That skirt the blue Horizon, doubtful, rise.

In *Autumn* (1730) the landscapes are well constructed, but less Italian; though they show " a serener blue with golden light irradiate," a " boundless prospect," a " mountain, horrid, vast, sublime," and one great pictorial map, a " broad cerulean scene," of

> . . . CALEDONIA, in romantic view;
> Her airy mountains, from the gelid main,
> Invested with a keen, diffusive sky,
> . . . her forests huge,
> Incult, robust, and tall, . . .
> . . . her azure lakes between, . . .
> . . . Winding deep, and green, her fertile vales;
> With many a cool, translucent, brimming flood
> Wash'd lovely. . . .

In 1730 Thomson, making the grand tour with young Talbot, developed into something of a virtuoso; at least he acquired ideas on painting, which he sets down in *Liberty*. He is oddly backward in decorating his heavy subject with pictures from his travels. Those he gives are such as he might almost have given without seeing the places, — brief and general beside Dyer's.

> In Umbria's closing Vales, or on the Brow
> Of her brown Hills that breathe the scented Gales . . .
> Or Baia's viny coast . . .
> Far-shining upwards to the *Sabine Hills* . . .
> . . . The rugged Appenines that roll
> Far thro' *Italian* bounds their wavy tops . . .
> The hollow-winding Stream, the Vale, fair-spread
> Amid an Amphitheatre of Hills . . .
> . . . Hung o'er amazing Rocks,
> The Mountain-Ash, and solemn-sounding Pine. . . .
> And high o'ertopping all the broken Scene,
> The Mountain fading into Sky. . . .

His interest in painting is shown by his giving twice over an account of its derivation:

> First elder *Sculpture* taught her *Sister Art*
> Correct Design; where great Ideas shone . . .
> Then the bright Muse, their eldest Sister, came;
> And bad her follow where She led the Way:
> Bad Earth, and Sea, and Air, in Colours rise;
> And copious Action on the Canvas glow:
> Gave her gay Fable; spread Invention's store;
> Inlarg'd her View; taught Composition high,
> And just Arrangement, circling round one Point,
> That starts to Sight, binds and commands the Whole.[8]

One picture which he gives is a Claude:

> As when the Shepherd, on the Mountain Brow,
> Sits piping to his Flocks, and gamesome Kids;
> Mean time the Sun, beneath the green Earth sunk,
> Slants upward o'er the Scene a parting Gleam:
> Short is the Glory that the Mountain gilds,
> Plays on the glittering Flocks, and glads the Swain.

In the edition of 1744 he added to his story of the arts a passage upon landscape painting, vividly suggesting visits to the various Roman Palaces which held the assembled works of Claude, Salvator, and the Poussins:

[8] *Greece,* 1735, p. 31. See also *Britain,* 1736, pp. 15–17.

> . . . to Rural Life,
> The softer canvas oft repos'd the Soul.
> There gayly broke the Sun-illumin'd Cloud;
> The less'ning Prospect, and the Mountain blue,
> Vanish'd in Air; the Precipice frown'd, dire;
> White, down the Rock, the rushing Torrent dash'd;
> The Sun shone, trembling, o'er the distant Main;
> The Tempest foam'd, immense; the driving Storm
> Sadden'd the Skies, and from the doubling Gloom,
> On the scath'd Oak the ragged Lightning fell;
> In closing Shades, and where the Current strays,
> With Peace, and Love, and Innocence around,
> Pip'd the lone Shepherd to his feeding Flock. . . .

In his account of the arts engraving has a place; and we recall his collection of prints:

> From *Rome*, awhile, how PAINTING, courted long,
> With POUSSIN came; *Ancient Design*, that lifts
> A fairer Front, and looks another Soul.
> How the kind *Art*, that, of unvalu'd Price,
> The fam'd and *only* Picture, easy gives,
> Refin'd her Touch, and thro' the shadow'd Piece,
> All the live Spirit of the Painter pour'd.

The Castle of Indolence (1748) is rich in bits of landscape sometimes rather vaguely given, as accords with that dreamy poem:

> In lowly Dale, fast by a River's Side,
> With woody Hill o'er Hill encompass'd round, . . .

" Sleep-soothing Groves and quiet Lawns between," " Lowing Herds along the Vale. . . . And vacant Shepherds piping in the Dale," a Castle " mid embow'ring Trees," " Gay Plains," woods that " imbrown the Steep, or wave along the Shore," " trees by Lightning scath'd." Of the larger pictures, one is a Salvator, one a Claude:

> Full in the Passage of the Vale, above
> A sable, silent, solemn Forest stood . . .
> And up the Hills, on either Side, a Wood
> Of blackening Pines, ay waving to and fro,
> Sent forth a sleepy Horror through the Blood;
> And where the Valley winded out below,
> The murmuring Main was heard, and scarcely heard, to flow.

. . . That fatal valley gay,
O'er which high wood-crown'd hills their summits rear . . .
Like a green isle, it broad beneath them spread,
With gardens round, and wandering currents clear,
And tufted groves to shade the meadow-bed. . . .

If for sixty or seventy years to come Claude is *soft*, Salvator *dashes*, and Poussin is *learned*, the responsibility is Thomson's. That stanza of his on landscape painting was a handy compendium of criticism for the general public:

Sometimes the Pencil in cool airy Halls
Bade the gay Bloom of vernal Landskips rise,
Or Autumn's varied Shades imbrown the Walls:
Now the black Tempest strikes the astonish'd Eyes;
Now down the Steep the flashing Torrent flies;
The trembling Sun now plays o'er Ocean blue,
And now rude Mountains frown amid the Skies;
Whate'er *Lorrain* light-touch'd with softening Hue,
Or savage *Rosa* dash'd, or learned *Poussin* drew.

To those three he adds one more,

No *Titian's* Pencil e'er could so array,
So fleece with Clouds the pure Etherial Space!

He would doubtless have been pleased to find himself compared to these four. " It has been affirmed in my hearing," says his critic More (whose adjectives here are not too discriminating), " by some whose profession and science give them a right to speak decisively, that the pieces of *Poussin* are not more uncommon, exotic and classical, the sketches of *Lorenese* more daring and sublime, or the descriptions of *Titian* more happy, natural, graceful, varied and charming, than his." And again, " The scenes of Thomson are frequently as wild and romantic as those of Salvator Rosa, varied with precipices and torrents, and ' castled cliffs,' and deep vallies with piny mountains, and the gloomiest caverns." [9]   " The *Seasons* of Thomson," says

[9] J. More, *Strictures, Critical and Sentimental, on Thomson's Seasons,* 1777, pp. 180, 182. The second sentence (quoted by More) is from Joseph Warton's *Essay on Pope.* Another writer of the same time objects to Thomson's painting as too realistic and harsh: " Had Art But soften'd the hard lines and mellow'd down The glaring tints." . . . (*A Poetical Epistle,* . . . [W. H. Roberts], 1773, pp. 8–9.

Joseph Warton, " have been very instrumental in diffusing a general taste for the beauties of *nature* and *landschape.*" [10]

Occasional descriptions of stage scenery in this period remind us that among the scene-painters were such imitators of Claude as George Lambert and Joseph Goupy. Perhaps that for the epilogue of *Tancred* was of such creation. " The back scene opens, and discovers a romantic Sylvan landskip; from which Mrs. Cibber, in the character of the Tragic Muse, advances slowly to music." The epilogue to *Alfred* (revised by Mallet and twice presented in the grounds of the Prince of Wales at Cliefden) shows " a beautiful valley, bordered on each hand by forest trees, rising irregularly; and forming from space to space, various groves. The prospect behind is a landschape of woodlands, and of mountains that ascend one above another, till the last seem to lose themselves in the sky. From the summit of the nearest hill a river pours down, by several falls, in a natural cascade."

While Thomson was writing *Summer,* Mallet, tutor to the sons of the Duke of Monstrose, was engaged on *The Excursion,* in which Thomson and Aikman expressed great interest. He went on the grand tour with his young pupils in 1727; but the pictures in his poems are more like pale reflexes of Dyer's and Thomson's than like anything caught in Italy:

> There spreads a green expanse of plains . . .
> And there, at utmost stretch of eye,
> A mountain fades into the sky;
> While winding round, diffused and deep,
> A river rowls with sounding sweep. . . .
>
> The boundless scene beneath, hill, dale and plains;
> The precipice abrupt, the distant deep . . .
> The river's crystal, and the meadow's green,
> Grateful diversity! allure the eye. . . .
>
> . . . how the sun
> Declin'd, hangs verging on the western main . . .
> A circling glory glows around his disk
> Of milder beams; part, streaming o'er the sky,
> Inflames the distant azure; part below
> In level lines shoots through the waving wood,
> Clad half in light and half in pleasing shade,
> That lengthens o'er the lawn. . . .

10 *Essay on the Genius and Writings of Pope,* 1782, II, 185.

Extent and amount of prospect were the main things with most of the poets who deal with landscape in this century. At just about this time Bridgeman's invention of the ha-ha, or fence concealed in a ditch, was beginning to " call in the country." For the enumeration of objects so frequently appearing, Milton was partly responsible,[11] just as he was accounted the true father of the English school of gardening. But when John Duncombe styled Milton " the great artist," and admired the " lively tints " with which he drew " Hill, dale, and shady woods, and sunny plains" (using Milton's own phrase) he showed how the idea of the painted landscape dominated his age. References to the painter's tools and the painter's art were the poetic convention in descriptions of landscape. " Landscapes rise, scarce *Lambert's* art can mend," — so Whitehead;

> *Nature* the Pallat holds, the Canvas spread,
> Filled with *her* colours, *Art* the Pencil guides,

says the author of *The Landscape* (1748), a poem in elegiac quatrains antedating Gray's published *Elegy* by three years. Young, in a Berkleian vein, reflects that our eyes

> . . . half create the wondrous World they see. . . .
> Ours is the Cloth, the Pencil and the Paint;
> Which Nature's admirable Picture draws.

Young has little landscape description; in one scene cities swell over vales and mountains, " And gild our Landschape with their glittering Spires." His idea of the use of nature is seen in his list of sublimities:

> Seas, Rivers, Mountains, Forests, Deserts, Rocks,
> The Promontory's Height, the Depth profound,
> Of subterranean, excavated Grots . . .
> Ev'n *these* an aggrandizing Impulse give;
> Of solemn Thought enthusiastic Heights
> Ev'n *These* infuse. . . .

Such a Miltonic list is Henry Brooke's, in *Universal Beauty* (1735):

[11] E.g. Rocks, caves, lakes, fens, bogs, dens, and shades of death, P. L. II, 621. Clear spring, or shady grove, or sunny hill, P. L. III, 28. Fortunate fields, and groves, and flow'ry vales, III, 569. Hill, dale, and shady woods, and sunny plains, VIII, 262. Of hill and valley, rivers, woods, and plains, IX, 116.

> . . . Landskip, Hill and Dale,
> The lowly Sweetness of the Flow'ry Vale,
> The Mount elate, that rises in Delight,
> The flying Lawns, that wanton from the Sight,
> The steepy Mountains, and luxurious Plains,
> Delicious Regions! Plants, Woods, Waters, Shades,
> Grotts, Arbours, Flow'rets, Downs and rural Shades;
> Arcadian Groves, sweet Tempe! Blest Retreats. . . .

The topographical landscape poem is frequent, imitating *Cooper's Hill* and *Windsor Forest,* but with more use of picture, and, as the development of grounds become fashionable, glorifying some improved estate. Often the pictures are consciously composed. Mrs. Elizabeth Thomas, in *Bereford* (1731), describes a " large and varied Prospect " including " Towns, Churches, Mountains, Pleasure Fields and Woods, Enamel'd Meadows and transparent Floods," and terminated by gently rising hills " which close the Landscape with complete Delight." John Whaley, writing of Tintern, shows a sense of " Views Romantic," — overhanging cliffs, sparkling brooks, gray ruins, thoughtfully gilded by a setting sun.[12] Dr. John Dalton is an early poet of the Lakes, inadequate, as Thomas Amory complains in *John Buncle.* " Tremendous rocks," " the rough rocks of dread Lodore," " the horrors of the scene," " Cragged cliffs, impendent wood, Whose shadows mix o'er half the flood," are the best descriptive phrases Dalton finds. His poems are important for relish of wildness:

> Horrors like these at first alarm,
> But soon with savage grandeur charm,
> And raise to noblest thoughts the mind . . .
> A pleasing, tho' an awful sight.[13]

" Delightful Horrors, hail! " sings John Cunningham, after a visit to Riponden, in Yorkshire. But the topographical poets belong more to landscape gardening than to poetry.

Walpole and Gray, travelling to Italy in 1730, were properly struck with the Salvatorial landscape of the Grande Chartreuse. Walpole expressed himself in a letter to West; Gray in a Latin poem for the album of the monastery, to the *Genius Loci:*

[12] *Poems and Translations,* 1745, p. 208.
[13] 1755, pp. 19–20.

APOLLO AND THE SEASONS.

Painted by Richard Wilson and engraved by Woollett and Pouncy.

Museum of Fine Arts, Boston, Massachusetts.

Numen habet, veteresque sylvas.
. . . Nativa nam certe fluenta

Praesentiorem et conspicimus Deum
Per invias rupes, fera per juga,
Clivosque praeruptas, sonantes
Inter aquas, nemorumque noctem.

Except for the prospect from Windsor, " th' expanse below Of grove, of lawn, of mead " through which Thames " wanders . . . His silver-winding way," it is Gray's only elaborate landscape in poetry, though his prose pictures of the Lakes were among the most famous of the second half of the century.

Gilbert West shows the influence of Thomson, in his *Canto in Imitation of Spenser* (1739):

> . . . in Prospect wide
> A spacious Plain the false Enchanter show'd,
> With goodly Castles decked on every side,
> And silver Streams, that down the Champaign flow'd, . . .
> And Groves of Myrtle; and the Lamp of Day
> His orient Beams display'd withouten Cloud,
> Which lightly on the glistening Waters play,
> And tinge the Castles, Woods, and Hills with purple Ray.
> So fair a Landscape charm'd the wond'ring Knight;

and of Dyer,

> Now look, how vast a space the Eye
> Has journey'd 'thwart the ambient Sky,
> O'er grove & park & woody dale,
> Up the high hill & down the vale,
> Till we come round th' Horizon wide,
> Back to where Thames fruitful tide
> Thro' meadow, field & garden fair
> Winds its clear current.[14]

Akenside in his *Pleasures of the Imagination* (1744) had earlier than Burke a theory of the sublime and beautiful; he first enumerates " three sister-graces, whom the painter's hand, The poet's tongue confesses; the *sublime*, The *wonderful*, the *fair*," and later contrasts the tastes for the vast and wild and for harmony, grace, and beauty. Taste with him is " a discerning sense

[14] *Correspondence of Gray, Walpole, West and Ashton.* Ed. Paget-Toynbee, I, 192–194.

Of decent and sublime," and in the revision of 1772 he names God as source " of beauteous and sublime." He likes to combine the two in his Thomsonian descriptions:

> For verdant valleys and surrounding trees,
> A solitary prospect, wide and wild,
> Rush'd on my senses. 'Twas a horrid pile
> Of hills and many a shaggy forest mix'd,
> With many a sable cliff and glitt'ring stream.
> Aloft recumbent on the dusky ridge
> The brown woods wav'd . . .
> . . . Now the western sun reveal'd
> Between two parting cliffs his golden orb,
> And pour'd across the shadow of the hills,
> On rocks and floods, a yellow stream of light,
> That chear'd the solemn scene.

> . . . Mark the sable woods
> That shade sublime yon mountain's nodding brow;
> With what religious awe the solemn scene
> Commands your stop! . . .
> . . . Behold th' expanse
> Of yon gay landscape, where the silver clouds
> Flit o'er the heav'ns before the sprightly breeze;
> Now their grey cincture skirts the doubtful sun;
> Now streams of splendor, thro' their opening veil
> Effulgent, sweep from off the gilded lawn
> Th' aerial shadows.

Collins, a poet more of ear than of eye, draws but few and slight landscapes: " some cliff, to Heav'n up-pil'd," " some wild and heathy Scene," " some Ruin 'midst its dreary Dells." His one " prospect " is of

> . . . the Hut
> That from the Mountain's Side,
> Views Wilds, and swelling Floods,
> And Hamlets brown, and dim-discover'd Spires.

The second-rate poets abound in " scenes ". There is one in Lyttelton, " Of verdant meads and cultivated fields," with winding stream, and " various tufts of rising wood," castle, cottage among trees, town in middle distance, and hills on far horizon. Beattie has plenty of prospects, sunrises, sunsets, lakes, long vales, craggy cliffs; and one large and elaborate composition, enthusiastically admired by the reviewers of *The Minstrel* as being " picturesque and romantic ":

> . . . Rocks on rocks pil'd, as by magick spell
> Fenced from the north and east this savage dell . . .
> Southward a mountain rose with easy swell,
> Whose long gay groves eternal murmur made;
> And toward the western sun a streamlet fell,
> Where, through the cliffs, the eye, remote, survey'd
> Blue hills, and glittering waves, and skies in gold array'd.

The " ingenious " Dr. Brown, whose pessimistic *Estimate* " rose like a paper-kite, and charm'd the town," has suggestions of the pictorial in his *Curse of Saul* (1763): the mountain's " rock-encumber'd Head," the torrent rolling " down his steep and shaggy Side," and winding " smooth and clear, along the fertile Plain " to the distant Sea; and a Claude-like sun that " steals into the golden Deep."

The Wartons, as would be expected, show strong leanings toward the picturesque. Thomas Warton writes of " daedal landscapes." and " sunny vales," and gives one sunrise scene, a mingling of Milton, Dyer, and paintings, of " Misty streams that wind below " " Groves and castled cliffs . . . invested all in radiance clear." [15]   The *Odes* (1747) of Joseph Warton offer several examples, chiefly Salvatorial. Such is the " vast, various landscape " in the *Ode to Fancy:*

> Say, in what deep and pathless vale,
> Or on what hoary mountain's side,
> 'Midst falls of waters you reside,
> 'Midst broken rocks, a rugged scene.

The *Ode to a Gentleman upon his Travels thro' Italy* abounds in Claude-like conventional images: rivers in mazy courses, ruined domes, mossy mouldering walls, storied temples, " Parian seats of Attic art defac'd." The park scene in *New Market* (1751) is pictorial:

> Here various trees compose a chequer'd scene,
> Glowing in gay diversities of green.
> There the full stream thro' intermingling glades
> Shines a broad lake, or falls in deep cascades.

[15] *Poems on Various Subjects,* 1791, pp. 128, 210.

The Enthusiast is full of scenery and of Thomson. In contrast to the artifices of Versailles are set

> . . . some pine-topt precipice,
> Abrupt and shaggy, whence a foaming stream,
> Like Anio, tumbling, roars; or some bleak heath,
> Where straggling stands the mournful juniper,
> Or yew-tree scath'd; while in clear prospect round,
> From the grove's bosom spires emerge, and smoke
> In bluish wreaths ascends, ripe harvests wave,
> Low, lonely cottages and ruin'd tops
> Of Gothic battlements appear, and streams
> Beneath the sunbeams twinkle.

The predilection of her sex for the Salvatorial is strong in Anna Laetitia Barbauld, whose *Corsica* (1773) has cascades, "Swelling mountains, brown with solemn shade," lofty pines, spreading chestnut,

> . . . lonely scenes
> Of unquell'd nature: precipices huge,
> And tumbling torrents; trackless deserts, plains
> Fenced in with guardian rocks.

Anna Seward found Dr. Darwin's *Botanic Garden* abounding "in Claude and Salvatorial sketches"; but the reader of today is put to it to find many of them. It is of interest that Miss Seward, who, however much she seems a fool, does represent (partly for that reason) a large section of the reading public of her time, recognizes the likeness to painting. Dr. Darwin certainly is composing his scenes with conscious art:

> . . . Grey precipices, and ivy'd towers,
> Long winding meads, and intermingled bowers, . . .

> So with long gaze admiring eyes behold
> The varied landscape all its lights unfold:
> High rocks opposing o'er the stream project
> Their naked bosoms, and the beams reflect;
> Wave high in air their fringed crests of wood,
> And checker'd shadows dance upon the flood;
> Green sloping lawns construct the sidelong scene,
> And guide the sparkling rill that winds between . . .
> Dim hills behind in pomp aerial rise,
> Lift their blue tops, and melt into the skies.

William Lisle Bowles sees landscape in this same manner, — as it carries out the art gallery. He seeks by preference for his *Sonnets, written chiefly on picturesque spots* (1789), grey battlements, forsaken towers, sunset light, " romantick " vales, rocks towering dark, rivers winding wild, castles gleaming on the distant shore. William Sotheby, making a poetic-picturesque *Tour through Parts of Wales* (1794), exclaims of the " loud-echoing crags " of Melincourt,

> Not bolder views Salvator's pencil dash'd
> In Alpine wilds romantic,

and at the view from Snowdon — vast and spreading — he invokes those who aspire

> to imitate the soft aerial hue
> That shades the living scene of chaste LORAIN.

2.

The greater familiarity with painting which the author both had himself, and assumed in his audience, after the middle of the century, is reflected in the practice just illustrated of describing landscape by means of the names of the artists. An early instance is found in Christopher Smart (who seems an unlikely subject for connoisseurship, yet who plainly relished pictures) apropos of the mimic landscapes which the virtuoso thought he could see in agate — " all the living landskip of the vale " — and drags in the admired Guido Reni, in a way which arouses suspicion that the names are not much more to him than names:

> In vain thy pencil, *Claudio,* or *Poussin,*
> Or thine, immortal *Guido,* wou'd essay
> Such skill to imitate.[16]

The author of *Verses Written in London on the Approach of Spring* deals likewise with the futility of art:

> Can rich Loraine mix up the glowing paint
> Bright as Aurora? Can he form a shade
> To strike the fancy with a gloom so solemn
> As every thicket, copse, or secret grove

[16] *On the Immensity of the Supreme Being,* Second ed., 1753, p. 9.

> At twilight hour affords? Can savage Rosa
> With aught so wildly noble fill the mind,
> As where the ancient oak in the wood's depth
> . . . deserted stands
> A barren trunk, while rude winds howl around . . .
> Such scenes awake Imagination's powers
> To sacred thought; such Rosa cannot paint:
> 'Tis his alone to show the shatter'd trunk. . . .[17]

So does W. Williams, in *An Essay on Halifax* (1761):

> . . . the beauteous mass
> Ting'd with the sanguine beams of setting day,
> Gives a refulgent harmony divine,
> And far, Lorain, beyond thy mimic skill.

Daniel Bellamy, in his *Ethic Amusements* [18] describes the works of " Painting's glowing hand," which

> . . . opens some ideal plain,
> On which, in all their bloom arise
> Perennial springs of Paradise,

" Oh! for a Claude to sketch the scene! " exclaims Richard Graves, describing a maiden fallen asleep by a spring.[19] The native painters are joined with the classic masters:

> . . . I wish'd
> The skill of CLAUDE, or RUBENS, or of HIM,
> Whom now on LORANT's banks, in groves that breathe
> Enthusiasm sublime, the Sister Nymphs
> Inspire,

says John Scott in *Aimwell* (1776), after he has spent some time in describing picturesque views, adding in a note: " Mr. George Smith of Chichester, a justly celebrated Landschape Painter, and also a Poet."

The widely read letter of Dr. John Brown, on the beauties of the Lakes, with its use of the names of Claude, Salvator and Gaspar Poussin, had many echoes. Richard Cumberland in the preface of his *Odes* (1776) expresses pain that Gray was moved

---

[17] Pearch, II, 156.

[18] Among the illustrations to this work, revised by Bellamy's son in 1768, appears one which is an adaptation of a seaport of Claude.

[19] *Euphrosyne*, 1773, I, 38.

to nothing more than a prosaic description by " this enchanting display of sublime and beautiful objects," and goes on to consider and quote from Brown's letter, and in one of the odes thus praises Ullswater:

> For neither Scottish LOMOND's pride,
> Nor smooth KILLARNEY's silver tide,
> Nor aught that learned POUSSIN drew
> Or dashing ROSA flung upon my view
> Shall shake thy sovereign undisturbed right. . . .

George Cumberland, who was or attempted to be, an artist himself, says in *Lewina the Maid of Snowdon* (1793),

> Words are but faint the image to pursue,
> SALVATOR's pencil, here, had trembled too!

— but goes on with a good many lines about rocks and cataracts.[20] Miss Seward uses the painters for scenes in her mind's eye; when " Poetic Fancy's plastic rays " dart on her spirit with full force,

> Then scenes arise in intellectual hue
> Gay, soft, and warm, as Claude or Poussin drew . . .
> Or sternly if she leads the mental sight,
> Where Horror scowls, beneath incumbent night,
> With all Salvator's savage dignity
> Scowl the dark, rugged rock, and lurid sky.

And when she follows her friend Whalley's tour, she fancies him seeing

> . . . rocks as bold as savage Rosa shows,
> And dales as soft a sunny Claude has gilt.

Her own feeble landscapes are created remotely after these models. Samuel Rogers has the paintings more clearly in mind than she, when he writes in *The Pleasures of Memory* (1792):

> These noble scenes SALVATOR's soul ador'd;
> The rocky pass half hung with shaggy wood,
> And the cleft oak flung boldly o'er the flood.

[20] The *Odes* are dedicated to Romney. He had another reference in *A Poem on the Landscapes of Great Britain,* written in 1780.
> Grand as POUSSIN, to whom ev'n Nature yields,
> And great as ROSA from CALABRIAN fields.

A belated topographical poem, *Richmond Hill* (1807), is very expressive of the treatment of landscape for the fifty years preceding. The Thames at Richmond was a favourite scene, the richness of the trees, the serpentine river, and the expanse of view bearing some likeness to the Italian paintings. The vale, says the poet, is called Frascati by " travelled bards." He apostrophizes Thomson and praises Brown in familiar comparison,

> A brighter, richer landscape lies display'd
> Then ever Poussin sketch'd, or Claude pourtray'd.

3.

Poets of more truly poetic quality do not beat out this old straw. Goldsmith, who in his essays makes slighting remarks on both connoisseurs and artists, sees " Campania's plain " with no illusions, as " A weary waste expanding to the skies." And though he does " Look downward where an hundred realms appear," he gives no intimation of seeing the " Lakes, forests, cities, plains extending wide " as a pictorial landscape, though one reviewer calls his description of Italy " picturesque and harmonious." He is nearer the picturesque in

> Woods over woods, in gay theatric pride;
> While oft some temple's mould'ring tops between
> With venerable grandeur mark the scene.

" The canvas glow'd, beyond even nature warm "; but it is not the canvas (which a poverty-stricken wanderer might not easily visit in the palace where it hung) which makes him write

> There in the ruin, heedless of the dead,
> The shelter-seeking peasant builds his shed,

nor does he view that object with the eye of a picturesque tourist. The graphic details in *The Deserted Village* are such as belong to Crome rather than to Claude; and Goldsmith sees in the rich man's park chiefly " a space that many poor supplied." According to his sentiments about landscape gardening

> The country blooms — a garden and a grave.

As for Cowper, the favorite poet of Constable, he dabbled in those little landscapes in India ink, about the merits of which he had no delusions. He did not like the grandiose and vast in landscape; even such an approach to it as Eartham, Hayley's estate in Sussex, made him uneasy. The stormy sea " Hoarsely and dangerously spoke " to him of his lost treasures. When he cries for " a lodge in some vast wilderness," it means only a desire to escape the cruelty of civilization. His pictures are of " Ouse, slow winding through a level plain," " hedge-row beauties numberless," " Green balks and furrow'd lands," " Downs that almost escape th' enquiring eye," —

> Scenes must be beautiful, which, daily viewed,
> Please daily;

though he grants that " desultory man " may find pleasures for a time in " forests, or the savage rock," it is only to return more happily to " snug enclosures in the shelter'd vale." His view of the relation of nature and art, especially exotic art, is strikingly set down in *The Task*:

> . . . Strange! there should be found, . . .
> Who, satisfied with only pencil'd scenes,
> Prefer to the performance of a God
> Th' inferior wonders of an artist's hand!
> Lovely indeed the mimic works of art;
> But Nature's works far lovelier. I admire —
> None more admires — the painter's magic skill,
> Who shows me that which I shall never see,
> Conveys a distant country into mine,
> And throws Italian light on English walls:
> But imitative strokes can do no more
> Than please the eye, sweet Nature ev'ry sense.

Burns and Blake are, of course, free from the artificial conception of landscape. Crabbe reproduces what is before his eyes, with the fidelity of a Dutch artist. In one of his last poems, *Selford Hall, or The Pictures*, he criticizes Salvator and Claude through the words of an unsophisticated country boy, visiting a grand house on an errand, and taken to the picture gallery. " But is this Nature? " is his exclamation at a scene of banditti, showing " rage, revenge, remorse, disdain, despair." " Corrupted Nature," says his guide;

She then displayed her knowledge. — "That, my dear,
Is called a Titian, this a Guido here,
And yon a Claude — you see that lovely light,
So soft and solemn, neither day nor night."

"Yes!" quoth the Boy, and "there is just the breeze,
That curls the water, and that fans the trees;
The ships that anchor in that pleasant bay
All look so safe and quiet. — Claude, you say?"

With Coleridge and Wordsworth we escape entirely from the conventional landscape forms; though in spite of their freedom from the Italian sway, it is clear that their poems are not wholly new and spontaneous growths in poetry, but connected with Thomson and Dyer, back in a long line of mediocre topographers, and observers of nature through the medium of art. Even Wordsworth did not escape wholly the obsession of Salvator in wild scenes. "William says that whatever Salvator might desire could there be found," says Dorothy, after describing to Coleridge the shattered tree, waterfall, and rocks of "a little slip of the river above Rydal."

VI

THE CREATION OF ITALIAN LANDSCAPE IN ENGLAND

The creation of beautiful landscape scenes in nature, with fields and hills, woods and water, for canvas, is an art peculiarly British in origin,[1] and of the eighteenth century in date. Of this their new art the British were aggressively vain, and looked with contempt upon Versailles and the villas of Italy. " It is well known to all Europe," says the *Critical Review,* apropos of the Count de Girardin's *Essay* (1783), " that the English were the inventors of the modern art of gardening. They have suffered all the scandal and ridicule which is the usual lot of discoverers; they have been considered as wild and visionary innovators, and now begin only to reap the reward. Till within these few years, the French have been their chief opponents . . . but . . . all those who wish, in their gardens, to realize the conceptions of the great landscape painters, imitate the English."[2] Indeed, the continent, about 1770, began to adopt widely the English, or as they sometimes called it, to the resentment of the English, the Anglo-Chinese fashion; and works in French and Italian were added to the copious literature of landscape gardening. So abundant is that literature, that a survey of the development of gardening in the eighteenth century is quite complicated enough without the additional confusion which arises from the survival of old modes alongside the new, according to the culture and sophistication of the gardener.

I

Just after the Restoration the influence of Versailles was predominant. French gardeners were employed in the royal

[1] " Nous appelons les jardins de l'ordre pictoresque *jardins anglais,* parce que les Anglais sont les premiers qui en adoptèrent le goût." M. Curten, aîné, *Essai sur les Jardins,* Paris, 1807.

[2] LVI, 159.

gardens, and if Le Nôtre himself did not accept the invitation of Charles II, some of his pupils certainly came over to direct the work at St. James' Park and Hampton Court, and at many a noble seat. The books on gardening published in the seventeenth century — and there were many — show that the interest was largely practical, and never picturesque. Evelyn does at times express pleasure in extended prospects; the chief beauty of Wilton for him " is its being so neere the downes and the noble plaines," and he admires Cliefden: " The grotts in the chalky rocks are pretty; 'tis a romantic object, and the place altogether answers the most poetical description that can be made of solitude, precipice, prospect, or whatever can contribute to a thing very like their imagination." He thinks the situation " somewhat like Frascati to its front, and on the platform a circular view to the utmost edge of the horizon, which with the serpentining of the Thames is admirable." But Evelyn's idea of a garden was really architectural and not pictorial; he dealt constantly with hedges. Sir William Temple also considered a garden as an enclosure, not too large. " I think from Five or Four, to Seven or Eight Acres, is as much as any Gentleman need design." What would he have said to Holkham and Stowe, with their eight hundreds!

Mistress Celia Fiennes chronicles gardens as they were under William and Mary. The Dutch taste then prevailing emphasized the artificiality of the French, often substituting grotesqueness for grandeur, especially by increasing the number of quaint water toys, and exaggerating the topiary work. Such things Celia Fiennes enjoys, — weeping statues, dripping urns, " cutt Trees "; and she enumerates with naïve delight the straight-cut rides and vistos, shaded alleys, grass and gravel walks, canals, fountains, statues, hedges, palisades, and iron gates. Walls and hedges were essential parts of gardens; only the open fences, or gratings in the gates, looking out into the adjoining country, marked the beginning of the new and more open style.

Shaftesbury slightly hints the coming reaction against formality. " I shall no longer resist the Passion growing in me for Things of a *natural* kind; where neither Art, nor the *Conceit* or Caprice of Man has spoiled that genuine Order, by breaking

PLAN FOR A GARDEN.

From *Systema Horti-Culturae,* by J. Woolridge, 1688.

in upon that *primitive State.*] Even the rude Rocks, the mossy Caverns, the irregular unwrought *Grotto's,* and broken Falls of Water, with all the horrid Graces of the Wilderness it-self, as representing NATURE more, will be the more engaging, and appear with a Magnificence beyond the formal Mockery of Princely Gardens." [3]   He speaks lovingly, however, of the finer Italian gardens, " with all those symmetries that silently express such order, peace and sweetness." [4]]

A translation of Rapin's Latin poem on gardens, made by James Gardiner, son of the Bishop of Lincoln, and published by Lintot in 1706, and again in 1718, with handsome plates in the old taste engraved by Kirkall, appeals to the older taste exclusively.   As one of the complimentary poems prefacing the work observes,

> But Nature's Charms are in Confusion sown,
> And want of Order marks 'em for her own.

Rapin commends well-ranged trees (" for Order is of Use "), elm-tree avenues, walks met in a center; but deprecates too elaborate cutting and twisting of paths.[5]   His account of water-toys gives a good idea of the taste from which Shaftesbury was revolting:

> Here a *Chimaera* opens wide her Jaws,
> And from her gaping Mouth a Torrent throws;
> In her wide throat the crowding Waters rise
> And foaming issue forth with horrid Noise. . . .
> There from a Dragon whirling round in Haste,
> On the Spectators gushing Streams are cast;
> Then with his Arms and watching of his Game,
> A brazen Huntsman stands and takes his Aim,
> To kill the Prey, but shoots a harmless Stream;
> A pleasing Cheat, at which the wondring Rout,
> At once with Laughter and Applauses shout.[6]

---

[3] *Char.,* II, 393–394.

[4] *Life,* ed. Rand, p. 246.

[5] He shows gallantry:
> If more extended Walks run round the Plain,
> Light Chairs should bear in State the Female Train;
> Yet trusting to their Feet, the younger Fair,
> Walk the long Circuit, and despise the Chair.

[6] To permit these practical jokes in gardening to be played without injury to fashionable garments, servants were employed as the victims to be splashed.

2

The most influential early advocate of the free and open prospect, and escape from the artificial in gardening, was Addison. His dream of Liberty, in 1710 (*Tatler*, No. 161), implies the landscape of the Roman painters, in its amphitheatre-like plain, and meandering river, unincumbered by fences and inclosures, and so the more delightful. In the same vein, praising freedom and suggesting Claude, is the *Spectator* (No. 412) of two years later:

Such are the Prospects of an open Champian Country, a vast uncultivated Desart, of huge Heaps of Mountains, high Rocks and Precipices, or a wide Expanse of Waters, where we are not struck with the Novelty or Beauty of the Sight, but with that rude kind of Magnificence which appears in many of these stupendous Works of Nature. Our Imagination loves to be filled with an Object, or to graspe at any thing that is too big for its Capacity. . . . The Mind of Man naturally hates everything that looks like Restraint upon it, and is apt to fancy it self under a sort of Confinement, when the Sight is pent up in a narrow Compass, or shortned on every Side by the Neighbourhood of Walls or Mountains. On the contrary, a spacious Horison is an Image of Liberty, where the Eye has Room to range abroad, to expatiate at large in the Immensity of its Views, and to lose it self amidst the Variety of Objects that offer themselves to its Observation. Such wide and undetermined Prospects are pleasing to the Fancy, as the Speculations of Eternity or Infinitude are to the Understanding. But if there be a Beauty or Uncommonness joyned with this Grandeur, as in a troubled Ocean, . . . or a spacious Landskip cut out into Rivers, Woods, Rocks, and Meadows, the Pleasure still grows upon us.

And a few days later (No. 414), he again encourages revolt against Le Nôtre and the Dutch. "The Beauties of the most stately Garden or Palace lie in a narrow Compass; the Imagination immediately runs them over, and requires something else to gratifie her; but in the wide Fields of Nature, the Sight wanders up and down without Confinement, and is fed with an infinite variety of Images." Though the painted landscapes seem unmistakably to lie behind his images, he alludes to them only once: "We find the Works of Nature still more pleasing the more they resemble those of Art. . . . We are pleased as well with comparing their Beauties, as with surveying them, and can represent them to our Minds, either as Copies or Originals. Hence it is that we take Delight in a Prospect which is well laid out, and diversified with Fields and Meadows, Woods and Rivers." The gardens of France and Italy he praises above those of England, because they are larger, and make more use of their neighbouring woodland, — a reason which the English thirty years later must have found puzzling. " Why may not a whole Estate be thrown into a kind of Garden by frequent Plantations? " he asks. " A Man might make a pretty Landskip of his own Possessions." A few months later he writes the charming paper (No. 477) on the irregular garden with " the little wandering rill," and compares the parterre makers to sonneteers, the contrivers of treillages and cascades [7] to romance writers, London and Wise to heroic poets; and the irregular garden described is, he says, " altogether after the *Pindarick* manner." To our minds, Addison's own gardening at Bilton was rather of the heroic style than the Pindaric; and so was Prior's at Down.

Addison's hint in 1712 about the " Modellers of Gardens " who had an interest in disposing of their evergreens, and his preference of a tree " in all its luxuriancy and diffusion of boughs and branches " to the cones, globes, and pyramids of London and Wise — " the pedantry of vegetation," as Thomas Warton described it [8] — was developed the next year by Pope in *The Guardian*. Such items in his catalogue as " Adam and Eve a little shattered by the fall of the Tree of Knowledge in the great storm. Eve and the Serpent very flourishing," " A Quickset Hog shot up into a Porcupine by being forgot a week in rainy weather," " A Lavendar Pig, with Sage growing in his belly," sent topiary work out of fashion; the death of London, its chief creator, that same year, doubtless contributed to its passing.

Bridgeman, " the next fashionable designer of gardens," as Walpole calls him, " enlarged his plans, disdained to make every division tally to its opposite; and though he still adhered much to straight walks with high clipped hedges, they were only his great lines; the rest he diversified by wilderness, and with loose groves of oak. . . . As his reformation gained footing, he ventured farther, and in the royal garden at Richmond, dared to

---

[7] He means the cascades over masonry, flights of stairs, etc.
[8] In his edition of Milton's *minor poems*, 1785, p. 70.

introduce cultivated fields, and even morsels of a forest appearance." Bridgeman's introduction of the ha-ha (so called to express the surprise of finding one's way checked by an obstacle unforeseen) was the "capital stroke" leading to the destruction of walls. By means of this device (of military and French origin) the outlying park, and even pastures and cultivated fields could be included in the general design. "What adds to the bewty of this garden," writes a traveller in 1724, "is, that it is bounded by no walls, but a Ha-hah, which leaves you the sight of a beautiful country, and makes you ignorant how far the high planted walks extend." "The walks are terminated by Ha-hah's," says another, writing of Hall Barn as Waller's grandson had improved it, "over which you see a fine country, and variety of prospects every time you come to the extremity of the close winding walks that shut out the sun." [9] Clearly the ha-ha was in 1724 still a novelty, and used chiefly at the ends of walks. A letter of the Duchess of Queensberry in 1731 implies openness of landscape, but no pleasure in uneven contour: "Did you ever see Brussels? The whole country round about it is like the best-natured ground that ever was seen, laid out by a Bridgeman some years ago. . . . Every blade of grass grows exactly to my mind."

The influence of Addison and Pope is perceptible in the works on gardening by Stephen Switzer and Batty Langley. Though Switzer received his training from London and Wise, he devoted a large section of his *Ichnographica Rustica* to "Rural and Extensive Gardening." In the Proemium to his second edition (1743) he says: "The Hours which many of the *Virtuoso's* in Gardening expended in observing the Colours of a *Tulip* . . . were better employed in open and extensive Views, with the Regularity of this Plantation, and the Wildness of another, in the sweet Meanders and precipitate Falls of a River, or the Rising of Hills or Promontories on each Side. . . . In this Way of Thinking I was encouraged by some of the greatest Genius's of the Times when these Tracts were wrote." A note explains that he means " The Authors of the *Spectator's, Tatlers,* and *Guardians*." He quotes approvingly Pope's lines, " Grove

[9] Mrs. Cecil, *History of Gardening in England*, ed. 1910, pp. 224, 232. Manuscript letters, quoted.

Artificial Ruins " after the old Roman manner."
From *New Principles of Gardening,* by Batty Langley, 1728.

nods at grove," etc. The *New Principles of Gardening,* by Batty Langley, " of Twickenham " (1728) describes, with many illustrative plates, " the Laying out and Planting Parterres, Groves, Wildernesses, Labyrinths, Avenues and Parks. . . . After a more Grand and Rural Manner than has been done before." There is nothing, he says, " more *Shocking* than a *stiff, regular* Garden." He gives numerous designs, obviously extracted from the painters, for " *Ruins of Buildings,* after the *old Roman manner,* to terminate such walks that end in *disagreeable objects;* which Ruins may either be *painted upon canvas,* or actually built in that Manner with Brick, and cover'd with *Plaistering* in Imitation of Stone." [10]

Pope influenced picturesque gardening through his poems, through his interest in gardens, and through his connection with Kent. " All gardening is landscape painting," he said. " You may distance things by darkening them, and by narrowing . . . towards the end, in the same manner as they do in painting." [11] Other evidence that he viewed gardening in a definitely pictorial light is the *Epistle* to Burlington (1731) *Of Taste:*

> Consult the *Genius* of the *Place* in all,
> That tells the Waters or to rise or fall,
> Or helps th' ambitious Hill the Heav'ns to scale,
> Or scoops in circling Theatres the Vale,
> Calls in the Country, catches opening Glades,
> Joins willing Woods, and varies Shades from Shades.
> Now breaks, or now directs th' intending Lines;
> *Paints* as you plant, and as you work *Designs.*

But the most influential passage and the most quoted, was probably that on the old regularity:

> On ev'ry Side you look, behold the Wall!
> No pleasing Intricacies intervene,
> No artful Wildness to perplex the Scene:
> Grove nods at Grove, each Ally has a brother,
> And half the Platform just reflects the other.

[10] Something like this — painted plaster walls giving the illusion of extended buildings — was employed in Italian gardening, and in the English gardens of Evelyn's time. " What is the vista or perspective? " says Shaftesbury, using the garden figuratively in *The Beautiful;* " a few sticks, a daubed wall, a cheat."

[11] Spence's *Anecdotes,* 1820, p. 144.

Yet the plan of his own garden seems to us to show slight trace of artful wildness or pleasing intricacies, and if grove does not nod at grove, mound faces mound.[12] However, it had, judging by Walpole's report, a picturesque effect: " A little bit of ground of five acres, enclosed with three lanes, and seeing nothing. Pope had twisted and twirled and rhymed and harmonized this, till it appeared two or three sweet little lawns opening and opening beyond one another, and the whole surrounded with thick impenetrable woods." Joseph Warton also is warmly appreciative of Pope's skill in impressing " such a variety of scenery on a spot of five acres," and wonders whether Rousham, which Kent laid out for General Dormer, had not Pope's garden for its model. His grotto, justified as an underground passage from house to garden, served a pictorial purpose, according to Pope's own account, by its use as *camera obscura,* and by the views which its entrances framed.[13]

Except as Salvator's natural arches and rocky caves may have affected its popularity, the grotto had little to do with Italian landscape, but much with that view of gardens so general in that century, as places for escape from facts into fiction, pastoral and Arcadian; which was also the prime motive in the copying of Italian pictures in English grounds.

[12] *A Plan of Mr. Pope's Garden . . .* by J. Serle his Gardener, 1745.

[13] A contemporary print shows this last very well. Reproduced in *Mr. Pope, His Life and Times,* by George Paston (Emily Symonds), 1909, II, 344. The grotto deserves a special word. Borrowed from the continent, where its purpose was coolness and shade, it became a favourite toy with the English. We hear of it from Evelyn. It afforded precious opportunities for moralizing, as Aaron Hill's account of his own extraordinary accumulation of grottos shows. (*Works,* 1753, I, 199–210.) He had Grottos of Power, Riches, Honour, Learning, a Cave of Content, a Temple of Happiness, a Hovel of Poverty, a Vault of Despair, if we may believe him: all painted, of course, with appropriate images. The grotto continued long in favour; Farington seriously describes one in 1793, — the Duke of Newcastle's, which took a man and his son five years to complete (*Diary,* I, 10). Pope's account shows the amazing decorations in vogue. Mrs. Delany's correspondence has many passages about collecting shells, bits of stone, etc., for adorning grots. Large sums of money were expended on them, as well as incalculable time; which for places to be damp in, in England, is hard to comprehend today.

3

No doubt the adoption of these Italian patterns would not have been so sweeping but for the appearance of William Kent, unsuccessful artist on canvas, infected with a passion for Italy, delighted with this new way of creating the landscapes which his pencil would not achieve, and associated with leaders of taste as devoted as he to the charms of Italy. Kent, one-time apprentice to a coach-painter at York, got the interest of some gentlemen who paid his way to Italy in 1710; there he met with Coke, future Earl of Leicester, and Burlington, and was their companion and protégé while they collected works of art and designs of architecture. On his return to England in 1719, or possibly a year or so earlier, he had rooms at Burlington's house, and made the acquaintance of Pope, who contributed to form his taste, says Walpole, and whose ideas at Twickenham he is said to have borrowed for Carlton House and Rousham. He was soon at work for Leicester on the eight hundred acres and the Palladian palace at Holkham. He became dictator of design in everything, from palaces to petticoats, but especially favoured for furniture and grounds.[14] Thanks largely to him and to his noble patrons, improvement of grounds was emphatically the mode. Bramston's *Man of Taste* (1733) includes it in his requisites:

> I'll have my Gardens in the fashion too,
> For what is beautiful that is not new?
> Does it not merit the beholder's praise,
> What's high to sink, and what is low to raise?
> Slopes shall extend where once a green-house stood,
> And in my horse-pond I will plant a wood.

[14] " So impetuous was the fashion that two great ladies prevailed on him to make the designs for their birthday gowns. The one he dressed in a petticoat decorated with columns of the five orders; the other like a bronze, in a copper-coloured satin with ornaments of gold." — *Anecdotes of Painting*.

Kent as royal painter was the object of some ridicule. Chesterfield made this epigram:

As to Apelles Ammon's son	Equal your envied wonders, save
Would only deign to sit,	This difference we see —
So to thy pencil, Kent, alone	One would no other painter have,
Will Brunswick's form submit.	No other would have thee.

Sir Thomas Robinson tells the Earl of Carlisle in 1734 that " a general alteration of some of the most considerable gardens in the kingdom is begun, after Mr. Kent's notions of gardening, viz. to lay them out, and work without level or line; it has the appearance of beautiful nature. The celebrated gardens of Clarmont, Chiswick and Stow are now full of labourers." [15] In 1743 Walpole writes: " Kent is now so fashionable that, like Addison's Liberty, he

> Can make bleak rocks and barren mountains smile."

The ha-ha of Bridgeman was laid hold of by Kent to create the extended prospects in which the new fashion delighted. Walpole speaks with rapture of his use of it, and of his painter-like conception of gardening:

At the moment of its creation appeared Kent, painter enough to taste the charms of landscape, bold and opinionative enough to dare to dictate, and born with a genius to strike out a great system from the twilight of imperfect essays. He leaped the fence, and saw all nature was a garden. He felt the delicious contrast of hill and valley, changing imperceptibly into each other, tasted the beauty of the gentle swell, or concave scoop, and remarked how loose groves crowned an easy eminence with happy ornament, and while they called in the distant view between their graceful stems, removed and extended the perspective by delusive comparison.

In all this the imitation of Claude and Gaspar is perfectly evident, and the art of the landscape painter in what follows: " The great principles on which he worked were perspective, and light and shade. Groupes of trees broke too uniform or too extensive a lawn; evergreens and woods were opposed to the glare of the champain; and where the view was less fortunate, or so much exposed as to be beheld at once, he blotted out some part by thick shades, to divide it into variety, or to make the richest scene more enchanting by reserving it to a farther advance of the spectator's step. Thus selecting favourite objects, and veiling deformities, . . . sometimes allowing the rudest waste to add its foil to the richest theatre, he realised the compositions of the greatest masters in painting. Where objects were wanting to animate his horizon, his taste as an architect

[15] H. Avery Tipping, *English Homes*, Period V, I, xxi.

THE TEMPLE OF ANCIENT VIRTUE, AT STOWE.

"Th' applauded work of Kent's judicious hands."

could bestow immediate termination. His buildings, his seats, his temples, were more the works of his pencil than of his compasses." " Kent's method of embellishing a field is admirable," says Lord Kames in *Elements of Criticism* (1762), " which is, to replenish it with beautiful objects, natural and artificial, disposed as they ought to be upon canvas in paintings."

We know, from the prints published by Arthur Pond in 1744, that Kent had in his collection examples of Italian landscape by Salvator and by Gaspar, at least, if no more. He was laughed at for carrying his imitations of painting so far as to insert dead trees at Kensington and Carlton Gardens, — evidently a Salvatorial inspiration which might have come from the example in his own collection; but his Italian temples and his management of water for picturesque effect were admired without reservation. Brown's enemy in the *Westminster Magazine* (1780) says that where Kent's designs have escaped Brown's hand " there is an easy grandeur which is at once striking and delightful." Kent's ideas were " but rarely great," says Walpole years after Kent's death, when the more magnificent improvements of Brown had become familiar; and the overwhelming domination of the serpentine so much derided by satirists seems to have been largely the responsibility of Kent, whose ruling principle was that " nature abhors a straight line." But at his best he seemed Claudian to his contemporaries. Walpole recalls at Stanstead, seat of the Earl of Halifax, a noble green avenue cut through woods; " the very extensive lawns at that seat, richly enclosed by venerable beech woods, and chequered by single beeches of vast size, particularly when you stand in the portico of the temple and survey the landskip that wastes itself in rivers of broken sea, recall such exact pictures of Claude Lorrain that it is difficult to conceive that he did not paint them from this very spot."

Of all his works Holkham was, according to Walpole, Kent's favourite; the admirers of Brown found its vistas magnificent, but formal. It inspired Robert Potter to write *Holkham: A Poem* (1759), which finds pen and pencil fail in describing its beauties:

> Can the verse paint like Nature? Can the power
> That wakes to life free Fancy's imag'd store.

Boast charms like her's? Or the creative hand
In blended tints such beauteous scenes command,
Tho' learned Poussin gives each grace to flow,
And bright Lorrain's ethereal colours glow?

The temples which he scattered with a liberal hand counted
for much in the impression of Italian scenery which the parks
designed by him conveyed. Stowe (where Vanbrugh had been
before him in buildings) showed notable examples, " The applauded Work of Kent's judicious Hands." [16]

O, how charming the walks to my fancy appear,
What a number of temples and grottos are here! [17]

was the sentiment of most visitors, at least before 1770. " Fields
where Art and Nature join," [18] " Where through one nobly simple
scheme Ten thousand varying beauties please "; [19]

Expence and Vanbrugh, vanity and show
May build a Blenheim, but not make a Stowe.

Walpole, visiting Stowe in 1770, at the entertainment given
by Lord Temple for the Princess Amelia, describes the view
through the arch erected in her honour, and looking toward
Kent's Palladian bridge, as " the most enchanting of all picturesque scenes. . . . You come upon it on a sudden, and
are startled with delight on looking through it; you at once see,
through a glade, the river winding at the bottom; from which
a thicket rises, arched over with trees, but opened and dis-
covering a hillock full of hay-cocks, beyond which in front
is the Palladian bridge; and again, over that, a larger hill,
crowned with the castle. It is a tall landscape, framed by
the arch, and the over-bowering trees, and comprehending more
beauties of light, shade and buildings than any picture of Albano's I ever saw." " If Stow had but half so many buildings
as it has," he had said before, " there would be too many;
but that profusion, that glut, enriches, makes it look like a fine
landscape of Albano's : one figures oneself in Tempe or Daphne."
Esher was Gray's favorite,

[16] Bell's *Fugitive Poetry*, II, 94. (Thomas Lisle.)
[17] *Stowe* . . . [By George Beckham], 1756.
[18] Ogilvie, *Poems*, 1762, p. 115.
[19] *An Ode*, Dodsley, II, 217.

The bowers, the temples and the groves
That Kent has planned and Pelham loves . . .
There (worthy ancient Greece or Rome)
Fair temples, opening to the sight,
Surprise each turn with new delight.[20]

" The scenes transporting, the trees, lawns, concaves, all in the perfection in which the ghost of Kent would joy to see them," says Walpole in 1765. Euston he found good twenty years before, " because Kent has a most absolute disposition of it," though he objected to the clumps of trees on so vast a stretch of lawn, as making it look " like a ten of spades." Rousham was, of all Kent's designs, Walpole's favourite.

Burlington, Leicester, Pelham, Bathurst, Temple, were leaders in a fashion which all gentlemen of landed property felt it incumbent on them to follow. " Every Man now," says *Common Sense* in 1739, " be his fortune what it will, is to be *doing something at his Place,* as the fashionable Phrase is; and you hardly meet with any Body, who, after the first Compliments, does not inform you, that he is *in Mortar* and *moving of Earth;* the modest terms for Building and Gardening. *One large Room,* a *Serpentine River,* and a *Wood,* are become the most absolute Necessaries of Life, without which a Gentleman of the smallest Fortune thinks he makes no Figure in his Country." Samuel Johnson refers to the fashion in *London* (1738):

There mightst thou find some elegant retreat,
Some hireling senator's deserted seat;
And stretch thy prospect o'er the smiling land . . .
Direct thy rivulet, and twine thy bowers.

Savage, addressing Frederick, Prince of Wales, in 1737, pursues the theme in his epistle *Of Public Spirit in regard to Public Works.* He speaks pictorially:

Up yon green slope a length of terrace lies,
Whence gradual landscapes fade, in distant skies . . .
Urns, obelisks, fanes, statues, intervene,
Now centre, now commence, or end the scene.

[20] Bell's *Fugitive Poetry*, II, 110, 113. (John Dalton.)

4

References to gardening and improvements are increasingly numerous; but only those showing the treatment of the garden as a picture-gallery concern us. *An Essay on Harmony, as it relates chiefly to Situation, and Buildings* (1739) shows Thomson very much deferred to as an authority on landscape; gardening is treated as both poetical and pictorial. Of Windsor the author says: " The Beauties are such, which more nearly approach to Solitude, and retirement; they are still images of Picteresque Romance, of silent Retreats, *rural,* and poetical." The Thames at Cliefden " spreads and divides itself into a Multitude of pleasing Forms, sufficient to afford many fine Picteresque Views, rather in Appearance romantick, than real." And realizing that his prose account is faint and languid, he quotes Thomson (" Young Day pours in apace ") as more nearly adequate.[21]

Kent's use of meadows and woods made a rural style manageable, and so evoked the *ferme ornée,* of which Wooburn Farm was the first notable example, and its designer and owner, Philip Southcote, the first of numerous gentlemen landscape gardeners to win fame, and, as Stephen Duck wrote, to fix the rule of taste:

> I see his lofty oaks advance their heads;
> I see the slope rejoice beneath their shades;
> The temple that adorns the rising brow,
> The lovely lawn-embracing stream below.[22]

A description published, with accompanying print, in 1761, speaks of one wide prospect " over a large extent of meadow, bounded by the river Thames, which winds through the fertile country in the most charming manner. . . . Within this elegant perspective are also ten or twelve villages, and several fine houses; and the bridge at Chertsey appears like a principal object." [23]

The Leasowes and Hagley were accounted *fermes ornées.*

[21] Reprinted in the *Oxford Magazine,* 1772, IX, 6–11.
[22] *Caesar's Camp,* 1755, p. 22.
[23] *Royal Magazine,* IV, 194. The print is also in the *Oxford Magazine,* 1772.

To those who sought rural " simplicity," the complicated efforts of Shenstone at the Leasowes were inspiring. Graves says that Shenstone got his ideas for grounds from Mickleton, in Gloucestershire, the owner of which in turn got his from Warleis, in Essex, in 1735. At any rate, Shenstone, who began work soon after 1745, was the most widely known of gentlemen amateurs in landscape designing. He spread the idea of making pictures in landscape, and erecting seats and summer-houses to ensure their being observed. He also, though Stowe had already made it familiar, struck the gently elegiac note by means of inscriptions; a literary treatment of the garden enormously popular later on with the French. Shenstone was famous for his skill in arranging gradations of foliage, size of trees, and buildings, to lengthen vistas;[24] so that he might well have been vexed at the Lytteltons (though Graves says he was not) for their introduction of visitors at the wrong end of a walk, as Johnson intimates. Dodsley's description of the Leasowes is like that of a picture gallery in its references to scenes, landscapes, and pictures viewed at various points of vantage. Hugh Miller, visiting the grounds (fallen into cureless ruin) in 1840, refers to Shenstone's making a picture gallery of his property. " In pursuance of our present taste in gardening," wrote Shenstone, " every good painter of landscape seems to me the most proper designer." " Objects should be less calculated to strike the immediate eye, than the judgment, or well-formed imagination, as in painting." He divided " garden-scenes " into the sublime, the beautiful, and the melancholy, or pensive; but though each scene was of a single tone, it " should contain enough variety to form a picture upon canvas."

His neighbour Lyttelton with the help of his cousin Pitt developed Hagley in the picturesque style. " You might draw, but I cannot describe the enchanting scenes of this park," wrote Walpole to Bentley in 1753. " Such lawns, such wood, rills, cascades, and a thickness of verdure quite to the summit of the hill and surmounting such a vale . . . extending quite to the Black Mountain in Wales, that I quite forgot my favourite

[24] *Cf.* Pope: " All the rules of gardening are reducible to three heads: — the contrasts, the management of surprises, and the concealment of bounds "; the *contrasts* meaning " the disposition of the lights and shades." Spence, p. 260.

Thames. . . . Then there is such a scene of a small lake with cascades falling down such a Parnassus! with a circular temple on the distant eminence, . . . and there is a hermitage, so exactly like those in Sadeler's prints, on the brow of a shady mountain . . . and there is such a pretty well under a wood, like the Samaritan woman's in a picture of Nicolo Poussin."

The most famous " object " at Hagley was the Gothic ruin, designed for Lyttelton by his friend Sanderson Miller, and still standing. " It has the true rust of the Barons' Wars," says the ardent Walpole. The ridicule directed against the artificial ruins in eighteenth century gardening fails to take account of the main intention of their designers: that they should supply a necessary part of the picture which was being painted in landscape. Shenstone is thinking of this when he writes of the ruin at Hagley, " They are going to build a castle in the park around the lodge, which, if well executed, will have a fine effect."

The ruin was both an " object " and a symbol, as were the classic ruins in Claude's pictures. This mixed view is manifest in a contemporary account of " this becoming object, " this eligible ruin," which adds much dignity to the scene, " and is valuable " not merely as an object only, to give a livelier consequence to the landscape, but for use; being a lodge for the keeper of the park. . . . To keep the whole design in its purity, to wipe away any suspicion of its being any otherwise than a real ruin, the large and mossy stones which have seemingly tumbled down from the tottering and ruinous wall are suffered to lie about the different parts of the building in the utmost confusion . . . while to throw a deeper solemnity over it . . . ivy is encouraged to climb about the walls and turrets." [25] Parts of this structure were genuine; the window-frames came from the ruined abbey of Halesowen.[26]

No wonder the elderly antiquary in Richard Graves' *The Spiritual Quixote* is concerned lest the artificial ruins introduce serious confusion in his study. The subject of ruins in gardens is elaborately discussed in *A Dialogue on Stowe* (1748). " Has not that Ruin a good Effect?" asks Callophilus. " The Sound of the Cascade, the Shrubs half-concealing the ragged view, and

[25] Joseph Heeley, *Letters on the Beauties of Hagley, Envil, and the Leasowes*, 1777, I, 173–175.
[26] Wyndham, *Chronicles of the Eighteenth Century*, 1924, I 179.

Inuentéta a Piero â Stéfano ŝtolan à.f. Zulano

LANDSCAPE ENGRAVED AFTER PAUL BRIL BY JOHANNES SADELER.

those dancing Fawns and Satyrs, I assure you, raise very roman-   (LOCKE)
tick Ideas in my Head." His friend Polypthon agrees: "There
is something so vastly Picturesque, and pleasing to the Imagination in such Objects, that they are a great Addition to any
Landskip." But he wonders why "we are more taken with Prospects of this ruinous kind, than with Views of Plenty and Prosperity?" His friend explains that there is a difference between
moral and imaginative pleasures; the latter may be given by a
rock "beautifully set off with Light and Shade, and garnished
with flourishing Bushes," and concludes, "Yon old Hermitage
gives us this sort of Pleasure; it is of the romantick kind."
Lord Kames, also, views these "objects" as sources of aesthetic
enjoyment: "A ruin, affording a sort of melancholy pleasure,
ought not to be seen from a flower-parterre; but to pass from an
exhilarating object to a ruin has a fine effect."

Sanderson Miller was the chief designer of ruins. By his castle
at Hagley he had "got everlasting fame," a friend tells him,
"so that I hear talk of nothing else."[27] Even Italian Holkham,
Lyttelton wrote him, "wants the view of Gothick Castle to
make it compleat, of which himself is so sensible that he had
desired me to make interest with you to come and give
him a Plan." Pitt (who talks of "that great Landskip Painter,
the Sun") calls upon Miller's imagination "for a very considerable Gothick Object which is to stand in a very fine situation on the hills near Bath," in the grounds of Allen. Lord
Chancellor Hardwicke has a mind for one. "Mearly the walls
and semblance of an old castle to make an object from the house.
. . . As the back will be immediately closed by the wood,
there is no regard to it, nor to the left side, but only to the front
and right side. . . . He would have no staircase nor leads
in any of the towers, but mearly the walls so built as to have
the appearance of a ruined castle." Sir William Chambers
introduced a Roman ruin — a triumphal arch — among the
Chinese adornments of Kew. The introduction of the generally
Gothic ruins [28] seems alien to Italian landscape; but the hint of
mingling classic and mediaeval came from Claude, if they needed
it. And the importance of ruins in pictures was certainly learned

---

[27] *Correspondence*, p. 135. (Written about 1748.)

[28] A volume containing designs for many ruins, generally with false fronts,

from Claude; indeed those buildings, as a critic of painting remarks, "are become in a manner naturalised to the trees and woods." [29]

> The broken arch,
> Or mouldering wall, well taught to counterfeit
> The waste of time, to solemn thoughts excite,
> And crown with graceful pomp the shaggy hill.

Thus in *Edgehill* Shenstone's friend Jago praises Miller's constructions. The poem is "a number of distinct scenes, corresponding to the different times of day, each forming an entire picture, and containing its due proportion of objects and colouring." Richard Jago was himself a gardener of his small plot, and his poem is made up of descriptions of the neighbouring seats and their improvements, with the conventional formula for landscape,

> . . . intermixture sweet
> Of lawns and groves, of open and retired,
> Vales, farms, towns, villas, castles, distant spires,
> And hills on hills, with ambient clouds enrob'd,
> In long succession court the lab'ring sight,
> Lost in the bright confusion.

He follows his friend Shenstone in assuming that " to plan the rural seat " is to copy " the well-form'd picture and correct design," and his favourite landscape involves a champaign country opening to the south, encircled by hills and woods, and with " chaste dome And fair rotunda " placed on " the swelling mount."

Richard Graves, another and more intimate friend of Shenstone, is a satirist of the gardeners. His best satire is his novel, *Columella*; but his early poem, *Love of Order,* is a revolt against excesses in irregularity. He ridicules the designers in miniature of grand and picturesque effects:

> Though P—tt in his Arcadian Views,
> Fair Beauty's waving line pursues;
> And, sketching with a Master's skill
> Contrasts each grove and rising hill;
> And, from variety of charms,

---

and intended to serve as cow-sheds, observation towers, etc., is Charles Middleton's *Decoration of Parks and Gardens,* [1800].

[29] *Town and Country Magazine,* XV, 527. (1783).

> With one grand *whole* our fancy warms;
> Yet let not us inferior folks
> Expose ourselves to great men's jokes,
> But *usefully* our ground dispose,
> By planting cabbages in rows.

The gardener's task he compares with the painter's:

> Discordant objects taught to join,
> Now form, now break, the varying line;
> From well-rang'd lights one mass compose,
> Till with full strength the landskip glows.

And he sees landscape in terms of picture:

> Amidst these circling woods, in chastest style,
> How sweetly rises yon majestic pile!
> The silver lake, from its meand'ring tides,
> Reflects each object which adorns its sides.
> The gently-rising slopes, the opening glades,
> The varied scenes of mingled lights and shades,
> A landscape form, which Claude well-pleas'd might view,
> Tho' none but Nature's pencil ever drew.[30]

Another poet influenced by Shenstone was Dodsley; the second part of his *Agriculture* has to do with landscape gardening:

> Genius of gardens! nature's fairest child!
> Thou who, inspir'd by the directing mind
> Of Heav'n didst plant the scenes of Paradise!
> Welcome, at length, thrice welcome, to the shore
> Of Britain's beauteous isle; there verdant plains,
> There hills and dales, and woods and waters join,
> To aid thy pencil, favour thy designs,
> And give thy varying landscape every charm.

In his lines on Wooburn Farm the idea of painting recurs:

> . . . Ornamented fields, where gay
> Variety, where mingled lights and shades,
> Where lawns and groves, and opening prospects break
> With sweet surprise, upon the wandering eye.[31]

[30] *Euphrosyne*, 1773, I, 7, 8; 19–21, II, 79.
[31] Other associates of Shenstone who wrote on gardening, but less in the pictorial manner, were Joseph Giles, and the cobbler poet, James Woodhouse, who was employed at the Leasowes and later by Mrs. Elizabeth Montagu. Perhaps Dr. Dalton, friend of Lady Luxborough, may be included.

Shenstone and Lyttelton were far from alone among amateur gardeners. At Enfield Chace Lyttelton's cousin, Pitt, studied picturesque effects; he made use of wild forest in contrast to inclosure, had a temple of Pan in " his Arcadian views," and, in advance of Uvedale Price, " a successful imitation of a bye-lane." [32] About the same time — 1750 — Charles Hamilton at Pain's Hill in Surrey and Mr. Morris (assisted by Richard Cambridge) at Persfield on the Wye undertook their extremely picturesque grounds. Stourhead was slightly later, at least in its more elaborate beauties.

5

In the period between 1750 and 1783 — the year of his death — Lancelot Brown reigned, but with not entirely undisputed sway, over the practice of landscape gardening. A kitchen-gardener at Stowe, he showed such a gift of foreseeing the " capabilities " of grounds, as his phrase was, that he gained the interest of Lord Temple, and was recommended to his friends. While still bailiff at Stowe, he was permitted to direct work elsewhere, and finally set up independently as improver, when he took over the changes at Blenheim. His improvements there brought him enormous fame, especially his management of the water. It was his boast that Thames could never forgive him for the glories of Blenheim; and all except a minority of the tasteful agreed. Brown had little education, but was shrewd, intelligent, honest, and able; " he had wit, learning, and great integrity," Walpole says, and seems to have had considerable artistic endowment, if limited in variety. Joseph Warton thought it " neither exaggeration or affectation to call Mr. BROWN a great painter; for he has realized

> Whate'er LORRAIN light-touched with softening hue,
> Or savage ROSA dash'd, or learned POUSSIN drew."

By captious gentlemen he was sometimes blamed for monotony and tameness, and for the lack of knowledge which made him alter old scenes without regard to historical and sentimental considerations; and blame falls on him heavily today for his destruction of avenues. He was certainly self-confident, and

[32] George Mason, *Essay on Design in Gardening*, 1795, pp. 116–117.

took his art with a seriousness which impressed both his admirers and his opponents. He liked to give his art a literary
turn. Mrs. Elizabeth Montagu speaks of her gardens and wood
at Sandleford as turning under his direction, into " sweet pastorals and gentle elegiacs. He is an agreeable, pleasant companion, as well as a great genius in his profession," she adds.
" I consider him as a great poet." [33] This was the year before
his death; about the time that he amusingly laid down his
ideas of composition to Hannah More, in the " very agreeable
two hours " which she spent with him:

> He promised to give me taste by inoculation. I am sure he has a
> charming one, and he illustrates every thing he says about gardening
> with some literary or grammatical allusion. He told me he compared
> his art to literary composition. Now there, said he, pointing his finger,
> I make a comma, and there, pointing to another part (where an inter-
> ruption is desirable to break the view) a parenthesis — now a full stop,
> and then I begin another subject.[34]

When, shortly before his death, a group of Irish noblemen made
him a lavish offer if he would supervise their improvements,
he refused, saying that he had not yet finished England. He was
once boasting to Richard Owen Cambridge of the changes he
had made in the face of the country, and of further plans.
Cambridge gravely remarked, " Mr. Brown, I very earnestly
wish I may die before you." " Why so? " asked the surprised
Brown. " Because I should like to see heaven before you had
improved it." A hostile critic in the *Westminster Magazine* for
1773 blames his extravagances of inversion. " No person can
execute his grotesque ideas, unless he has a pond full of mountains." [35]

But this hostility was not general. From the time of his
earliest improvements, at Croome and Blenheim, there arose a
continuous eulogy for his development of " the capabilities "
of the chief seats of England. Walpole speaks favourably of
Warwick in 1751, as " well laid out by one Brown, who has set
up on a few ideas of Kent and Mr. Southcote "; and characteristically adds, " one sees what the prevalence of taste does;

[33] *Mrs. Montagu, " Queen of the Blues,"* ed. Blunt, 1924, II, 123.
[34] *Memoirs,* ed. Roberts, 1834, I, 267.
[35] I, 590–591. See also VIII, 249–254.

since Brook, who would have chuckled to have been born in an age of clipt hedges and cockle-shell avenues, has submitted to let his garden and park be natural." William Whitehead has some extravagant lines *On the Late Improvements at Nuneham,* in which Nature and Brown encounter, and Brown has the best of it. The lady, a pettish goddess, demands to know how he can take credit for the results there. He replies:

> Who drew o'er the surface, did you or did I,
> The smooth-flowing outline, that steals from the eye,
> The soft undulations, both distant and near,
> That heave from the ground, and yet scarcely appear?
> Who thinn'd, and who group'd, and who scatter'd the trees?
> Who bade the slopes fall with such elegant ease?
> Who cast them in shade, and who plac'd them in light?
> Who bade them divide, and who bade them unite?
> The ridges are melted, the boundaries gone.[36]

" The place is more Elysian than ever, the river full to the brim, and the church, by one touch of Albano's pencil, is become a temple, and a principal feature of one of the most beautiful landscapes in the world," writes Walpole of Nuneham in 1780.

> Varied woods and lawns and streams combine
> With one loud voice, to prove a BROWN's design,

says the poet of *Richmond Hill* (1807).

The praise and growing dispraise of Brown take up a large part of the discussion of gardening for the last half of the century; particular comment belongs to individual names. For our purpose it is important to observe that in his emphasis on water, and his treatment of it, in his use of the clump, and particularly in his effects of space, he appears to have followed Claude and the painters, though less closely than his picturesque critics would have had him.

6

How great was the interest in gardening in the middle of the century is seen in that periodical paper written by and for men

---

[36] Anderson's *Poets*, XI, 951. See also XI, 593, for Edward Lovibond's licentious lines on Clermont.

of fashion, *The World* (1753-1756). There are essays concerned with gardening by Francis Coventry, Richard Owen Cambridge, and Horace Walpole. Coventry has a brief history of English Gardening (No. 15, April 12, 1755), especially as shown by the country adjacent to London, which is "usually new created once in twenty or thirty years." "Our present artists in GARDENING far exceed the wildness of nature, and pretending to improve upon the plans of Kent, distort their ground into irregularity the most offensive that can be imagined. A great comic painter has proved, I am told, in a piece every day expected, that the line of beauty is a S: I take this to be the unanimous opinion of all our professors of horticulture." For the serpentine, which was the object of so much satire, we may hold not only Kent but to some extent Claude, responsible; later, the Chinese influence helped it along, together with the zigzag.

Richard Owen Cambridge, himself an amateur improver, wrote in ridicule of the rage for alteration (No. 76), and of the modern art of laying out ground (Nos. 118, 119). "Whatever may have been reported, whether truly or falsely, of the Chinese gardens, it is certain that we are the first of the Europeans who have founded this taste." But the new art laid great demands on the gardener, who must study all the arts, "and since it has been thought necessary to embellish rural scenes with all the varieties of architecture, from single pillars and obelisks, to bridges, ruins, pantheons, and even castles and churches," the designer of gardens must rival Solomon in knowledge of building.

The first of the papers touching gardening was Walpole's (No. 6) on the daily progress toward nature, in gardens as in other things. "There is not a citizen who does not take more pains to torture his acre and half into irregularities, than he formerly would have employed to make it as formal as his cravat. Kent, the friend of nature, was the Calvin of this reformation, but like the other champion of truth, after having routed tinsel and trumpery, with the true zeal of a founder of a sect, he pushed his discipline to the deformity of holiness." Walpole himself practiced gardening on a small scale; in 1748 and 1749 it was, he says, his great delight. In 1750 he was sure that Mann would be pleased with the liberty of taste that had been developed; " the country wears a new face; every-body is improving their places." How Italian were some of them is seen in his account of Mereworth, Lord Westmoreland's, in 1752, the house itself on a Palladian plan: " A wood that runs up a hill behind the house is broken like an Albano land-scape with an octagon temple and a triumphal arch." Of Went-worth Castle, three years later: " There is a beautiful (artificial) river, with a fine semi-circular wood overlooking it, and the temple of Tivoli placed happily on a rising toward the end." By 1760 he was out of temper with excessive alteration, and " wondered, with the rage of taste which now reigns, that nobody has laid a plan before the Society for the Reformation of Manners, with a proposal for altering and improving the New Jerusalem in the modern style, upon consideration that *nobody one knows* could bear to go into so old-fashioned a town." Walpole's *Essay*, the most important except perhaps Whately's of the host of works on gardening, is better reserved for discussion in its place.

Gray, too, was a lover of gardening, though he lacked the op-portunity of practicing it which was enjoyed by his friends Walpole, Mason, and Norton Nicholls. He ridiculed Batty Langley, and admired Mr. Southcote's Paradise, but Esher was his favourite; though he evidently found Kent too classic, and thought that he had not read the Gothic classics with attention. Lord Radnor's he called " a laughing scene." Mr. Greathead at Guy's Cliff — " a fat young Man with a head & face much bigger than they are usually worn " — provoked Gray to lament the outrages done upon nature by the tasteless, — a frequent theme for the person comfortably assured of taste:

It was naturally a very agreeable rock, whose Cliffs cover'd with large trees hung beetleing over the Avon, wch. twists twenty ways in sight of it . . . but behold the trees are cut down to make room for flower-ing shrubs, the rock is cut up, till it is as smooth & as sleek as sattin; the river has a gravel-walk by its side; the Cell is a Grotto with cockle-shells and looking-glass; the fountains have an iron-gate before them, and the Chantry is a Barn . . . even the poorest bits of nature, that remain, are daily threatened, for he says (& I am sure, when the Great-heads are once set upon a thing, they will do it) he is determined it shall be all new.

7

The second half of the century produced works on gardening in great abundance, in both verse and prose. In the vanguard of the garden-poets was the Reverend Stephen Duck, whose *Caesar's Camp* (1755) gives an artistic Druid's appreciative prophecy of the Thames valley, as it will appear under the improvements of the Duke of Cumberland (famed for his gardening at Cranbourne Chace), the Prince of Wales, " nature's children, Hamilton and Spence," Ligonier, Newcastle, Pelham, and others. The descriptions, while vague and similar, follow the pictorial and " natural " ideas of gardening.

Mr. William Chambers, later, thanks to his Swedish order, Sir William, produced his large and elegant *Designs of Chinese Buildings* in 1757, and in the appended description of Chinese gardening — largely from hearsay, as he admits — gave briefly the ideas of " the pleasing, horrid and enchanted," the last being " what we call romantic," in Chinese gardening. The only trace of that jealousy of Brown which seems to have inspired his later *Dissertation* is the conclusion that Chinese gardening is quite beyond the range of a " person of narrow intellect." For the account of Chambers' extravagantly picturesque ideal for gardens, we may wait; only noticing the impressive list of subscribers to his large and sumptuous volume, which included many of the noble and gentle amateurs of gardening, — Hamilton, General Conway, Sir James Lowther, Earl Temple, Horace Walpole.

In 1767 appeared a history in verse of *The Rise and Progress of the Present Taste in Planting Parks, Pleasure Grounds, Gardens, &c. From Henry the Eighth to King George III*, dedicated to Viscount Irwin. The author remained anonymous, even to Walpole. All the important English gardens and gardeners are noticed. Sir William Temple is condemn'd because of lack of taste

> . . . for undulating hills,
> Bustles of oak, fine vales, and murmuring rills;
> Extensive lawns, and close embracing shades,
> Long lakes, bright spiry rocks, and opening glades.

The true art consists

In showing Nature great in every part,
Which chiefly flows from mingled lights and shades,
In lawns, and woods, hills, rivers, rocks and glades;
For only happy 's that assemblage made
Where force of light contends with force of shade.

High honours are paid to Brown, who is the climax of gardening; in terms that are pictorial, as indeed they are throughout this poem, but here with a dash of the literary:

At Blenheim, Croom and Caversham we trace
Salvator's wildness, Claud's enlivening grace,
Cascades and Lakes as fine as Risdale drew,
While Nature's vary'd in each charming view.
To paint his works wou'd Pousin's Powers require,
Milton's sublimity and Dryden's fire. . . .
Born to grace Nature, and her works complete;
With all that's beautiful, sublime and great!
For him each Muse enwreathes the Laurel Crown,
And consecrates to Fame immortal Brown.

The first edition of the Reverend George Mason's *Essay on Design in Gardening* (he was not related to William) appeared anonymously in 1767, and got little attention except an unfavourable notice in the *Gentleman's Magazine*; though the author in his expanded edition of 1795 asserted that succeeding writers had " silently adopted " his sentiments. He evidently meant Thomas Whately, literary critic and member of the House, whose *Observations on Modern Gardening* (1770) was the text-book of the gentleman gardener, in both England and France. A second edition that year, and four more before the elaborate one with plates by Woollett in 1801 indicate its popularity; and there was an important French translation in 1771.

" They have translated Mr. Whately's book, and the Lord knows what barbarism is going to be laid at our door," says Walpole, whose opinion of French taste in gardening was low. Walpole thought the work ingenious and carefully executed, though he was a little jealous at Whately's having got before him into print. Whately considered gardening " as superior to landscape painting as a reality to a representation." But he shows the influence of the painters. He prefers concave ground, " as the more elegant shape " (the Claudian amphitheatre), and likes bridges, sometimes, as Claude has them, more than one in a scene. He has a section " Of Picturesque Beauty "; *picturesque* being " a denomination in general expressive of excellence, but which by being too indiscriminately applied may be sometimes productive of errors." The relation of pictures and nature meets his approval: " We are delighted to see those objects in the reality, which we are used to admire in the representation; and we improve upon their intrinsic merit, by recollecting their effects in the picture." But he would use the pictures " as studies, not as models; for a picture and a scene in nature, though they agree in many yet differ in some particulars." He likes the idea of representing a scene or object celebrated in description or familiar in idea. " Artificial ruins, lakes, rivers, fall under this denomination; the air of a seat extended to a distance, and scenes calculated to raise ideas of Arcadian elegance, or of rural simplicity." He suggests, however, in preference to classic temples for British forest scenes, "the semblance of an antient British monument " made of brick or plastered timber, as " an object to be seen at a distance, rude and large, and in character agreeable to a wild view"; but nothing that might not really belong to such a situation. " The fine effect of a dark green tree, or groupe of trees, with nothing behind it but the splendour of a morning, or the glow of an evening sky, cannot be unknown to any who was ever delighted with a picture of Claude, or with the beautiful originals in nature."

Horace Walpole's *Essay on Gardening* was first published in 1771, at the end of the fourth edition of *Anecdotes of Painting*; and again in 1785, with the translation by the Duc de Nivernois. Magazines quoted it, cultivated persons referred to it familiarly; it was in all polite hands. Though brief, it was the best historical account of the subject which had appeared. It covered only the time up to the age of Brown, who, since he was yet living, received only a graceful gesture of approval. As would be expected of a connoisseur, Walpole holds Milton and Claude Lorrain to be the true prophets of English gardening: " The description of Eden is a warmer and more just picture of the present style than Claud Lorrain could have painted from Hagley or Stourhead." Kent is named as the founder of the style, which, since it was founded on landscape painting, Walpole would call landscape gardening. He introduces the term as if it were new, though Shenstone had suggested the connection.[37] " We have given the true model of gardening to the world," says Walpole; " let other countries mimic or corrupt our taste, but let it reign here on its verdant throne, original by its elegant simplicity, and proud of no other art, than that of softening nature's harshnesses, and copying her graceful touch." He glows with enthusiasm:

How rich, how gay, how picturesque, the face of the country! The demolition of walls laying open each improvement, every journey is made through a succession of pictures. . . . Enough has been done to establish such a school of landscape as cannot be found on the rest of the globe. If we have the seeds of a Claud or a Gaspar among us, he must come forth. If wood, water, vallies, glades, can inspire a poet or a painter, this is the country, this is the age, to produce them.

Yet when at last the painters came, it was not from Stourhead or Hagley or Persfield, but out of the low-lying, " fenny " east country, and from London.

In 1772 Sir William Chambers published his much-talked-of *Dissertation on Oriental Gardening*, elaborated from his description of 1757, and more directly aimed at Brown. The jealousy which the royal architect and designer of the pagoda at Kew felt toward the royal gardener and improver of Richmond Park was, as a *Monthly* reviewer implies, common gossip.[38] According to Chambers, the gardens of Brown and his disciples " differ very little from common fields . . . so little variety in the objects, such poverty of imagination in the contrivance, and of art in the arrangement, that these compositions rather appear the offspring of chance than of design." The visitor on entering

is treated with the sight of a large green field, scattered over with a few struggling trees, and verged with a confused border of little shrubs, and flowers; upon farther inspection, he finds a little serpentine path, twining in regular esses amongst the shrubs of the border, upon which

---

[37] Others are slow to accept the term, and cling for years to such nomenclature as " rural ornamentation," " embellishment of grounds," etc., especially those who are pro-Brown, and opposed to the assumption that the gardener must follow the painter.

[38] Cf. *The Estate Orators*, 1774:

" *Brown*, in quaint art whom *Chambers* may excel, But ne'er could capabilitate so well."

he is to go round, to look on one side at what he has already seen, the large green field. . . . From time to time he perceives a little seat or temple stuck up against the wall; he rejoices at the discovery; sits down, rests his wearied limbs, and then reels on again, cursing the line of beauty.

In such monotonous reiterations of the scant materials of nature — water, plants, and ground — says Chambers, with something like a sneer, " it matters not who are the gardeners; whether a peasant or a Poussin. But wherever a better style is adopted . . . gardeners must be men of genius, experience, and judgment; quick in perception, rich in expedients, fertile in imagination, and thoroughly versed in all the affections of the human mind." " Chambers' book is written in wild revenge against Brown," writes Walpole to Mason; " the only surprising consequence is, that it is laughed at, and is not likely to be adopted as I expected; for nothing is so tempting to fools as advice to deprave taste."

The account of Chinese gardening, as Chambers admitted, was more from hearsay than from observation; [39] though delivered with great authority of tone. Its " pleasing, terrible, and surprising " scenes have little to do with Claude, but have a hint of Salvator, and still more of wax-works. They are certainly pictorial, as well as allegorical. Thus, in the autumnal scenes, the foliage is carefully arranged for effect of colouring; and dead trees, pollards, and stumps are mingled (a notion for which Kent was derided) both for pictorial and for moral meaning.

The buildings with which these scenes are decorated are generally such as indicate decay, being intended as mementos to the passenger. Some are hermitages, and almshouses, where the faithful old servants of the family spend the remains of life in peace, amidst the tombs of their predecessors. . . . Others are ruins of castles, palaces, temples, and deserted religious houses; or half-buried triumphal arches [such, perhaps, as Sir William had erected at Kew?] and . . . whatever else may serve to indicate the debility, the disappointments, and the dissolution of humanity; which, by co-operating with the dreary aspect of autumnal nature, and the inclement temperature of the air, fill the mind with melancholy, and incline it to serious reflections.

[39] As reviewers did not fail to point out, it is strongly reminiscent of the translation from Attiret, by Spence (under the name of " Sir Harry Beaumont ") published in *Fugitive Pieces,* 1754.

A little hard on the faithful old servants, these gardens are not easy on the " passenger " ; who is sometimes " hurried by steep descending paths to subterraneous vaults . . . where lamps, which yield a faint glimmering light, discover the pale images of antient kings and heroes," or after wandering in a dusky forest, " finds himself on the edge of precipices, . . . with cataracts falling from the mountains . . . or at the foot of impending rocks, in gloomy vallies overhung with woods."

There is evidence that this didactic and alarming style was occasionally practised, even though it was generally derided. Arthur Young tells of a threatening rock, in some grounds near Bath, which came near to annihilating the passengers it was supposed to menace harmlessly. In the *Scots Magazine* of 1767 is an engaging account of the pleasure-gardens (if that is not a misnomer) belonging to Mr. Tyers, proprietor of Vauxhall. These gardens near Dorking seem to connect with Chambers' theories, though if he inspired them, it must have been through his description of 1757. The very walks were instructive, " in some parts easy, smooth, and level, in others rugged, and uneven," — " a proper emblem of human life," — and they were decked with flags inscribed with moral sentiments. At the entrance of " the Valley of Shadow of Death " (wherein, by the same hand that had adorned Vauxhall, were depicted the latter ends of saint and sinner) instead of columns stood two stone coffins, bearing moral admonitions " proper to the different sexes," and atop of each a human skull. The skulls were agreeably believed to be those which had in life appertained to a noted highwayman and a celebrated courtesan; and were represented as uttering respectively the warnings that " *Men, at their best state, are altogether vanity*," and that " *Favour is deceitful and beauty is vain.*" Incidentally, these gardens had the usual " prospects " of extensive vale and meandering river.

Chambers did not escape ridicule. William Mason attacked him in the anonymous *Heroic Epistle* (1773), which circulated more widely by far than the essay which evoked it. Mason had personal reason; he held a brief for Brown in Book I of *The English Garden,* which had been published in 1772. He also decidedly held a brief for the garden which took the landscape painter for model. Considering his highly artificial precepts,

Mason's invocation to divine Simplicity is surprising. But simplicity is a relative term; and, as one of his critics observed, formed part of the " macaroni cant " of that day. Mason makes the customary boast of landscape gardening as a British art; and warns British youth that the Latian plain will afford their taste no aid, except that their eyes

> Shall catch those glowing scenes, that taught a CLAUDE
> To grace his canvas with Hesperian hues:
> And scenes like these on Memory's tablet drawn,
> Bring back to Britain; there give local form
> To each idea; and if Nature lend
> Materials fit for torrent, rock or shade,
> Produce new TIVOLIS.

Shortly he calls on the muse of Painting — whom, it should be remembered, he followed — " to teach the docile pupil " of his song the elements of gardening:

> Of Nature's various scenes the painter culls
> That for his fav'rite theme, where the fair whole
> Is broken into ample parts, and bold;
> Where to the eye three well-mark'd distances
> Spread their peculiar colouring. Vivid green,
> Warm brown, and black opake the foreground bears
> Conspicuous; sober olive coldly marks
> The second distance; thence the third declines
> In softer blue, or less'ning still, is lost
> In faintest purple.

If a scene can be found bearing these gradations distinctly, the pupil is to apply his colours, and develop the picture.

The names of the great three stare in capitals from a single page:

> O great POUSSIN! O Nature's darling, CLAUDE!
> What if some rash and sacrilegious hand
> Tore from your canvass those umbrageous pines
> That frown in front, and gives each azure hill
> The charm of contrast! . . .

Such harm is done by the ill-judging planter who uproots trees, or plants the wrong ones and in the wrong places:

> . . . So should art
> Improve thy pencil's savage dignity,
> SALVATOR! If, where, far as eye can pierce,
> Rock pil'd on rock, thy Alpine heights retire,
> She flung her random foliage, and disturb'd
> The deep repose of the majestic scene.
> This deed were impious. Ah, forgive the thought,
> Thou more than Painter, more than Poet! HE,
> Alone thy equal, who was " Fancy's child."

Again he urges the gardener to turn for guidance to " the masters of correct design," whose works have broad contrasts and careless lines in place of " Dull uniformity, contrivance quaint, or labour'd littleness." To the argument that Nature must be a better guide than the copyists of nature, he replies by citing Raphael, and his recourse to Greek sculpture as superior to living bodies. The proved authorities are best:

> . . . the favour'd few, whom heav'n has lent
> The power to seize, select and reunite
> Her loveliest features; and of these to frame
> One archetype complete of sovereign grace.
> Here Nature's sees her fairest forms more fair.

He runs through the history of English gardening, with approval for Bacon (whom he misunderstands) and hard words for Temple. He praises Pope, who " Waves the poetic brand o'er Timon's shades," and his associate

> KENT, who felt
> The pencil's power; but, fir'd by higher forms
> Of beauty than that pencil knew to paint,
> Work'd with the living hues that Nature lent,
> And realiz'd his landscapes.

Southcote and Shenstone he commends; and last,

> HIM too, the living leader of thy powers,
> Great Nature! . . .
> . . . Bards yet unborn
> Shall pay to BROWN that tribute, fitliest paid
> In strains the beauty of his scenes inspire [sic].[40]

But though the gardener imitates the painter, the " sons of Claude " are the more blest, for the outline of their pictures stays where they put it, while the gardener's is constantly chang-

[40] He wrote an epitaph for Brown, " the Christian, Husband, Father, Friend." *Works*, I, 143.

THE GROTTO AT AIMWELL.

From *Poetical Works of John Scott, Esq.*, 1782.

ing. This last observation is in Part II, in 1777. Parts III and IV appeared in 1779 and 1782. The specific instructions in Books II and III (as to painting fences green and other practical matters) and the story of Alcander in Book IV (though that has much to say to artificial ruins) add little regarding imitation of pictures.

An *Essay on the Different Natural Situations of Gardens* (1774), reprinted with Whately in 1801, is said [41] to be by Samuel Ward. The author considers Nicolas Poussin and Salvator Rosa the two greatest landscape painters; Salvator for " terrible and noble natural situations," with blasted trees and scarce a sign of life, and Poussin for views of temples, palaces on hillsides, and rich verdure. For general outline, he says, " Perhaps the landskips of Poussin are the best instructor which a gardener of genius and taste can follow."

The Honorable Daines Barrington desisted a moment from archaeology and science to approve the new style, in 1785.[42] The " more particular aera of taste in gardening " at which England had arrived, was owing, he thought, chiefly to Kent. Kent realized the beautiful descriptions 'of the poets, " for which he was peculiarly adapted by being a painter; the true test of perfection in a modern garden is, that a landscape painter would choose it for a composition." He speaks politely of Brown; " but I conceive that in some of his plans I see rather traces of the gardens of Old Stowe than of Poussin or Claude Lorraine."

In all this discussion of gardening and shifting of taste, the situation of the amateur, especially if of limited means, was distressing. Poor John Scott of Aimwell developed his few acres, about 1765, according to the mode as then understood, and showed them proudly to his guest, Dr. Johnson, who delighted his host by kindly remarking that " none but a poet would have such a garden." The grotto, said the Doctor, might well be called Fairy Hall; for it was fit for the Queen of the Fairies to dwell in. But the literature of gardening poured down, and Scott found his little garden all wrong:

[41] By the Hon. Mrs. Evelyn Cecil, *History of Gardening in England.*
[42] *On the Progress of Gardening.* In *Archaelogia,* VII. Reprinted in the *European,* VIII, 15–16.

> This long straight walk, that pool's unmeaning round,
> These short curv'd paths that twist beneath the trees,
> Disgust the eye, and make the whole displease.
> "No scenes like this," I say, "did Nature raise,
> Brown's fancy frame, or Walpole's judgment praise;
> No prototype for this did I survey
> In Woollett's landscape, or in Mason's lay."

Ridiculous imitation in little gardens of elaborate effects is the theme of many a satire. One, *The Parsonage Improved,* is by that forgotten Laureate, Pye. He wrote also *Farington Hill,* addressed to Bathurst, and *The Progress of Refinement* (1783), which deals with gardening, the art

> To teach the wave in graceful bends to flow,
> To crown with wood the mountain's heathy brow,

whereby Britain is glorified more than by other arts;

> Secure her fame unhurt by time shall stand,
> Since *Mason's* verse records what *Brown* has plann'd.

Among other references to picturesque gardening, we may notice Goldsmith's accounts of Chinese gardening (founded on Chambers, apparently) and of the Leasowes, which also heightens facts into fiction. His friend Cradock was one of the opponents of Brown, regretting the uniformity caused by the domination of one man's taste over most of the grounds in England. Cowper, another foe of Brown and his works, sighs for the "fallen avenues," thanks his friend Throckmorton (who was one of the clients of the improver) for sparing him yet "the obsolete prolixity of shade," and refers disparagingly to "clumps and lawns, and temples and cascades." Not the least interesting comments are those which the Wartons contrive to introduce into their critical writings, as Joseph does in the *Essay* on Pope, and Thomas in his edition of Milton's minor poems.

The picturesque tourists belong to the next chapter. They generally praise the works of Brown, and talk much of "scenes," "views," and "landscapes" in the grounds they visit. As the century nears its end, they show less innocent readiness to take pleasure in the efforts of gentlemen amateurs, and of Brown as well. By that time most of them were themselves gardeners, presumably. Young disapproved of Brown's treatment of ancient ruins; Gilpin, in spite of the admiration which his patrons Mason and Walpole bestow on Brown, was inclined to carp; and Price and Knight, as we shall see, were at open war with Brown and his inheritors, especially Repton.

Some of the grounds which are most often described and most lavishly praised should be mentioned, in addition to those already noticed. Mr. Charles Hamilton definitely planned his grounds at Pain's Hill, near Cobham in Surrey, " from the pictures of Poussin and the Italian masters," according to Mitford; who adds that a waterfall at Bowood was modelled by Mr. Hamilton after a picture of Gaspar's. He laid out the grounds of other gentlemen; notably of his friend Charles James Fox, who was very much an amateur of the picturesque. Hamilton is said to have hired an old man of venerable appearance to enliven his picture by acting as hermit in the hermitage at Pain's Hill; but the hermit, wearying of numerous visitors, resigned his position.[48] Studley Park, near Ripon, was the work of the wealthy Aislabie, whose efforts were variously regarded by various visitors. The later connoisseurs, like Young and Gilpin, condemned his clearing away of the debris about Fountains Abbey. The grounds as they survived into the early twentieth century certainly showed strongly the Italian influence, circular temple, winding stream, wooded banks, points of observation, and arrangement of the path with regard to the ruin. Stourhead, designed by Colt Hoare, was much decorated with classic buildings. " I have never beheld the beauties of nature so well set off by a judicious taste of ornament, as here," wrote John Wilkes to his daughter: " Wood, lawn, water, hill, plain, form this beauteous landscape, happily joined." " The imagination could not invent a more picturesque scene," said Edward Jerningham. Persfield, Mr. Morris's seat on the Wye, which Richard Cambridge assisted in designing, was another picturesque seat. " The united talents of a Claude, a Poussin, a Vernet and a Smith would," according to Arthur Young, "scarcely be able to sketch its beauties." [44]   Admiration of gardening was a social

43 J. T. Smith, *Book for a Rainy Day*, ed. 1905, p. 289, note.
44 *The Register of Folly;* 1773, has a flattering reference. Other topo-

convention to which even James Boswell bowed. " Even in the midst of all that surrounded us at Ugbrook, . . . a cloudiness damped my mind. But I had been exhausted by riding all the forenoon, and expatiating upon rural beauties which I did not much feel." [45]

8

In 1794 broke out that may be called the paper war between the Picturesque School and the Brownists. For over forty years it had been preparing, in the resentment of the gentleman gardener (who was inevitably a connoisseur as well) at having his avocation dominated by the one-time under-gardener at Stowe. Brown had been dead ten years, but his disciples were continuing his methods, and his mannerisms; and one of them, Humphry Repton, recognized heir to his documents and his position as leading improver, was a gentleman, an amateur landscape painter, even an author of essays, and known to have in preparation a work on gardening. The picturesque theorists, connoisseurs, and landed gentlemen, Uvedale Price and Richard Payne Knight, old friends of Repton, took alarm lest his rule spread yet more widely what they considered the insipidity of Brown, and the preference of mere utility to picturesque beauty. They were amateur gardeners themselves, especially Price — Wordsworth did not altogether approve his creations — and Knight was a notable collector and general arbiter of the arts.

Price had been for some time preparing a work on the theory of the picturesque and had often discussed his notions with Knight — indeed, with Repton too. Knight preceded his friend in print — it was assumed by collusion — with *The Landscape* (1794) which he styled " a didactic poem," and dedicated to Price. The first of Price's *Essays on the Picturesque* followed shortly. Repton answered the two attacks with an open letter to Price; Price published a letter in reply to Repton. Others of the Brownists leaped to Repton's defence; an anonymous satire in verse, *A Sketch from the Landscape* (1794), was addressed to Knight;

---

graphical and picturesque poems on grounds are *Paradise*, by John Ogilvie, in *Poems*, 1769; *Ugbrooke Park*, 1776; *Needwood Forest*, 1776, by H. C. Mundy; *Netherby*, and *Hagley*, by Thomas Marriott, in *Poems*, 1779; *Grove Hill*, 1779, by Thomas Maurice. These are but examples.

[45] *Letters*, ed. Tinker, I 238.

LIBER VERITATIS, *No. 89.*

Engraved by Richard Earlom.

and William Marshall, a professional improver, author of *Rural Ornament* (1785), issued a sharp *Review of the Landscape,* and a reply to Price (1795). Repton's *Sketches and Hints* on landscape gardening, a costly work, published by subscription, came out in 1796. The copious reviews given to Knight and Price, and even to Marshall, show how great was the literary interest in this subject. The main point of the whole controversy was that which Shenstone had brought up years before: whether a landscape painter was indeed the proper guide of a landscape gardener, — whether the designer of grounds ought to model his work after Claude, Gaspar, and Salvator.

Knight was vigorous in maintaining that he should, and used strong terms in assailing the mere practitioners who thought less highly than did he of Salvator Rosa as a guide in gardening:

> Curse on the pedant jargon, that defines
> Beauty's unbounded forms to given lines! . . .
> Or when, Salvator, from thy daring hand
> Appears in burnish'd arms some savage band, —
> Each figure boldly pressing into life,
> And breathing blood, calamity, and strife,
> Should coldly measure each component part,
> And judge thy genius by a surgeon's art.

Claude, however, held highest place with him; of whose drawings, indeed, Knight owned perhaps the best collection in England, as we are reminded in reading the poem. Titian and Rubens, to be sure, preceded Claude in time (Knight notices that landscape is a modern art)

> But both their merits, polish'd and refin'd,
> By toil and care, in patient Claude were join'd:
> Nature's own pupil, fav'rite child of taste!
> Whose pencil, like Lycippus' chisel, trac'd
> Vision's nice errors, and with feign'd neglect,
> Sunk partial form in general effect.

He is catholic in his admirations; but his precept of the three distances is, as with Mason, founded on Claude:

> To make the landscape grateful to the sight,
> Three points of distance always should unite;
> And howsoe'er the view may be confin'd,
> Three mark'd divisions we shall always find:

> Not more, where Claude extends his prospect wide,
> O'er Rome's Campania to the Tyrrhene tide,
> (Where tow'rs and temples, mould'ring to decay,
> In pearly air appear to die away,
> And the soft distance, melting to the eye,
> Dissolves its forms into the azure sky)
> Than where, confin'd to some sequester'd rill,
> Meek Hobbima presents the village mill: —
> Not more, where great Salvator's mountains rise,
> And hide their craggy summits in the skies;
> While towring clouds in whirling eddies roll,
> And bursting thunders seem to shake the pole;
> Than in the ivy'd cottage of Ostade,
> Waterlo's copse, and Rysdael's low cascade.

His precepts are mainly based on Claude. For bridges he commends

> The stately arch, high rais'd with mason'd stone,
> The pond'rous flag, that forms a bridge alone,

and refers to the *Liber Veritatis* for authority. Instead of the " clump " of the improvers he would have " loose and vary'd groupes " of trees, such as Claude arranged, " The foreground of some classic scene to grace." And he sighs regretfully for the pearly air of Italy, despite its miasmic origin, whose tints " Melt the tender distance to the eye." [46]

Among the passages in his poem which enraged the Brownists the worst was the tasteless apostrophe:

> Hence, hence, thou haggard fiend, however call'd,
> Thin, meagre genius of the bare and bald;
> Thy spade and mattock here at length lay down,
> And follow to the tomb thy fav'rite Brown.

Price, milder than Knight, was insistent, in his *Essays*, on the picturesque. " Near the house," he conceded, " picturesque beauty must in many cases be sacrificed to neatness; but it is a sacrifice, and one that should not wantonly be made." He admits that a sheep-track is not just the model for a carriage-drive; yet thinks it may offer useful hints. For the thistles and

---

[46] He opposes the artificial ruin, however, and advises British artists to copy British scenes in their pictures, not " blindly follow some preceding guide," or copy crudely what they never view.

docks with which the painters deck their foregrounds, ornamental plants may be substituted. But the painter is the true guide. " Quam multa vident pictores in umbris, et in eminentia, quae nos non vidimus," he quotes from Cicero on his title-page, and repeats the story of Salvator's reproof to the layman, — " O pensa quel tu diresti se tu la videsti con gli occhi di Salvator Rosa." To the anticipated objection that if pictures, which are copies of nature, are good, nature itself will be better as guide, he answers that the copies are made by men of enlarged and liberal minds, and are to be regarded by the layer-out of grounds as so many beautiful experiments by men most skilled in the grouping of trees, water, and buildings. The great principles of the two arts are the same; for general composition, grouping, harmony of tints, unity of character, effect of light and shade. He contrasts at some length the methods of the Brownists and of Claude, by imagining how the improver would treat a picture of Claude's — clumping trees, clearing away thickets, smoothing surfaces, defining the edge of the pool, smartening buildings.

For the gentleman-gardener — for Shenstone and Hamilton — he has great respect. They took pictures as their models in gardening. " It may be said with much truth, that the reformation of public taste in real landscape, more immediately belongs to the higher landscape painters," he says. " There is a natural repugnance in him who has studied Titian, Claude, and Poussin, and the style of art and nature they studied, to copy the clumps, the naked canals, and no less naked buildings, of Mr. Brown." The *Essays* examine in great detail all the constituents of gardening — trees, water, ground, buildings — with the recurring phrase, " we find in nature or in Claude."

Repton met the attacks in the *Letter* (1794) which preceded his *Sketches and Hints*. This latter elaborate work, a collection of his various " Red Books " prepared from designs for the grounds he had improved, had a delightful device of " slides," or overlapping plates, the lower showing the scene before improvement, the upper, folding over it, the changes proposed. Repton stoutly and sensibly insisted that " *Utility* must often take the lead of beauty, and *convenience* be preferred to picturesque effect, in the neighbourhood of man's habitation." Rather unfairly — but the unfairness of Knight justified him

— he chose to construe the admiration of Salvator as a recommendation of that " wild " artist for an exact model; and quoted a letter from " a Right Honourable Friend " (Windham): " A scene of a cavern, with banditti sitting by it, is the favourite subject of Salvator Rosa; but are we therefore to live in caverns, or encourage the neighbourhood of banditti? "

Repton's other works on gardening were published after 1800. His *Observations on the Theory and Practice of Landscape Gardening* (1803) has a strong note of resentment; but he is eager to deny that he follows the errors of Brown. He explains elaborately just why a painter is not a satisfactory guide for a gardener, yet exhibits a tendency to follow Claude wherever possible, — for example, in his fondness for the amphitheatre outline in grounds, for arrangements of water and trees, and for crowning " the summit of a naked brow " with a temple " such as the temple of the Sybil or that of Tivoli."

William Marshall, " rural ornamentalist," entered the conflict in *A Review of the Landscape* (1795). He lost his temper more than did Repton, who under great provocation retains his gentlemanly demeanour. " He is a madman, who would look up to Claud, in preference to Brown, for *practical* ideas in Rural Ornament," Marshall asserts; and thinks that " a mere Connoisseur in painting," if taken to view the scenes painted by Claude, would find them " insipid." Not that he does not admire " the Prince of Landscape Painters," whom he cites on his side, for Claude chose beautiful, not ruined, trees, and often cleared their stems, and smoothed the turf about them. " Many of his paintings differ much more, in style, from the works of Salvator Rosa, than they do from the present style of Rural Ornament." Salvator is his abhorrence. " Who, but a student in painting — one who had been accustomed to see dead stumps sticking out of canvass — could have thought of planting dead trees in a living landscape? " he queries, contemptuous of Kent; and suggests that if Salvator had been born without eyes or hands, " it would have been a private misfortune, and partial [*i.e.*, private] evil universal good."

Most of the reviewers, under the literary influence of Gilpin, inclined to the literary side in this argument. The *Critical* was especially picturesque in its tastes, and anxious lest the whole of England be rendered " insipid." Only the *Monthly*, its rival, was strongly Reptonist, but even the *Monthly* found Marshall, however sound in ideas, very improper in tone toward gentlemen of fortune and talents. Miss Seward was warmly a partisan of Repton, her friend and correspondent; naturally he did not escape her tribute epistolary and poetical. She thought Knight's poem " the Jacobinism of taste." Mason also resented it in two sonnets, which show Taste rising indignant " from his polish'd lawn," and the serpentine path an " emblem pure of legal liberty." Mathias, in *The Pursuits of Literature*, notices the quarrel:

> With Price and Knight grounds by *neglect* improve,
> And banish use, for naked Nature's love,
> Lakes, forests, rivers, in one landscape drawn,
> Thy park a county, and a heath thy lawn.

Not that the critics do not have moments of belittling the fray. " To an indifferent reader who may prefer a beefsteak to a landscape," says the *Critical* after a while, " the warmth of this writer on a theme of taste will appear ridiculous." The greatest oddity, to a modern reader, is to find Price and Knight accounted the representatives of nature.

In 1795 George Mason republished his *Essay on Design*, enlarged, with his word on the controversy. He has no high opinion of Brown, " an egregious mannerist, who from having acquired a facility in shaping surfaces grew fond of exhibiting that talent without due regard to nature." But he would not blame Brown for all the faults of his successors. He mentions with approval another designer, contemporary with Brown, a gentleman named Wright. Of Kent he has a higher opinion than was then general. " According to my own idea, all that has since been done by the most deservedly admired designers, by SOUTH-COTE, HAMILTON, LYTTLETON, PITT, SHENSTONE, MORRIS, for themselves, and by WRIGHT for others, all that has been written on the subject . . . have proceeded from KENT." He rejects the artificial ruin (of which books of designs were published as late as 1800), nor does he agree with Price and Knight as to following pictures. " Every landscape painter puts blinkers on the spectator." Ideas may be gained from the painters; but study of Shenstone's and Hamilton's gardens will do more. Claude

" the most ornamented of the great masters," is more misleading
than Gaspar as model; his pictures seem rather wonderful combinations of objects by effort of genius than what were likely
to have existed together anywhere in reality. " *Tussocks* of
rushes may have a very good effect in one of Claude's landscapes,
. . . but in land in any state of cultivation they would be pre-
posterous."

John Trusler's *Elements of Modern Gardening* (1800?) follows the picturesque school unintelligently. He appears to take
Mason seriously, would have ice-house and dairy take on Gothic
shapes, and recommends " when a romantic scene is studied," a
stone bridge of two or three arches, broken down in the middle,
" the vacancy supplied by a plank or two, with a hand rail."
A ruin should not only serve picturesque effect, but have " some
beautiful emblematical character " ; it is best to copy " some
beautiful fragment of an ancient castle or abbey."

9

The theory of gardening was an important branch of aesthetics
in the eighteenth century. Lord Kames has a chapter on
gardening and architecture. " To paint in the gardening way,"
he says, requires more genius than to form a landscape on canvas. A landscape " ought to be confined to a single expression."
Straight lines and formality he dislikes; Versailles is a monument of depraved taste. The right sort of landscape swells the
heart, and arouses emotions of grandeur. " The spectator is
conscious of an enthusiasm, which cannot bear confinement,
nor the strictness of regularity and order; he loves to range
at large; and is so enchanted with magnificent objects, as to
overlook slight beauties or deformities." Alison's explanation
that Italian landscape is the inspiration of English gardening
has been cited previously.[47] He develops the notion at some
length: the English at first copied Italian scenes, with much
use of temples, ruins, and statues, but later arrived at more
correct imitation of natural scenes, in the spirit of the painters.
Like Warton, Alison attributes the increased delight in natural
scenery to the influence of Thomson. Another writer on garden-

[47] Introduction, p. iii.

DESIGN FOR CATTLE SHED AND GOTHIC RUIN.

From *Decorations for Parks and Gardens,* by Charles Middleton.

"So shall each part, tho' turn'd to rural use,
　　Deceive the eye with those bold feudal forms
　　That Fancy loves to gaze on."
　　　　　　　　William Mason: *The English Garden,* Bk. IV.

ing is Dr. John Aikin, an opponent of the picturesque school, impatient with Mason, and agreeing with Cowper in love of avenues.[48] We should recall the remarks of Wordsworth on the devastation wrought by pretentious and tasteless persons upon the scenery of the Lakes, and his advice to the Beaumonts regarding their garden; and Scott's *Essay on Landscape Gardening*.[49] Though with these we are far into the next century, it is impossible to neglect the tale which Sir Walter tells of a pupil of Brown, one Robertson, who in laying out the ground of Duddingstone, near Edinburgh, refused to allow a sight of the ruins of Craigmillar Castle, because, being visible over all the countryside, it " was a common prostitute "; and excluded Duddingstone Loch, because " it did not fall within his lordship's property."

10

The English garden on the continent must be briefly noticed. Montesquieu had one at La Brède by 1750, probably in the manner of Kent; at least the description so implies.[50] The Elysée of Rousseau's Julie evoked many an imitation. Claude Henri Watelet, of whose *ferme ornée* Walpole had a low opinion, published his *Essai sur les Jardins* in 1764. The *caractères* possible for parks he classifies as *Le Pittoresque, Le Poétique,* and *Le Romanesque*. Landscape gardening with him is slightly more literary than pictorial; he separated the art of painter from that of gardener. Walpole, visiting France in 1771, found that English gardening had gained prodigiously owing to the translation of Whately in that year, but was practiced with more zeal than taste; " I have literally seen one that is exactly like a tailor's paper of patterns." Melchior Grimm, in England that same year, was moved to tender enthusiasm by the sight of English gardens: " On ne peut sortir d'un jardin anglais sans avoir l'âme aussi affecté qu'en sortant d'une tragédie." The Count de Girardin, protector of Rousseau, produced in 1777 his essay *De la Composition des Paysages, ou Les Moyens d'embellir la Nature autour des Habitations, en joignant l'agréable à l'utile.*

---

[48] *Letters from a Father to his Son,* third ed., 1796, pp. 149–152.
[49] *Quarterly,* March, 1828.
[50] E.g., *Memoirs of Michael Clancy,* Dublin, 1750, II, 51; Montesquieu, *Essai sur le Goût.*

This goes even beyond Mason in advocating the use of painting as guide. Milton is not neglected; the title-page is adorned with the motto, " Ahappi rural seat of different views." Count de Girardin found it surprising that when painters and poets provide us with so many representations of the beauties and simplicity of Nature, no "homme de bon sens (car c'est du bon sens que le goût dépend) " had sought to realize their pictures. In view of the variety of landscape-painters, it is possible to find models of all sorts, for " paysages héroiques, nobles, . . . riches, élégantes, voluptueux, solitaires, sauvages, sévères, tranquilles, frais, simples, champêtres, rustiques." His essay was translated into English in 1789, and somewhat annoyed the English because neither author nor translator accorded due recognition to English accomplishment in this sort of gardening. Girardin's own park, which consisted " of three distinct water scenes " in one of which the central theme was Rousseau's tomb, was a favourite resort of British travellers before the Revolution.

Whately's *Observations* was the text-book for French imitators of English gardens. The translator was a student of the subject, who respected Kent, " le premier en Angleterre qui ait osé s'écarter vers l'année 1720, des règles de Le Nôtre, dans la composition des bosquets d'Esher." That the mode was far developed by 1775 is implied in the *Epître sur la manie des jardins anglais* of that year by Michel-Paul-Gui de Chabanon.

The Abbé Delille exhibits the " mania " in *Les Jardins* (1782), much admired by English devotees of gardening. Well might it be, for in it English gardens were complimented elaborately in a long *catalogue raisonnée*. " Un jardin, à mes yeux, est un vaste tableau," he says; and urges in consequence, " soyez peintre,"

> Et ce qu'à la campagne emprunta la peinture,
> Que l'art reconnoissant le rende à la nature.

There are two sorts of gardening: one, " de la nature amant respectueux," the other, " despote orgueilleux."

> Je ne décide point entre Kent et Le Nôtre.
> L'un, content d'un verger, d'un bocage, d'un bois,
> Dessine pour le Sage, l'autre pour les rois,

a description which would not greatly have flattered the designer of the magnificent Holkham; and Whately must have been startled to find his Matlock risen to Alpine heights; "Whateli, je te suis; viens, j'y monte avec toi," cries the ecstatic Abbé.

The translation of Walpole's *Essay* by the Duc de Nivernois in 1785 was much read and increased the followers of the fashion, who ranged from royalty to bourgeoisie. Arthur Young, in 1787, found Marie Antoinette's English garden showing more of Sir William Chambers than of Brown, "more effort than nature, and more expence than taste. It is not easy to conceive any thing that art can introduce into a garden that is not here; woods, rocks, lawns, lakes, rivers, islands, cascades, grottos, walks, temples, and even villages." One protesting note against the English style is raised by Madame de Genlis, who, in *Les Veillées du Chateau*, writes of the mountains and precipices of Savoy, that they would rouse disgust for "ces froids jardins à l'anglaise, où l'on a voulu follement imiter de semblables effets." But the Revolution (of which the natural garden was in its way symbolic) came to end the gentle pastimes of queen and nobles.

In Belgium the Prince de Ligne followed the fashion, with reservations, at Beloeil. He published in 1778 *Un Coup d'Oeil sur Beloeil, et sur une grande partie des jardins de l'Europe.* Of English seats he admired most those in the grand style — Blenheim, Wilton, Kew — and was impatient of mock-ruins and pseudo-Gothic. "Quand on voit la Grécie de plusieurs Anglais, et la Gothie de Mr. Walpole, on est tenté de croire que c'est le délire d'un mauvais rêve qui a conduit leur ouvrage. J'aime autant son château d'Otrante; celui de la Tamise est tout aussi fou, et n'est pas plus gai."

The French fashion of English gardens was copied in Germany. Continental gardeners could not go quite so far as Price and Knight. "Nous n'adopterons pas tout à fait . . . l'idée de ces jardins entièrement pittoresques et romantiques de la création de *Salvator Rosa*," says the author of a work published in Leipzig at the opening of the nineteenth century; [51] and continues with a contrasting reference to the charms which a Claude and a Poussin gave to nature. In a footnote is brief reference to the controversy between Gilpin, Price, and Knight,

[51] *Descriptions Pittoresques de Jardins du goût le plus moderne,* second edition, Leipzig, 1805.

who have adopted Salvator Rosa as a model, and the more
" grand artiste *Repton*."

Italy was late in taking over the taste, but partly adopted
it in the last decade of the century. Arturo Graf gives a list of
dissertations, poems and other works, including a comedy and
a sermon in verse, either in eulogy or in ridicule of the mode.[52]

It may be doubted whether the garden was ever in any century a more constant subject of literary treatment than in the
eighteenth, and whether it ever before or since so mingled the
functions of library, picture gallery, and even pulpit; so Edward
Barnard writes, in *The Entertainments of the Garden*:

> Then say; were ever rising Landskips giv'n
> Only to gaze on? No! for higher End —
> To lead the intellectual Mind to trace
> Eye and admire Perfection infinite —
> Heav'ns matchless Skill, Benevolence, and Pow'r![53]

[52] *L'Anglomania e l'influsso inglese in Italia nel secolo XVIII*, Torino,
1911, pp. 343–350.
[53] *Virtue the Source of Pleasure*, 1757, p. 122.

VII

THE CULT OF THE PICTURESQUE

I

" Le Pittoresque," said Henri Beyle in *Mémoires d'un Touriste*, " nous vient d'Angleterre; un beau paysage fait partie de la religion comme de l'aristocratie d'un Anglais; chez lui c'est l'objet d'un sentiment sincère." The sentiment was scarce a century old in England when Beyle wrote this; it really does not appear there until 1740, when the collecting of pictures had been fashionable for a score of years. It rises into frequency by 1760, is general after 1780, and ridiculously hackneyed after 1800. The word, despite its frequent occurrence, and its appearance as early as 1705, holds an anomalous position to the very opening of the nineteenth century. As Steele used it in *The Tender Husband*, it is almost a synonym for *graphic*.[1] Pope, who regards it as French in 1712, uses it again in a note to the *Iliad*, 1715; but both times in the meaning, *pictorial*;[2] which is also slow to receive recognition in dictionaries.[3] The French Academy did not admit *pittoresque* until 1732; *pittoresco* was in common

---

[1] *Niece.* I would be drawn like the Amazon *Thalestris*, with a Spear in my Hand, and an Helmet on a Table before me. . . . At a distance behind me let there be a Dwarf, holding by the Bridle a Milk-white Palfrey. . . .
  Clerimont. Madam . . . if you please, there shall be a Cupid setting away your Helmet, to shew that Love should have a Part in all gallant Actions.
  Niece. That Circumstance may be very Picturesque.
  Act IV, Sc. ii. *Dramatick Works*, 1723, p. 141.
[2] Pope to Caryll, Dec. 21, 1712. *Works*, ed. Croker, VI, 178. " Mr. Phillips has two lines, which seem to me what the French call *Picturesque* . . .
  ' O'erlaid with snow, in bright confusion lie,
  And with one dazzling waste fatigue the eye.' "
. . . The marshy Spot of Ground where *Dolon* is killed, the Tamarisk . . . upon which they hang his Spoils, and the Reeds that are heap'd together to mark the Place, are Circumstances the most Picturesque imaginable." Pope's *Iliad*, 1715, III, 140. Note liv, Book X. *Cf.* Spence's *Anecdotes*, p. 11: " That idea of the picturesque, from the swan just gilded with the sun amidst the shade of a tree over the water."
[3] Blount, 1661, gives *pictorical, pictorian,* and *pictural;* in which he is followed by Coles, 1701.

Italian use in the seventeenth century, but meaning *painter-like,* not *picture-like.*

Gray used the word in 1740. " You cannot pass along a street," he writes from Rome, "but you have views of some palace, or church, or square, or fountain, the most picturesque and noble one can imagine." The same combination of adjectives returns when he writes of Dover Cliffs, 1766: " noble and picturesque." His friend Dr. Brown makes use of it in the famous letter on Keswick, of which more later. It is common in Arthur Young's *Tours,* from about 1766 on. Its first appearance in Gilpin's work is on the title-page of his *Essay on Prints* (1768), " the Principles of Picturesque Beauty," the stock phrase which recurs on the title-page of each of his later descriptive works. The phrase, as he says, is little understood, and vaguely used. He means by it precisely " that kind of beauty which *would look well in a picture.*" [4]

The word is never recognized by Johnson with a definition, yet he uses it to define one sense of *prospect,* in the fourth edition of the Dictionary, 1773; "A view delineated; a picturesque representation of a landscape." This is of course the sense of *in picture.* Neither Rider, 1759, nor Ash, 1775, gives the word; nor Walker, 1794. " *Pictoresque,* fr. like a picture," appears in Martin, 1754. Sheridan's fourth edition, 1797, gives *picturesque,* " suited to the pencil, though destitute of regular beauty," showing the influence of Gilpin, Price, and Knight; as does Entick, the same year, " exhibiting a picture, variegated." Barclay, 1799, has " Fine, beautiful, like a picture." George Mason, in his *Supplement* to Johnson, 1801, has a half-column of meanings and illustrations (borrowed largely from Mason's *Memoirs* of Gray), with a note at the close calling attention to Johnson's use of it in definition. The senses Mason gives are: (1) What pleases the eye; (2) remarkable for singularity; (3) striking the imagination with the force of painting; (4) to be exprest in painting; (5) affording a good subject for a landscape; (6) proper to take a landscape from. Undiscriminating as are some of his definitions, their very number shows how vague was the employment of the word, and also how frequent, — in short, how like slang.

[4] *Western Parts,* p. 238.

Salvator Rosa was generally agreed to be, as Price says, remarkable beyond most painters " for picturesque effects." We may consider him largely responsible for the common identification of the picturesque with the irregular and wild. " In no other master are seen such abrupt and rugged forms, such sudden deviations." Salvator himself had such a sense of the picturesque as his admirers in England had; theirs grown partly out of their admiration of him. He goes to Loreto in 1662, " et il viaggio è assai più curioso e pittoresco de cotesto di Fiorenza senza comparazione, attesochè è d'un misto cosi stravagante d'orrido, e di domestico, di piano e di scosceso, che non si puo desiderar di vantaggio per lo compiacimento dell'occhio." He goes out of his way to visit the waterfall of Terni; and finds for it a phrase which foreshadows many an utterance of the eighteenth century: " cosa da far spiritare ogni incontentabile cervello per la sua orrida bellezza." The association of beauty and horror was frequent in what were accounted *sublime* scenes; and it was Salvator who helped to establish this conjunction. Not that the picturesque was of necessity sublime; a thatched cottage, a rustic mill, a shaggy ass, were picturesque. But almost inevitably the picturesque was, as these too were held to be, *romantic,* whether or not that word of shadowy meaning accompanied the description.

2

It is surprising to see how suddenly and how powerfully the conception of the picturesque comes into fashion. Addison finds the scenery of Cassis " romantic," and does not wonder that poets have written of it; but he does not see it as picture. Lady Mary Montagu describes a " prodigious prospect of mountains covered with eternal snow, of clouds hanging far below our feet, and of vast cascades tumbling down the rocks with a confused roaring"; but not picturesquely. Edward Wright, passing along the shore to Genoa, comes nearer, but indistinctly: " The Eminence I rode along, gave me a variety of distant Prospects; and many of them not disagreeable; the nearer ones often romantick enough, and would have been fine Situations for enchanted Castles."

The first instance I know of true picturesque vision in the eighteenth century is Dr. Thomas Herring's impression of a Welsh valley. In 1738 Dr. Herring, Bishop of Bangor, and later Archbishop of Canterbury, made a diocesan journey through part of Wales, romantic and also perilous, as he pronounced it in retrospect, and was so much impressed by " the magnificence of nature" that he feared the sight of Stowe afterwards would have made him smile, and he would have " beheld with contempt an artificial ruin " after having been " agreeably terrified with something like the rubbish of a creation." The valley which he recalls picturesquely had rocky walls, woods, a foaming stream, with a rude bridge, a cataract down the mountain which shut in the valley, flocks and herds, and peasants coming home at evening with full pails. " All these images together put me much in mind of Poussin's drawings, and made me fancy myself in Savoy, at least, if not nearer Rome." [5]

Young Walpole, in 1739, views Savoy as picturesquely as possible: " Precipices, mountains, torrents, wolves, rumblings, Salvator Rosa. . . ." And he goes on painting appropriate details: " But the road, West, the road! Winding round a prodigious mountain, and surrounded by others, all shagged with hanging woods, obscured with pines, or lost in clouds! Below, a torrent breaking through cliffs, and tumbling through fragments of rocks! Sheets of cascades . . . hasting into the roughened river at the bottom! Now and then an old footbridge, with a broken rail, a leaning cross, a cottage, or the ruin of a hermitage! This sounds too bombastic and too romantic to one that has not seen it, too cold for one that has."

The sentiments of Walpole were doubtless reinforced by those of Gray, who may be considered the pioneer of the picturesque school. Gray, in 1739, ridicules Versailles and is intoxicated with the sublimities of the Grande Chartreuse; the hanging woods of pine-trees, the monstrous precipices, the torrent thundering below, concurred " to form one of the most astonishing scenes I ever beheld," " one of the most poetical scenes imaginable." " I do not remember to have gone ten paces without an exclamation, that there was no restraining: Not a precipice, not a torrent, not a cliff, but is pregnant with religion and poetry.

[5] *Letters from the late reverend Dr. Thomas Herring*, 1777, pp. 39–42.

St. John Preaching in the Wilderness.

From a painting by Salvator Rosa in the Collection of the Earl of Chesterfield.
Drawn by Richard Earlom, engraved by John Brown, 1768.
Fogg Art Museum, Harvard University.

There are certain scenes that would awe an atheist into belief.
. . . One need not have a very fantastic imagination to see
spirits there at noon-day."

Women are among the first to perceive the picturesque; perhaps
because so many of them copied prints, sketched, or painted.
A magazine writer of 1766 complains, to be sure, that " the
fair, in general, are not qualified for conversation, nor blessed
with a relish for sentimental pleasures. . . . They never contemplate on nature, and are insensible to her beauteous works.
. . . With vacant eye they pass the pleasing landskip, whose
variegated prospects display the evidence of an all-perfect and
all-bountiful Creator."[6] This passage affords evidence that a
sentimental enjoyment of landscape was then assumed as part
of the cultured endowment. But no complaint of vacant eye
could hold against Lady Hertford, or Mrs. Montagu, or her
friends Mrs. Delany and Mrs. Carter. Lady Hertford shows
her artistic proclivities as she travels, in 1740. Of her many
picturesque descriptions one will serve. Crossing the Apennines
she observes hermitages

as if stuck on the clefts of the rock, and old ruined fortresses that have
scarcely left a name. Below, the firs and cypresses . . . made a gloomy
retreat for the torrents that fell roaring from above; and the evening
sun gave a lustre to the whole, which finished in a rich and delightful
plain, where the rising grain, the gentle murmur of the river, the green
meadows, the elms twined round with vines, the solitary chapels, with
here and there some broken piece of ancient sculpture . . . both soothed
and waked the soul, to find and adore the Great Creator.

Mrs. Delany is a notable example of the gentlewoman actively
interested in various arts, and because of her study of painting,
sure to observe scenery and grounds with a picturesque eye.
She sketches scenes in the grounds of her friends. Her slight
descriptions are numerous; one passage which shows her
following the usual rule is an apology for not describing:
" Could I have attended to the beauties en passant between
dear, sweet Ilam and [Sudbury], I should present my dearest
Mary with such a mixture of pastoral delights as would have
served a Claude or a Shenstone for their whole lives." She
helped Mr. Delany to plan Delville, which was the first attempt

[6] *Universal Magazine*, 1756, p. 269.

in Ireland in the new style of gardening. Her account of an Irish ball shows how landscape entered even the ball-room, in 1752: " The *room represents a wood,* and there is room left down the middle enough for thirty couple to dance; at one end is a portico on Doric pillars, lighted by baskets of flowers, the candles *green wax,* so that nothing appears but the flame." There is a jessamine bower, a Gothic temple (serving as sideboard), a grotto " extremely well exprest," in which sit musicians garbed as shepherds and shepherdesses. " The trees are *real trees* with *artificial leaves,* but when all is done, it will be too much crowded to be agreeable, and most dangerous if the spark of a candle should fall on any of the scenery, which is all painted paper." [7]

The Blues, considerably younger than Mrs. Delany, were all picturesque enthusiasts, in varying degrees. Mrs. Elizabeth Montagu, their leader, being daughter of a distinguished amateur landscape painter, was prepared to judge of scenery. At Tunbridge in 1754 she went on what might be called a picturesque picnic, along with Pitt, and presumably Lyttelton, his friend Bower and the Wests.

> We drank tea yesterday in the most beautiful rural scene that can be imagined, which Mr. Pitt had discovered in his morning's ride. . . . He ordered a tent to be pitched, tea to be prepared, and his French horn to breathe music like the unseen genius of the wood. The company dined with us; and we set out, number eight. After tea we rambled about for an hour, seeing several views, some wild as Salvator Rosa, others placid, and with the setting sun, worthy of Claude Lorrain.[8]

Visiting Spa in 1763 she is happy to view the " noble and sublime " prospects in a violent hurricane on a mountain top, accompanied by deep thunder; " this circumstance, which wd have spoiled the amenity of a little scene, added dignity to this solemn and majestick character." [9] From the mountain one morning, she and Mrs. Carter watch the Cordeliers carrying

---

[7] Mrs. Chapone has an amusing letter, in 1776, about an *al fresco* picturesque entertainment by Beckford, the Arcadian beauties of which were painfully blasted by the northeast wind. Mrs. Cornelys' rooms were decorated in a style to convey ideas of rural landscape, as appears from some descriptions.

[8] *Letters,* 1809, III, 315–316.

[9] *Mrs. Montagu, Queen of the Blues,* I, 53–54.

the host in procession, and their thoughts fly to Thomson; also, it is clear, to Gaspar Poussin if not to Salvator Rosa: " Their solemn step, lugubre habit, and the base voice of their chaunting deepen'd the murmur of the falling floods, and shed a browner horror on the woods. The dreary desert, the woods, the rocks, the cascades, and all the objects we look'd upon borrow'd from, and lent solemnity to this religious ceremony."

Mrs. Montagu's dear friend, the celebrated Mrs. Carter, who accompanied her on some of the expeditions to Tunbridge, was " fond of every view of nature, from the soft landscapes of a vernal evening to the awful beauty of a stormy sky." She is one of the best examples in her time of the sentimental treatment of nature; an attitude with her perfectly sincere and unaffected. " The sublime views of wild uncultivated nature, the silence of a desert, and the melancholy repose of a ruin, strikes the imagination with awful and affecting ideas. In such a situation the soul expands itself, and feels at once the greatness of its capacities, and the littleness of its pursuits." She loved to take long walks, especially by moonlight, over the hills, along the shore, among the ruins of an old abbey, " in all that composure of pleasing melancholy which scenes like these so naturally inspire." It offended her taste that the country about Battle Abbey was " too pastoral and riant to suit the ideas which belong to such a spot " ; she would have liked " to have the ground planted with yew and cypress . . . and restore the scrub oak and ravens." " Savage beauty," the " idea of the sublime and terrible " which Mrs. Vesey's letters from Wales provided, thrilled her; but she lamented that the intrepid lady was obliged to go so far out of her way to find a spot capable of amusing her with the danger of breaking her neck. " Safety and convenience are very agreeable circumstances in a place of abode; though the sublime objects of untamed nature afford so high an entertainment for the imagination of a poetical traveller." But this was at the age of fifty-six. Studley and Fountains Abbey she admired, untouched by the artistic scruples which affected William Gilpin and even Arthur Young. " Such scenes as these are certainly admirably adapted to raise the imagination to sublime enthusiasm, and to soften the heart by poetic melancholy; but sublime enthusiasm and poetic melancholy are too high an exer-

tion for our intellectual powers to be long continued without
pain and langour," (she was at this time sixty-five, if it is fair
to speak of years with one so perennially young) " and are quite
unconnected with the general temper that qualifies us for social
life." With the soft and agreeable wildness about Tunbridge
she was pleased; the country near the rocks was " the most perfectly romantic I had ever seen, except in the descriptions of
poets, or the paintings of Salvator Rosa. . . . All was wild
spontaneous beauty, and what Mr. Mason finely calls ' the lone
majesty of untamed nature.' " They drank tea in this wild
region after sunset, and then waited " to see the effect of moonlight on so solemn a scene."

Mrs. Chapone, another of the Blues, writes to Mrs. Carter in 1770 even more enthusiastically: " At Taymouth indeed every conceivable beauty of landscape is united with the
sublime. Such a lake! such variegated hills rising from its
banks! such mountains and such cloud cap'd rocks rising behind them! such a delicious green valley to receive the sweet
winding Tay! such woods! such cascades! — in short, I am
wild that you and all my romantic friends should see it; for
even a Milton's pen, or a Salvator Rosa's pencil would fail to
give you a complete idea of it."

That admired friend of these literary ladies, Lord Lyttelton,
journeyed to Wales with his protégé, the undeserving Bower,
in 1756, and described the sights as a connoisseur of scenery,
especially of parks. He thought the mountains rising at a
distance gave "a magnificence and grandeur to the scene, without
giving you any horror or dreadful ideas," when so far off that
their outlines were softened. But the prospect from Berwin
struck his mind with awful astonishment. " Nature in all
her majesty is there, but it is the majesty of a tyrant, frown-
ing over the ruins and desolation of a country." The admired
vale of Clwydd has great beauty, but lacks majesty; whereas
in Montgomeryshire, " as in the mind of our friend the *Madona* "
(thus Lyttelton and Bower styled Mrs. Montagu) " the soft and
agreeable is mixed with the noble, the great, and the sublime."
To Lord Lyttelton's son, the " wicked Lord," some of this innocent enjoyment of scenery must have descended. Mrs.
Montagu was struck with his youthful descriptions of the

Highlands: "His views of Scotland appear as the scenes of Salvator Rosa would do, were they copied by Claude, whose sweet and lovely imagination would throw fine colours on the darkest parts, and give grace to the rudest objects."

3

The most important connection of Lyttelton with the picturesque was his being the correspondent to whom " the ingenious Dr. Brown " of the *Estimate* wrote a letter about Keswick which apparently everyone read; for it is referred to frequently in the periodicals as familiar. It was printed in Pearch's *Supplement* to Dodsley's *Miscellany* in 1768, as a note to Dr. Dalton's *Descriptive Poem*. This letter played a part in making the lake scenery famous; and appears to be the first important published work on the picturesque. Printed at Newcastle in 1767, it must have been written before 1760, the date of Brown's quarrel with Lyttelton, and probably before 1756, when he had not yet been appointed to the living in Essex, but was still in the Lake region. The description contains the favorite elements of romance, horror, Thomson, and painting;

At Keswick you will, on one side of the lake, see a rich and beautiful landskip of cultivated fields, rising to the eye in fine inequalities, with noble groves of oak happily dispersed; and clinging to the adjacent hills, shade above shade, in the most various and picturesque forms. On the opposite shore, you will find rocks and cliffs of stupendous height, hanging broken over the lake in horrible grandeur, some of them a thousand feet high, the woods climbing up their steep and shaggy sides. . . . A variety of waterfalls are seen pouring from their summits, and tumbling in vast sheets from rock to rock, in rude and terrible magnificence, while on all sides of this mimic amphitheatre the lofty mountains rise around, piercing the clouds. . . .

. . . The full perfection of Keswick consists of three circumstances, beauty, horror, and immensity united. To give you a complete idea of these three perfections . . . would require the united powers of Claude, Salvator and Poussin. The first should throw his delicate sunshine over the cultivated vales, the scattered cots, the groves, the lakes and wooded islands. The second should dash out the horrors of the rugged cliffs, the steeps, the hanging rocks and foaming waterfalls, while the grand pencil of Poussin should crown the whole, with the majesty of an impending mountain.

. . . I would point out the perpetual change of prospect: the woods, rocks, cliffs, and mountains, by turns vanishing or rising into view: now gaining on the sight, hanging over our heads in their full dimensions, beautifully dreadful; and now . . . assuming new romantic shapes. . . .

Another bit of evidence for the increasing picturesque vision is a plate in the *British Magazine* for June, 1761, of the view from the Star and Garter at Richmond, with accompanying *Reflections*, beginning thus:

> The assemblage of objects, known by the name of landscape, is so interesting to the eye, and affecting to the imagination, that when nature did not supply sufficient variety to regale the faculty of sight and the power of fancy, the most eminent painters have employed their talents in exhibiting artificial views and prospects in which the great and sublime, the gay and agreeable, objects of inanimate nature are variously combined, so as to furnish an infinite fund of entertainment, according to the different dispositions of the human mind. At one moment the imagination loves to contemplate the awful scenes of solitary nature, such as stupendous rocks, gloomy forests, and louring skies; sometimes to survey the terrible . . . the tumbling ruin, the oak up-torn, the blackening cloud, and gleaming lightning. Those are scenes that strike the soul with a kind of pleasing horror, and fill it with sublime ideas of greatness and immensity. Such were the subjects that employed the pencil of the celebrated Salvator Rosa, in contra-distinction to the more mildly pleasing scenes which rose from the labours of a Poussin and Claude Lorrain, according to those lines of the poet,
>
> > Whate'er *Lorrain* light touch'd with soft'ning hue,
> > Or savage *Rosa* dash'd, or learned *Poussin* drew.

The appearance of Burke's *Inquiry into the Origin of our Ideas of the Sublime or Beautiful* (1756, second enlarged edition 1757) had a good deal of influence in arousing aesthetic perception of scenery, though Burke does not enter into discussion of the *picturesque*. But his remarks upon *smoothness* as perhaps the most essential attribute of the beautiful, with the necessary corollary that *roughness* belongs to the sublime, had great effect on Gilpin and Price.

In 1760 the influence of Salvator was reinforced by that of Ossian. The descriptions in Ossian are brief and hazy, but the dark woods, lonely heaths, mountain streams, green hills, mossy rocks, gray torrents, and storm-bent trees are impressive from sheer repetition. Isaac Taylor's vignettes in the first editions are very suggestive of Salvator's influence. How impressive was Ossian to the sentimental soul we may learn from Miss

THE CASCADE.

Engraved by Vivares after the painting by Gaspar Poussin in the Houghton Collection.

Seward. " In my sixteenth year," says she, " I first read Ossian.
If I did not dance for joy . . . I wept for joy." But she could
not proceed with it long at a sitting; for the imagination " will
not bear the protraction of unrelieved sublimity." She prides
herself on possessing sublimity as birthright. " Born amidst
the highest of the Peak mountains, and passing the first seven
years of my life surrounded by the wild grandeur of that scenery,
it seized my first affection. Hence the landscapes of Ossian
charm me more than those of more cultivated, more luxurious
countries." " The first objects that met my infant glance, and
impressed me with their lonely and romantic grandeur, were
the mountains, the rocks, and the vales of Derbyshire. . . .
Poetic descriptions and pencilled resemblances please me best
when they take the Salvatorial style. This early established
predilection steeps my eyes in the dews of pensive transport,
when they stray over the pages of Ossian." But she would
not have them stray long at a time. " We should look attentively at his landscapes, but not consider them for a much
longer time than we could, without weariness, gaze at a landscape of Claude's, or Salvator's."

She is constantly viewing scenery through the medium of
pictures. Her native village, Eyam, " boasts a Salvatorial dale
and glen " ; again, she wishes " for a Claude, and Salvatorial
pencil, to delineate " her native rocks and hills, their romantic
beauties and sterner graces." We hear of " the Salvatorial
features of Mr. Roberts' situation," and " the Claude-landscapes
of Langollen's vale." The vale of Stow " glows sunny through
the Claude-Lorain-tint, which is spread over the scene like blue
mist over plumb." When her friend Whalley travels in Switzer-
land and sends back the usual descriptive letter, she thanks him
fervidly: " Oh, my beloved friend, through what magnificent
and beautiful scenery do you lead me! Were Claude, Poussin
and Salvator now living, and were they also my partial friends;
for my amusement were they to employ their magic pencil,
and throw the scenes through which you have passed on their
breathing canvas, . . . my imagination could not more forcibly
receive the distinct ideas of their glowing beauty and astonishing
sublimity." Her friend Major André evidently catches the
contagion; he sends a poetic account of an autumn walk:

" Gilded hills, variegated woods, glittering spires, ruminating brook, bounding flocks, all combined to enchant the eyes." [10]

It is indicative of the general taste for scenery that we find in 1765 such different persons as Smollett, Joseph Warton, and Wilkes writing impressions of it. Smollett is ill-pleased with Italian gardens. An Englishman looks to see in a park " a number of groves and glades intermixed with an agreeable negligence," lawns, ponds, cascades, streams, clumps of trees, arbours, grottos, hermitages, temples, alcoves. The gardens of Italy lack the effect of rural simplicity which English gardens are designed to produce. He visits the waterfall at Terni, " an object of tremendous sublimity," though it loses effect from lack of a proper point of view. Joseph Warton, visiting Derbyshire, finds Matlock " of all earthly places the most exquisite and romantic, and beyond any possible description." John Wilkes, travelling in Italy, notices " picturesque " views, recalls the beauty of his native greensward, though he admits that " in England it is scarcely known what a fine blue arch of heaven is here, pure, serene, and unclouded," and visits the Grande Chartreuse. There he writes in the album: " I had the happiness of passing the entire day of July 24, 1765, in this romantic place, with the good fathers of the Grande Chartreuse, and I reckon it among the most agreeable of my life." So far we might assume merely the politeness of the conversable Wilkes; but his closing lines show how he too lay open to the sentiments of the picturesque-sublime: " The savageness of the woods, the gloom of the rocks, and the perfect solitude, conspire to make the mind pensive, and to lull to rest all the turbulent guilty passions of the soul." [11] It is easy to conceive of a modern politician as unscrupulous as Wilkes, and possible to think of one as clever, but to imagine one thus spreading his soul on the pages of a visitor's book is an effort which brings sharply to mind the change in sentimental fashions.

Another proof of this lies in the *Tours* of Arthur Young, who travelled for purposes economic and agricultural, but seems most to enjoy describing scenery and visiting picture galleries; he is

[10] Seward, *Poet. Works*, II, 97–98.

[11] *Correspondence*, 1805, II, 183–184. Fox was also " a very exquisite judge of the picturesque "; as well as something of a landscape gardener. Thomson, *Recollections of Literary Characters*, 1854, I, 120.

commended by the critics for his attention to the polite arts. He is something of an artist himself, though his cascades in the Northern *Tour* do look rigid. It is amusing that the predecessor of Gray in picturesque touring should be one whose primary interest was in crops. But even from " Mr. Tucker's cabbage field " he can see a view; " I would at any time with the utmost pleasure, ride forty miles to view such another. . . . Three rivers wind through it, . . . lost in some places among the trees, and break upon the eye in others, in a stile of picturesque elegance." Young's first *Tour*, through the southern counties, was published in 1768. The descriptions of scenes are largely views of grounds. Mr. Hamilton's park at Cobham is manifestly in the style of Gaspar Poussin, though Young does not say so. He describes a view through an artificial ruined arch: " The river appears winding in a proper manner; that is, dark and gloomy, around a rough piece of grass, which has a consistent appearance. But what hurt me very much, was the contradiction of emotions, raised by the scene behind; . . . elegant and agreeable; a smooth water, and sloping banks, closely shaven, with a little island in it, are all *agreeable* objects; and by no means affect the spectator in unison with the ruin of *Grecian* architecture, and the gloomy objects around." He finds this place one of *beauty*; but Persfield, on the Wye, is *sublime*. He describes it at length, apologizing for inadequacy: " A landscape too beautiful for such a daubing pencil as mine to paint; Mr. *Dodsley*—with his dingells, *and such expressive terms*, might make amends for the want of a Claud Loraine." At one view, his pen drops from his hand: " No, my good friend, the eyes of your imagination are not keen enough to take in this point, which the united talents of a *Claude*, a *Poussin*, a *Vernet*, and a *Smith*, would scarcely be able to sketch." After his enthusiastic account he suggests a few deficiencies, chiefly the want of contrast: " For the general emotions which arise on viewing the rocks, the hanging woods, and deep precipices of *Persfield*, are all those of the *sublime*; and when that is the case, the *beautiful* never appears in such bewitching colours, as those it receives from contrast: to turn suddenly from one of these romantic walks, and break full upon a beautiful landscape, without any intermixture of rocks, distant prospect, or any object that was *great* or *terrible,* . . . would be a vast improvement here." What he would like would be " Small elegant buildings, in a light and airy taste, rising from green and gently swelling slopes, . . . and situated so that the sun may shine full upon them," — in other words, a Sibyl's temple or so.

The *Tour of the North,* taken in 1768, has more descriptions of natural scenes, along with the ornamented grounds. One of the last is clearly Italian in style, with " an Ionic temple, commanding a noble variety of prospect and landscape ; The former is seen to the left picturesquely, broken by large trees near the temple itself : A little to the right of that a vast extent of country ; then you look down upon a valley, winding at the bottom of a noble amphitheatre of hanging woods, . . . and at the other end of the terrass, a tuscan colonnade temple. . . . The valley . . . the meanders of the river, . . . the cascade almost overhung with the pendant wood, . . . the tuscan temple crowning a bank of wood, form together a distant landscape in which every object is such as the warmest fancy could wish for, or the correctest taste approve." The Yorkshire moors give him many pleasing encounters with " the terrible sublime." Once he finds an enchanting landscape " as if dropt from heaven in the midst of this wild desart. . . . Would to heaven I could unite in one sketch the chearfulness of *Zuccarelli,* with the gloomy terrors of *Pousin* [*sic*], the glowing brilliancy of *Claud,* with the romantic wildness of *Salvator Rosa.*" At Studley he digresses on the subject of ruins. A ruin ought to be in a retired, neglected spot, half filled with rubbish, the habitation of bats, owls, and wild beasts. " This horrible wildness greatly strengthens the idea raised by falling walls, ruined columns, and imperfect arches : both are awful, and impress upon the mind a kind of religious melancholy." Ruins generally appear best at a distance ; and approach to them should be difficult ; in fact, to some parts, impossible, so that the imagination may have room to range in. As for an artificial ruin, it should be in exact imitation of a real one ; for this reason it should never serve a festive purpose, but should be allowed to inspire ideas of melancholy unimpeded.

How consciously he viewed scenes with a picture-making eye
is shown by his account of Hackfall, Mr. Aislabie's other estate:
" the outline of the picture is noble; but the filling up of the
canvass adds a colouring more than equal to the pencil of
a *Claud*." One little amphitheatre scene " may not be admired
by those who are fond only of the *great,* but to such as are
pleased with the soft tints of nature's pencil, — with the mild
glow of *Vernet* as well as the majesty of *Poussin,* this landscape
will yield pure enjoyment." Near Cocken (where two of Salvator's landscapes were to be seen in the house) " the wild
imagination of *Salvator* has scarcely pictured any thing more
striking, or in a more splendid stile, than this variety of wood
breaking forth from the craggy clifts and chasms of these noble
rocks. This intermixture of rocks and wood is truly romantic
and picturesque." The Lake country moves him to impassioned
raptures. The boldly indented shore of Winandermere is
" skirted with spreading trees, an edging as elegant as ever fancied by *Claud* himself."

His *Eastern Tour,* published in 1771, gives many descriptions
of grounds. Newstead Abbey has a fine lake, with *two* castles
on its banks, " uncommon, tho' picturesque; it seems rather
unfortunate that the cannon should be levelled at the palace
windows." He fears that Brown's improvements at Roche Abbey
may spoil the effect by raising a cheerful idea. As Young saw
them, the cliffs " are spread with thick woods that throw a
solemn gloom over the whole, and *breathe a browner horror* on
every part of the scene. All is wild, and romantic. . . . Every
part unites to raise melancholy ideas; perhaps the most powerful, of which the human soul is capable." The *Tour in Ireland*
suffered by the loss of Young's notes; though it would never be
guessed from his full and frequent descriptions of landscape.
His Travels in France have less to do with scenery; but he gets
much pleasure from the Pyrenees, and finds at Montauban features " which *Claude Lorain* would not have failed transfixing
on his canvass."

Gray, though his work on the subject was but the rough notes
of a fortnight's walking tour in the Lakes in 1769, was more
influential upon the picturesque tourist than Young with all
his thirteen volumes. The notes, published with Gray's other

letters in 1775, were read by every person of taste, and played no little part in making the Lake country fashionable touring ground. Already it was the haunt of artists; the eccentric Chatelain had copied it, and Gray tells of being at the same inn where Vivares, Smith, and Bellers had stayed. As sole companion, after Wharton fell ill and failed him, Gray had his Claude-glass, " a plano-convex mirror, of about four inches diameter, on a black foil, and bound up like a pocket-book." [12] The reflections of scenery in this, from the convexity and dark ground, showed the objects as if painted, with composition and lowered tone. Foliage and rocks are especially effective in the Claude-glass. Nothing is more characteristic of Gray, or of his age, than his thus translating Keswick and Borrowdale into the four-inch darkened picture of his glass, in order to have fullest pleasure from them. He refers to it several times:

On the ascent of the hill above Appleby, the thick hanging wood & the long reaches of the Eden . . . winding below with views of the Castle & Town gave much employment to the mirror. . . .

Cross'd the meadows obliquely, catching a diversity of views among the hills over the lake & island and changing prospect at every ten paces . . . near the food of *Walla-crag* . . . the most delicious view, that my eyes ever beheld. behind you are the magnificent heights of *Walla-crag;* opposite lie the thick hanging woods of Ld Egremont, & Newland Valley, with green & smiling fields embosom'd in the dark cliffs . . . to the left the turbulent chaos of mountain behind mountain roll'd in confusion; beneath you . . . the shining purity of the *Lake,* just ruffled by the breeze enough to shew it alive, reflecting rocks, woods, fields, & inverted tops of mountains, with the white buildings of *Keswick, Crosthwait*-church & Skiddaw for a back ground at a distance. oh! Doctor! I never wish'd more for you; & pray think, how the glass play'd its part in such a spot.

At Kirkstall Abbey, where ivy, and roots of sturdy trees encroach upon the ruins, " the gloom of these ancient cells, the shade & verdure of the landscape, the glittering & murmur of the stream, the lofty towers & long perspectives of the church, . . . detain'd me for many hours, & were the truest subjects for my glass I have yet met with." Once he fell down with the glass open in his hand; but luckily broke only his knuckles. It is not necessary to give more of his pictures; they are well

---

[12] Mason's note, 1775, p. 352.

known. Always he shows a sense of pictorial composition, and
of light and shade, strongly suggestive of the paintings of the
Italian landscape school.

The next summer he spent six weeks with Norton Nicholls in
a tour of the border counties, "five of the most beautiful
counties in England," and went down the Wye in a boat; "its
banks are a succession of nameless wonders! one out of many
you may see not ill described by Mr Whateley [*sic*] in his
Observations on Gardening under the name of the New *Weir*;
he has also touched upon two others, *Tinterne-Abbey*, and
Persfield." Of the five regions of Britain most haunted by
the lovers of the picturesque, Gray noticed four. (He does
not describe North Wales.) The Peak he did not like, "a
country beyond comparison, uglier than any other I have seen
in England, black, tedious, barren, & not mountainous enough
to please one with its horrors." As to the Highlands, he writes
to Palgrave in 1758: "I congratulate you on your new acquaintance with the *savage,* the *rude,* and the *tremendous.*
Pray, tell me, is it anything like what you had read in your
book, or seen in two-shilling prints?" In 1765 he went there
himself: "The mountains are ecstatic, and ought to be visited
in pilgrimage once a year. None but those monstrous creatures
of God know how to join so much beauty to so much horror.
A fig for your poets, painters, gardeners and clergymen" (he
is writing to Mason, who is all four) "that have not been among
them; their imagination can be made up of nothing but bowl-
ing-greens, flowering shrubs, horse-ponds, Fleet ditches, shell
grottoes, and Chinese rails."

4

The Reverend Mr. Gilpin made his picturesque tour of the
Wye the same year that Gray made his. It was the encouragement of Gray, and later of Mason, that finally induced the
timid and impecunious gentleman to publish his remarks and
sketches, some fifteen years after he made the first of them.
His *Essay on Prints,* printed in 1768, ten years after it was
written, had been received with warm approbation. In the
meantime he was each year adding to his accumulation, made

in his vacation pilgrimages to the various parts of Britain. There is something engaging about Gilpin: his anxiety that the study of picturesque beauty shall not be deemed unsuitable to the vocation of a clergyman, his deference to his critics, at the same time that he holds firmly to certain opinions, as for example that upon the character of Charles II, his conscientious alterations of nature to bring it more into accord with the principles of the picturesque, his very oddities of style, such as the constantly recurring *it's* and the quaint distribution of italics. " A humane, tolerant, ingenious, benevolent man," his friend Samuel Pratt calls him. He was a schoolmaster of excellent ideas; and when he received from his former pupil, the historian Mitford, a living at Boldre in the New Forest, he set about to remedy the conditions of ignorance and squalor which he found among his parishioners by establishing a school. It was this school which the profits of his books went to support; his desire to help it overcame his fears of failure. For a number of years his remarks and sketches were passed about, in manuscript, under the supervision of Mason. Walpole, Mrs. Delany, the Duchess of Portland, the Reverend Michael Tyson, are among those who were interested. Tyson industriously copied the sketches, which he admired, though he could not see that they resembled their orginals. He thought the remarks admirable, " but yet a book *only* of Picturesque Beauty is to me as palling as a Dinner made up of Plumb-cake, Trifle, and Caraway Comfits. But mark me, I had rather have Gilpin's Plumb-Cake than Pennant's hard Dumplings." For more than ten years Gilpin's work had only such private circulation. " I wish I *cou'd steal* (for fear I shall never influence)," sighs Mrs. Delany, " out of the mischievous banks at the gaming tables four or five hundred pounds, and bestow it upon a work that wou'd do honour, not only to the very worthy and ingenious author, but to the country which he lives in." The Duchess of Portland offered to assist in the publication, but Gilpin, sensitive in his poverty, would not accept her generosity.

At last, encouraged by his friends, especially by Mason, he began to publish, by Mason's advice taking first a small volume, the *Observations on the River Wye*, made in 1770, rather than one of his more elaborate works. The attempt, in 1782, was successful; by 1800 the book had gone into a fifth edition, and appeared besides in a small form suitable for a guide-book. There followed the series of elaborately printed volumes on the Lakes, on the Highlands, on the New Forest, and forest scenery, on the southwest counties, the Isle of Wight, the southern coast, the eastern counties, and north Wales. Two of the volumes appeared after Gilpin's death in 1804. The fact that the early editions were small, and quickly exhausted may have helped to enhance his reputation. "The first edition of this elegant work," says the *Monthly Review*, of the *Observations* on the Lakes, "eluded the vigilance of our collector by the rapidity of its sale, the whole impression having been bought up in a few days." [13]

By picturesque beauty Gilpin means, as has been said, simply "that kind of beauty which *would look well in a picture*." In arriving at decisions as to what scenes are "correctly picturesque," it is clear that he has in mind the landscape art which is most admired by his age. Nature and picturesque considerations sometimes clash; he is generous enough to suggest that this is due to the vast scale on which nature works. The artist, on the other hand, "is confined to a *span*; and lays down his little rules, which he calls the *principles of picturesque beauty*, merely to adapt such diminutive parts of nature's surface to his own eye as come within its scope. — Hence, therefore, the painter who adheres strictly to the *composition* of nature, will rarely make a good picture." [14] The confusion between *picturesque*

[13] Gilpin's picturesque works are:
Observations on the River Wye and several Parts of South Wales, &c. relative chiefly to Picturesque Beauty, 1782.
Observations on . . . the Mountains and Lakes of Cumberland and Westmoreland . . . 1786.
Observations on Several Parts of Great Britain, particularly the High-lands of Scotland, . . . 1789.
Remarks on Forest Scenery . . . illustrated by Scenes of the New Forest, . . . 1791.
Three Essays: On Picturesque Beauty; on Picturesque Travel; and on Sketching Landscape, 1792.
Observations on the Western Parts of England. . . . Remarks on the Isle of Wight . . . 1798.
Observations on the Coasts of Hampshire, Sussex, and Kent . . . 1804.
Observations on . . . the Counties of Cambridge, Norfolk, Suffolk and Essex. . . . Also on several Parts of North Wales . . . 1809.
[14] *Wye*, fifth ed., pp. 30–31.

and *romantic* he attempts to clear in his remarks on Arthur's Seat, which is " romantic but not picturesque," — for it is " odd, misshapen, and uncouth; and a view with such a staring feature in it, can no more be picturesque, than a face with a bulbous nose can be beautiful." To distinguish the beautiful from the picturesque he finds the principle of *roughness*, following Burke.[15] Though he had not travelled abroad, he was sure that England " exceeds most countries in the variety of its picturesque beauties." River-views were his favourites. If perfect, they had " four grand parts: the *area*, which is the river itself; the *two side-screens*, which are the opposite banks, and lead the perspective; and the *front screen*, which points out the windings of the river." He had fixed views on the grouping of cattle. Two cows will hardly combine. " With three, you are sure of a good group, except indeed they all stand in the same attitude and at equal distances." Price tells of a person of picturesque proclivities, who, when his prudent wife suggested that two of their three cows would suffice for their needs, replied, " Lord, my dear, *two* cows you know can never group."

Gilpin made some use of Claude Lorrain glasses. He seems to have known a different kind from that used by Gray, and still employed; he describes them as " combined of two or three different colours; and if the hues are well sorted, they give the object of nature a soft, mellow tinge, like the colouring of that master," as well as greater depth to the shades. This seems to be the kind that Scott refers to in *Redgauntlet*, " which spreads its own particular hue over the landscape you see through it." But Gilpin used the mirror, also, and especially enjoyed its changing pictures, when he was riding in a chaise. " They are like the visions of the imagination; or the brilliant landscapes of a dream. Forms, and colours in brightest array, fleet before us; and if the transient glance of a good composition happen to unite with them, we should give any price to fix and appropriate the scene."

Gilpin does not often compare real landscapes to painted ones, though he plainly has in mind the painted ones in admiring

---

[15] Sydney Smith was probably thinking of this in his famous distinction: " The rector's horse is *beautiful*, the curate's is *picturesque*." Lockhart's *Life of Scott*, Chap. XV.— Mr. W. P. Ker, in *The Art of Poetry*, 1923, notices these passages in the definition of *romantic* and *picturesque*, p. 78.

real ones. The withered and shattered tree is justified as picturesque by Salvator Rosa's use of it; and the chestnut " is consecrated" by adorning his foregrounds. Berghem is a favourite, of whom he is reminded at Windermere, by cattle standing before a rock, and at Kenilworth, where " cattle and ruins adorn each other." The influence of the Italian painters shows in his preference for river views, either grand, or as the " scene of rural pleasure " ; for sharp contrasts of light and shade, chiaroscuro; for darkened foregrounds; for an extensive distance, " one of the greatest beauties of nature " ; and especially for banditti as ornaments to landscape. The approach to Dunmail Raise is unhappily without these last adornments, though so " well adapted to the perpetration of some dreadful deed." The gentle clergyman sighs that " moral and picturesque ideas do not always coincide."

In a moral view, the industrious mechanic is a more pleasing subject than the loitering peasant. But in a picturesque light, it is otherwise. . . . The lazy cowherd, resting on his pole, . . . may be allowed in the grandest scene; while the laborious mechanic, with his instruments of labour, would be repulsed. . . .

The characters, which are most *suited to these* scenes of grandeur, are such as impress us with some idea of greatness, wildness, or ferocity; all which touch on the sublime. Figures in long, flowing draperies; gypsies; banditti; and soldiers, not in modern regimentals; but as Virgil paints them, "Longis adnixi hastis, et scuta tenentes; ". . . For the truth of all these remarks, I might appeal to the decisive judgment of Salvator Rosa.

Gilpin has a comical fashion of treating nature as an artist of genius, but untrained and requiring correction. " She touches every object with spirit. Her general colouring, and her local hues, are exquisite. In composition only she fails." To be sure, the seeming failure may be explained because she works on so vast a plan. But it is generally necessary for the human artist to use his imagination, to cull from nature the most beautiful parts, and remove the offensive. Even if you wish for the picture of a particular scene, you must allow the artist to make certain changes, especially such as might be made in the actual objects, like planting or removing trees, or changing the course of a road. Thus in representing Conway Castle and the scenery about it, where nature's composition is incorrect, you should introduce only part of the castle, cut down the heavy wood, and plant a tree or two in the foreground. Castles are rarely found just as they should be for picturesque purposes; in spite of the efforts of Cromwell upon which Gilpin makes a mild jest: "What share of picturesque genius Cromwell might have had, I know not; — I have seen many pieces by this master, executed in a very grand style." Rarely Gilpin remarks on a natural scene "correctly picturesque," as is Goodrich Castle, on the Wye.

He has much to say of the embellished scene, though he accounts it unfit for picturesque representation. The number of his descriptions shows how prevailing was the taste for landscape gardening, and his frank strictures on such as seem to him in poor taste, like Studley and Ford Abbey, forecast the severity of Price and Knight. He stands between them and Walpole and Mason in his view of Brown. When Brown deals with a ruin, as at Roche Abbey, Gilpin protests. As to artificial ruins, he is open-minded. He seems to approve of ruins placed at a distance, to make an object in a picture, but ruins near at hand, and to be walked around, are risky ventures. "When it is well done, we will allow that nothing can be more beautiful; but we see everywhere so many absurd attempts of this kind, that when we walk through a piece of improved ground; and hear the next of being carried to *see the ruins* . . . we dread the encounter."

Gilpin's fondness for a high style (of course he admired Ossian), and his mixture of poetic vocabulary with technical jargon of side-screens, foreground, and distances, was found ridiculous by some readers, even in his own time. But his descriptions, if flowery, are often admirably vivid and painter-like; for example:

Our approach to Wells, from the *natural* and *incidental* beauties of the scenery, was uncommonly picturesque. It was a hazy evening; and the sun, declining low, was hid behind a purple cloud, which covered half the hemisphere, but did not reach the western horizon. Its lower skirts were gilt with dazzling splendor, which spread downwards, not in diverging rays, but in one uniform ruddy glow; and uniting at the bottom with the mistiness of the air, formed a rich, yet modest tint, with which Durcote-hill projecting boldly on the left, the towers of

THE PANTHEON AT STOURHEAD.

Aquatint by Gilpin.

Wells behind it, and all the objects of the distance, were tinged; while the foreground, seen against so bright a piece of scenery, was overspread with the darkest shades of evening. The whole together invited the pencil, without soliciting the imagination. But it was a transitory scene. As we stood gazing at it, the sun sunk below the cloud, and being stripped of all its splendor by the haziness of the atmosphere, fell, like a ball of fire, into the horizon, and the whole radiant vision faded away.

Though Gilpin's works did not begin appearing till 1782, they had considerable influence, as has been intimated, through their circulation in manuscript. On their appearance, they were greeted with warm enthusiasm. The reviewers treat Gilpin with a respectful deference which must have delighted his anxious soul, and such occasional carping as is found directs itself against the costliness of his productions and the doubtful value of the numerous aquatints which caused the costliness. These aquatints are to us the best evidence, in their quaint and rather delightful unreality, of the distinction he made between "the principles of Picturesque Beauty" and the reality of nature. Even the costliness of his volumes — they were usually thirty-one shillings, for the larger works — is appropriate; for the picturesque view was mainly a luxury of the leisure class, an elegant accessory of life; and if the price added to the sums which Gilpin was gathering for his school at Boldre in the New Forest, so much the better.

5

Gilpin's *Observations* were largely made in the seventies, a period when the pleasures of the picturesque were confined to a more limited circle than later, after he was publishing. But it was a rapidly increasing circle, even then. He did not so much create a taste as satisfy a taste already existing. Not a few minor poets, of whom John Scott of Aimwell is representative, were pointedly picturesque. Scott writes in *Aimwell: a Descriptive Poem* (1776):

> How various is yon view! delicious hills
> Bounding smooth vales, smooth vales by winding streams
> Divided, that here glide thro grassy banks
> In open sun, there wander under shade
> Of aspen tall, or ancient elm, whose boughs

> O'erhang grey castles, and romantic farms. . . .
> How picturesque the view! where up the side
> Of that steep bank, the roofs of russet thatch
> Rise mix'd with trees, above whose swelling tops
> Ascends the tall church tow'r, and loftier still
> The hill's extended ridge: how picturesque!
> Where slow beneath the bank the silver stream
> Glides by the flowery isle . . .
>   . . . How picturesque
> The slender group of airy elm, the clump
> Of pollard oak, or ash, with ivy brown
> Entwin'd,

and calls on the artists to picture these scenes under the rays of rising or of setting sun, though it require

> The skill of CLAUDE, or RUBENS, or of HIM [*i.e.*, George Smith]
> Whom now on LORANT'S banks, in groves that breathe
> Enthusiasm sublime, the Sister Nymphs
> Inspire.

Anthony Champion, pupil of Walter Harte, wrote in 1772 a poem comparing Wales and the Highlands. As for the Highlands,

> Claud's colours there, and Virgil's style are faint —
> Let Churchill's pen, and Rosa's pencil paint;

whereas in Wales

> How elegant the woods, the streams and shades. . . .
> Yon villa's site, Italia's taste might please. . . .

Though they do not use the word in describing their travels — Boswell is fonder of *romantic* — both Boswell and Johnson show symptoms of picturesque vision. To be sure, Boswell says *he* had little taste for " rural beauties," and thought that Johnson had not much. But Boswell enjoys castles and ruins, though from literary and historical rather than pictorial associations. He visited the falls of Terni (perhaps in company with Wilkes) [16] and his journey to Corsica is " romantick," if not picturesque as well. He takes " romantick " satisfaction in beholding his great friend in Macbeth's castle; Dunvegan, he thinks, lends a rude magnificence to the scene; Roslin is " ro-

---

[16] This is Mr. Tinker's suggestion.

mantick " ; and as for Auchinleck, he cannot figure a more romantick scene." " The sullen dignity of the old castle," was Johnson's phrase. Johnson went to Scotland decidedly in picturesque mood; he sought " wild objects, — mountains, — waterfalls, — peculiar manners." He is amiably disposed to grottos, though he refuses to visit the park of Lord Findlater. He thinks the situation of Slanes Castle the noblest he has ever seen — nobler even than Mount Edgecumbe — and would willingly have beheld from it " the terrifick grandeur of the tempestuous ocean." At the Fall of Fiers, he says: " the country at the bridge strikes the imagination with all the gloom and grandeur of *Siberian* solitude " ; and the Buller of Buchan rouses agreeable horrors. " But terror without danger is only one of the sports of fancy, a voluntary agitation of the mind, that is permitted no longer than it pleases." Nor are objects of terror the only ones to entertain him; he expresses " a pastoral pleasure on seeing the goats browzing."

The few notes of his journey into Wales the next summer have more talk of scenery than the pages of both the *Journal* and the *Journey*; suggesting that even Johnson was subject to the contagion of picturesque enthusiasm felt by his companions. Mr. Thrale " loved a prospect " ; and as loving prospects was a fashionable sentiment, of course Mrs. Thrale did. Though Johnson teased Thrale by insisting that a blade of grass was always a blade of grass, whether in one country or another, and though his sight was defective, he could attend to scenery; witness the account of Ilam which he gave to Boswell. His fearful joy in wild scenes is shown at Sir Rowland Hill's, " a region abounding with striking scenes and terrifick grandeur." He notices " the extent of its prospects, the awfulness of its shades, the horrors of its precipices, the verdure of its hollows, and the loftiness of its rocks; the ideas which it forces upon the mind are, the sublime, the dreadful and the vast. . . . He that mounts the precipices at Hawkestone . . . has not the tranquillity, but the horror, of solitude; a kind of turbulent pleasure, between fright and admiration." The castles please him. Ruthin is " a very noble ruin." Beaumaris " corresponds with all the representations of romancing narratives." Regarding his friend Dr. Taylor's artificial ruins, at Ashbourn, he seems to have preserved discreet silence. There were two, a hovel faced with stone, representing a castle; and a smaller castle on a hill, backed by an old tree, to " terminate the prospect." These were placed according to the rules of perspective, we are assured by one R. J. in the *London Magazine* for 1778; and had a most pleasing effect. It is a pity we have not Dr. Johnson's ideas regarding them. His pleasure in castles, and precipices, was more poetical than pictorial; but then, much of the picturesque tourist's pleasure was, and, as I have said, no little of the pleasure felt in landscape painting itself.

6

In a style even more florid and poetic than Gilpin's is William Hutchinson's *Excursion to the Lakes* (1776). Hutchinson is an example of the combination of antiquary and picturesque observer. He and his brother, who drew his pictures, were collecting material for an antiquarian volume; but they revelled in scenery. They had Dr. Brown's letter in hand before visiting Keswick; and the influence of its manner is strong upon Hutchinson. He too paints in words, like Gilpin, Gray, and Brown; witness this sunrise sketch in the manner of Claude:

As the sun advanced, he gave various beauties to the scene, the beams streaming through the divisions in the mountains, shewed us their due perspective, and striped the plain with gold — the light falling behind the castle, presented all its parts perfectly to us — through the broken windows distant objects were discovered; — the front ground lay in shadows; — on the left the prospect was shut in by a range of craggy mountains, over whose steeps shrubs and trees were scattered; — to the right a fertile plain was extended, surmounted by distant hills; over their summits the retiring vapours, as they fled the valley, dragged their watery skirts, and gave a solemn gloom to that part of the scene. Behind the building, the lofty promontory of Wilbore Fell lifted its peaked brow, tinged with azure hue, and terminated the prospect.

His account of Lodore introduces Thomson ("Smooth from the shelving brink,"); Mason ("Vivid green, Warm brown and blake opake the foreground bears"); Claude (who "in his happiest hour never struck out a finer landskip; it has every requisite which the pencil can demand, and is perhaps the only view in England which can vie with the sublime scenes from which that painter formed his taste"); and Salvator: "Mountain behind mountain, and rock behind rock, fell here in fine perspective, and brought to our minds those astonishing scenes which characterize the pencil of Salvator."

His taste is for the grand manner of the Italian landscape:

> When the long protracted shades the mountains cast upon the bosom of the lake, shewed the vastness of those masses from whence they proceeded; and still as the moon arose higher in the horizon, the distant objects began to be more illumined, and the whole presented us with a noble moon-light piece, delicately touched by the hand of nature; and far surpassing those humble scenes which we had often viewed in the works of the Flemish painters.

It is plain that he was something of a painter himself; and even more an admirer of paintings. He takes his cue from Brown thus:

> The lake of WINDERMERE differs very much from those of ULS-WATER and KESWICK;— . . . The paintings of POUSIN [*sic*] describe the nobleness of ULS-WATER; — the works of SALVATOR ROSA express the romantic and rocky scene of KESWICK; — and the tender and elegant touches of CLAUDE LORAINE, and SMITH, pencil forth the rich variety of WINDERMERE.

Somewhat coldly, the *Monthly* remarks: "The scenes here described are, indeed, worthy of all the powers which the pen or the pencil could contribute toward their due celebration; but the hand in which either is held, ought to be guided by the genius of a Titian, a Poussin, or a Claude."

Richard Cumberland, in his *Odes* (1776), refers to Gray, with astonishment that "this enchanting display of sublime and beautiful objects could extort nothing more than a prosaic description from a poetical pen," and clearly thinks that Dr. Brown is Gray's superior, since to his famous letter he added a poem. Cumberland refers to the painters in his own description of Ulswater:

> For neither Scottish LOMOND's pride,
> Nor smooth KILLARNEY's silver tide,
> Nor aught that learned POUSSIN drew,
> Or dashing ROSA flung upon my view
> Shall shake thy sovereign undisturbed right.

Exaggerated echo of this comes from William Cocker, in an *Ode to the Genius of the Lakes,* which was "thrown in the way of tourists" :

> Though CLAUDE and ROSA join their utmost art,
> Though greater BROWN his rich invention strain. [17]

A *Guide to the Lakes,* which was extremely popular (it went to a seventh edition in 1799) was published by Thomas West in 1778. "To *make the Tour* of the Lakes, to speak in fashionable terms," says the *Monthly,* "is the ton of the present hour." West begins by attributing the great interest in the Lake country to interest in landscape painting; makes use of all the other writers on the Lakes, — Young, Pennant, Hutchinson; gives the letter of Brown, Gray's Journal, Dr. Dalton's *Descriptive Poem,* Cumberland's *Ode to the Sun,* and other literature about the region. He recommends the use of the glass; in fact, of two glasses, one on dark foil for sunny days, and one on silver for cloudy weather. Perhaps of these two kinds were the "Claude Lorrain glasses" found in the pocket of that hapless Charles Gough, dashed to pieces in the descent from Helvellyn, who, with his faithful dog, furnished a poetic subject for Wordsworth and for Scott. West plans his route so that it leads "from what is pleasing, to what is surprising; from the delicate touches of *Claude,* verified on *Coniston*-lake, to the noble scenes of *Poussin,* exhibited on *Windermere*-water, and from there, to the stupendous romantic ideas of *Salvator Rosa,* realized in the lake of *Derwent*." Again, "the conic summits of Langdale-pike — the far-extended mountain of Troutbeck . . . form as magnificent an amphitheatre and as grand an assemblage of mountain, dells, and chasms, as ever the fancy of *Poussin* suggested, or the genius of *Rosa* invented."

There was also the *Survey of the Lakes* (Penrith, 1787) by James Clarke, which was more critical of the flowery language of Hutchinson and Young, and gave Gray the credit of the best, because least pretentious, account; though he was blamed by the author for missing some of the best scenery, because of too great timidity. Another handbook was Joseph (later Palmer) Budworth's *Fortnight's Ramble to the Lakes* (1792). "It is now

---

[17] *The Rural Sabbath,* 1805, p. 148.

so meritoriously the fashion to make this tour," is his excuse for publishing his trivial volume, " I dare almost say it will be thought want of taste not to be able to speak about it."

Books of picturesque tours were numerous in the last quarter of the century. It may be that the French Voyages Pittoresques helped to set the fashion for England, but it was a fashion in which the Englishman was at home. The various works of Thomas Pennant lack the " glowing scenes " of the truly picturesque writer; a defect which was often brought against them. But most of the other volumes of tours show the pictorial sense strongly developed; as the antiquarian Bray's tour of Derbyshire and Yorkshire (1777); William Thompson's tour of northern England and Scotland (1788); Hassell's tour of the Isle of Wight (1790); the Reverend Stebbing Shaw's tour of western England (1788); Skrine's tours of Wales and of Scotland (1795); and such works on counties as *The Kentish Traveller's Companion*, which gives under *Prospect* in the index nineteen references, and that enormous folio, *The New British Traveller*, by George Augustus Walpoole, with numerous plates.

Shaw refers to Gilpin's work on the Wye as being so scarce at that time as to be hard to procure. He got it afterward, and thought " the hints and occasional descriptions of such a companion were highly desirable, and would have been of infinite assistance." Hannah More, journeying down the Wye with the Wilberforces in 1789, has Gilpin's book as companion as she writes to Walpole of " sailing down the beautiful river Wye, looking at abbeys, and castles, with Mr. Gilpin in my hand to teach me to criticise, and talk of foregrounds, and distances, and perspectives, and prominences, with all the cant of connoisseurship, and then to *subdue* my imagination, which had been not a little disordered with this enchanting scenery." " I had rather wander in Forests with such an Author, than accompany a modern novel writer's adventures," wrote Mrs. Elizabeth Montagu, in 1792.

William Thompson's *Tour of England and Scotland* (1788) refers to painting and to Thomson in right picturesque vein, describing " the romantic region of Borrowdale, where there is such a mixture of the tremendous and beautiful scenery as perhaps no other spot on earth can exhibit. To describe the component parts which form the wonderful whole, would require the genius of a Thomson or Salvator Rosa." J. Hassell, in his *Tour through the Isle of Wight* (1790), is yet more a deliberate copyist of Gilpin, in price, in use of aquatints, and in language; in the last not successful, for he overdid the florid, and is reprehended by the reviewer for it, since such a book would "probably fall into the hands of females," but too ready to accept its style as their model. Hassell compares the scenes he views with the paintings of De Loutherbourg, Morland, and Gainsborough, showing an attempt to depart from the conventional formula; but once he goes back to Claude, describing a sunset over water.

The English visitor to the continent carried the memory of the painters with him. So James Smith, the botanist, found at Ermenonville "scenes where even Salvator Rosa might have taken hints of wildness," observed in travelling from Florence "several very rich and extended landscapes . . . with quite a Claude's sky"; near Capua passed through woods "which would have made an admirable subject for Berghem, and the scenery around was worthy of the pencil of Ruysdael or Claude Lorraine"; and at Tivoli thought: "Nothing can be more charming than these scenes; no wonder they are so celebrated. Sometimes the landscape with the buildings of Tivoli, the temple, and the vast plain of Rome beyond, resembles a picture of Poussin's; in other points of view, with the noble cascades and rocks, and the towering mountains above, it recalls the more majestic scenes of Salvator Rosa." [18] Thomas Watkins saw in Altdorf and Urseren such a contrast as between "the rich fancy of Claude Lorrain" and "the romantic genius of Salvator Rosa. If either of these great masters of painting had added anything, the one would probably have introduced a distant view of the sea with shipping, and the other gibbets of Banditti on an eminence." [19] Mrs. Radcliffe at Cologne beheld a sunset landscape, "in tints so soft, so clear, so delicately roseate, as Claude only could have painted." [20]

[18] *Sketch of a Tour on the Continent*, 1793, I, 323–324, II, 132–133, 291–292.
[19] *Travels*, 1792, I, 48.
[20] *Journey*, second ed., 1795, II, 177.

7

It is amusing among the raptures of the amateur to come upon that disappointing experience which Dr. Adar and certain ladies had with Burns, whom they escorted to the Caldron Linn, and watched hopefully, to see a poet inspired by picturesque beauty. But Burns did not perform well. " I am surprised that none of these scenes should have called forth an exertion of Burns' muse," observed the Doctor; " but I doubt if he had much taste for the picturesque." The ladies were unhappy " at his not expressing in more glowing fervid language his impressions of the Caldron Linn scene, certainly highly sublime, and somewhat horrible."

Coleridge would have satisfied the ladies better. When he took his walking tour in Wales, in 1794, he found the scenery " most wild and romantic." In the ruined castle at Denbigh he wandered for two hours on a still evening, " feeding on melancholy." Two other travellers entered, " well-dressed men." Said one, " I will play on my flute; it will have a romantic effect." — But let the deceived poet proceed with the story:

" Bless thee, man of genius and sensibility," I silently exclaimed. He sate down amid the most awful part of the ruins; the moon just began to make her rays predominant over the lingering daylight; I preattuned my feelings to emotion; and the romantic youth instantly struck up the sadly pleasing tunes of *Miss Carey, The British Lion is my Sign,* and *A roaring trade I drive.*

Wordsworth attacked abuse of picturesque theory in *The Prelude,* Book XII:

> . . . Even in pleasure pleased
> Unworthily, disliking here, and there
> Liking; by rules of mimic art transferred
> To things above all art;

but characteristically congratulates himself on having escaped the worst of its effects:

> . . . For this
> Although a strong infection of the age,
> Was never much my habit, — giving way
> To a comparison of scene with scene,
> Bent overmuch on superficial things,
> Pampering myself with meagre novelties
> Of colour and proportion.

8

In the last decade of the century appeared several works on the theory of the picturesque. Uvedale Price's *Essays* (1794) — chiefly directed toward picturesque gardening — have been noticed earlier. He attempts to establish for the theory aesthetic principles more definite than Gilpin's. His main thesis, that the picturesque is a distinct quality from either the sublime or the beautiful (as to these he follows Burke with fidelity), he naturally finds some trouble in making clear. It is, he says, between the two. Roughness and sudden variation are its " most efficient cause." Thus, Gothic architecture is picturesque, Grecian beautiful; but Grecian in ruins, picturesque. The picturesque differs from the sublime in having nothing to do with dimension, or with awe. Price has a not unnatural difficulty in making his distinctions clear, since he insists on finding the quality inherent in the object, rather than in the beholder's eye.

Price neglected Alison's *Essays on the Nature and Principles of Taste* (1790), probably because his first work was already written before those appeared. Alison's theory of associations better explains the picturesque:

> The effect . . . produced by associations, in increasing the emotions of sublimity or beauty, is produced also, either in nature, or in description, by what are generally termed Picturesque Objects. — An old tower in the middle of a deep wood, a bridge flung across a chasm between rocks, a cottage on a precipice, are common examples. If I am not mistaken, the effect which such objects have on every one's mind, is to suggest an additional train of conceptions.

Price's friend Knight seems to have taken note of Alison in his *Analytical Inquiry into the Principles of Taste* (1805). He has an elaborate discussion of the word *picturesque,* and its Italian original *pittoresco:*

> This very relation to painting, expressed in the word *picturesque,* is that which affords the whole pleasure derived from association; which can, therefore, only be felt by persons, who have correspondent ideas to associate; that is, by persons in a certain degree conversant with that art. Such persons, being in the habit of viewing, and receiving pleasure from fine pictures, will naturally feel pleasure in viewing those objects in nature, which have called forth those powers of imitation. . . . The objects recall to the mind the imitations, . . . and these again recall to

the mind the objects themselves, and show them through an improved medium — that of the feeling and discernment of a great artist.

Knight distinguishes between the "merely" picturesque, and the picturesque which is also beautiful:

The mouldering ruins of ancient temples, theatres, and aqueducts, . . . as they appear in the landscapes of Claude, are, in the highest degree, picturesque; but the magnificent quays and palaces, adorned with porticos and balustrades, and intermixed with shipping, which enrich the seaports of the same master, are likewise picturesque; though in a less degree.

There is a species of scenery "in which every object is wild, abrupt, and fantastic. . . . This sort of scenery we call *romantic;* not merely because it is similar to that usually described in romances, but because it affords the same kind of pleasure, as we feel from the incidents usually related in such of them as are composed with sufficient skill to afford any pleasure at all."

Dr. John Aikin was annoyed by the affectations which Gilpin so easily provoked. In his *Poems* (1791), is a *Picturesque Fragment,* intended to be in the manner of Cowper, to which Aikin appends this explanation:

The author is by no means insensible to the fund of genuine taste, as well as the uncommon powers of description, possessed by the admirable writer here alluded to; but he thinks he clearly discerns, that a habit of looking at nature merely with reference to its affording objects for the pencil, has, at times, given a fastidiousness to his feelings, and led him away from the perception of those beauties of a superior order which charm the simpler lover of the country. If this has at all been the effect upon the accomplished *master* of the picturesque school, what must be that upon many of his disciples, the vulgar herd of imitators.

> New follies spring; and now we must be taught
> To judge of prospects by an artist's rules,
> And PICTURESQUE's the word,

begins his satire on *The Prospect-Critic:*

> And is it thus the handmaid Art presumes
> To rule her mistress? Thus would she confine
> The maker's hand to suit the copyist's skill?

He would rather see a mountain, though of form disapproved by Gilpin, "than own whatever Claude or Poussin drew." Aikin

would confine the taste " for what is properly called *picturesque,*
or a reference of the natural scene to its imitations and improvements by the pencil," to the artist; otherwise he would " apprehend that more might be lost by opening an inlet to fastidious
nicety, than would be gained by viewing things with a more
learned eye."

One last fling [21] at the picturesque tourist was William Combe's
Tour of Dr. Syntax, in Search of the Picturesque (1812), which
had the effrontery to set upon its title-page *Ut pictura poesis,*
etc.   Dr. Syntax is unmistakably derived from Gilpin, at least in
the beginning.   The schoolmaster has inspiration for a profitable
vacation:

> I'll make a TOUR — and then I'll WRITE it. . . .
> I'll ride and write, and sketch and paint,
> And thus create a real mint;
> I'll prose it here, I'll verse it there,
> And picturesque it ev'rywhere.

He follows (at a distance) Gilpin's rules:

> I'll make this flat a shaggy ridge,
> And o'er the water throw a bridge:
> I'll do as other sketchers do —
> Put any thing into the view. . . .
> Thus, though from truth I haply err,
> The scene preserves its character. . . .
> He ne'er will as an artist shine,
> Who copies Nature line by line:
> Whoe'er from Nature takes a view,
> Must copy and improve it too.

Though Knight and Price — he was then Sir Uvedale — lived
respectively to 1824 and 1829, no new works of theirs on the
picturesque were published after this poem.   Not that the picturesque tourist died out; but when admiration of the picturesque
had become vulgarized, it ceased to gratify the exquisite.   As
Knight complained in 1794,

> . . . Keswick's favour'd pool
> Is made the theme of ev'ry wandering fool.

21 Of importance, that is.   In *The Album* (1822) is a satirical essay *On
the Taste for the Picturesque,* which describes it as highly artificial; and cites
Salvator Rosa and the admiration felt for his banditti, as an example.

VIII

THE LANDSCAPE ARTS AND THE PICTURESQUE IN THE NOVEL OF THE EIGHTEENTH CENTURY

As THE novels of an age are mirrors (often distorting) of its tastes and sentiments, so those of the eighteenth century reflect the development of taste for landscape, for the arts of landscape, and for the picturesque. These reflections in the novel sometimes remain after the objects themselves have disappeared. Connoisseurship and landscape gardening were amusements of the genteel few as early as 1740, — of the genteelest few still earlier; but the novel is somewhat slow to take much account of these aristocratic matters. The *cit's* belated apprehension of taste in pictures and in gardening was the butt of many a jest, as in *The World*.

The faint Arcadian images of the romance-writers, though ridiculed by dramatists, make little figure in the novels of the early eighteenth century. Steele has in *The Tender Husband* (1705) a sentimental heroine with head " full of Shepherds, Knights, Flowery Meads, Groves, and Streams"; and Fielding, in *Love in Several Masques* (1727), refers to the dangers of " woods and purling streams . . . when a beauteous grove is your theatre, a murmuring cascade your music, and nature's flowery landscape your scene." But such things are infrequent in the novels. Mrs. Manley has but the vaguest and most conventional traces in *The Agreeable Variety* (1717), which speaks of the fine prospect from a hill-top showing " a View of the Inclosures of *Kent,* and the open lands of *Surrey*." With Defoe a hill " rises very steep and high," [1] a country is " very pleasant and fruitful," or " green and pleasant," an African cataract shows " the water tumbling down the rock from one stage to another in a strange manner," [2] and the Andes give " such a prospect of horror, that . . . it was frightful at first to look on the stupendous altitude of the rocks,

[1] *Robinson Crusoe, Works,* 1840, I, 62 (1719).
[2] *Captain Singleton, Works,* 1840, III, 27; 81: 89 (1720).

— every thing above looking one higher than another was amazing." [3]

The concern of the early novel is incident or intercourse; description of nature figures just a little more than not at all. Mrs. Elizabeth Rowe, herself something of a painter, has a little interest in scenery. The few celestial scenes in her *Letters from the Dead to the Living* (1733) bear a vague resemblance to the pictures of Claude and Gaspar, in their " delectable Vales and flow'ry Lawns, . . . bright Cascades and chrystal Rivulets." [4] In *Letters Moral and Entertaining* she describes " a prospect of the most beautiful valley imaginable; it was full of woods, and waters, and water'd with a large river; in some places it run very streight, in others it was more contracted, and flow'd in a thousand windings; sometimes it was lost among the flow'ry lawns." Her ideal ladies employ their time after prayers " with musick or painting."

An epistolary novel by Mrs. Mary Collyer, *Felicia to Charlotte* (1744–1749), shows considerable sense of the picturesque, and is topographical as well. The author, fearful lest the descriptions should be thought " romantic," explains that the " landscapes are actually situated near Nottingham." There is a prospect of " spacious meadows and fields " extended to " an inconceivable distance, where our sight was only bounded by a clear sky that seemed to meet the ground, and in some places by hills, which could hardly be distinguished from the gilded clouds in which they wrapped themselves." The plain is " agreeably diversified " by villages, rising among the trees, and a meandering river. But the specific turns to the usual literary vagueness. A park belonging to Lord M. is described, an " intermixture of dusky groves and lightsome plains," making a " landscape the most pleasingly rural." The vistos are plainly in the old manner; and Felicia's garden has hedges like walls, arches, alcoves, knots of flowers; though she and her husband change this, dismissing the " fantastical," their ideas are certainly not advanced to the true " new manner." [5]

[3] *Voyage Round the World, Works,* 1840, VII, 257 (1725).

[4] *Friendship and Death,* 1733, pp. 7–8.

[5] This novel I have not been able to procure, but am indebted for the information about it to the article by Miss Helen Sard Hughes in the *Journal of English and Germanic Philology,* XV, No. 4.

Leonora, or Characters Drawn from Real Life (1745), of anonymous authorship, testifies to the increasing interest in landscape, and in gardening, though the garden is in the antiquated mode. The scenery described is unreal, derived from pastoral poetry, apparently enhanced by Claude:

> This Place, sacred to Solitude, was situate on a rising Ground, which every Way entertain'd the Sight with a Variety of Silvan Scenes. *There* opening Lawns where happy Shepherds on their oaten Pipes play'd artless Lays of Love; whilst their tender Flock crop'd the verdant Herbage. *Here* purling Streams play'd in their wild Meanders through the flowery Landscape, and shone between the Hills, which bounded the View, that else would have been lost in the immense space of Air. . . . The Sky flush'd with the last Gleams of departing Day.

As a later novelist remarks, " Poetry or Love gives an agreeable Enthusiasm to the Imagination, and presents all Objects in a different Light from that which they appear in to vulgar Eyes. To the latter, Trees are only Trees, and Water, Water; but to the former, they are Woods, and Groves, and purling Streams." [6] To Poetry and Love as modifiers of language was soon added Picturesque Enthusiasm.

By this enthusiasm Richardson is but slightly affected. Mr. B.'s garden in *Pamela* (1740) seems vaguely old-fashioned, having a canal, a fountain, and walks; the " cascade " does not imply the new mode, since there were cascades of masonry in the older style. Clarissa Harlowe (1748) takes delight (in a brief footnote) in the view from her Ivy Summer-house, " a pretty variegated landscape of wood, water, and hilly country; which had pleased her so much that she had drawn it; and had the piece hanging up, in her parlour, among some of her other drawings." Sir Charles Grandison (1753) has likewise his interest in nature expressed in a footnote, but a longer one, describing his grounds, which are suitably adorned with cascade, winding stream, and ledge of rock-work " rudely disposed." His park " is remarkable for its prospects, lawns, and rich-appearing clumps of trees. . . . Alcoves, little temples, seats, are erected at different points of view; the orchard, lawns, and grass-walks, have sheep for gardeners; and the whole being bounded only by sunk fences, the eye is carried to views that have no

[6] *The History of Miss Lucinda Courtney*, n. d., II, 33.

bounds." In this park the Lady Clementina pledges her friends to visit Italy; and in the spot where the pledge was given, is erected a little temple: "The orangery on the right hand; that distant clump of oaklings on the left; the villa, the rivulet, before us; the cascade in view; that obelisk behind us."

It seems at first strange that Tom Jones, Peregrine Pickle, and Matthew Bramble are more sensitive to scenery than Clarissa, Anna Howe, or Sir Charles Grandison. But Fielding and Smollett were more adaptable and more in the current of things than the prim little bookseller, in his grotto with the admiring ladies. Fielding, too, was a visitor at Hagley and at Prior Park. Tom Jones (who is in love, and therefore "romantick") has true relish for prospects. He longs for the view from the top of a hill, by moonlight; "for the solemn gloom which the moon casts on all objects is beyond expression beautiful, especially to an imagination which is desirous of cultivating melancholy ideas." He is contrasted in this matter with the humble Partridge, afraid to be abroad by night, whose blood runs cold at his talk. When Thomas mounts Masard Hill at sunrise, "one of the most noble prospects in the world presented itself to their view, and which we would likewise present to the reader, but for two reasons: first, we despair of making those who have seen this prospect admire our description; secondly, we very much doubt whether those who have not seen it, would understand it." Fielding speaks with warmth of Esher, Stowe, Wilton, Eastbury, and Prior Park, where "days are too short for the ravished imagination while we admire the wondrous power of Art in improving Nature. In some of these Art chiefly engages our admiration; in others, Nature and Art contend for our applause; but, in the last, the former seems to triumph. Here Nature appears in her richest attire, and Art, dressed with the modestest simplicity, attends her benignant mistress." The compliment to Allen which follows is a slighter echo of the elaborate one which makes Allen into Allworthy, and Prior Park into Allworthy's grounds. The description of these is a combination of Gaspar — we are reminded of *The Cascade* which Mason engraved in 1744 — and of Claude:

. . . A plentiful spring, gushing out of a rock, covered with firs, and forming a regular cascade of about thirty feet . . . tumbling down in

a natural fall over the broken and mossy stones till it came to the bottom of the hill, then running off in a pebbly lake. . . . Out of this lake,
which filled the centre of a beautiful plain, embellished with groups of
beeches and elms, and fed with sheep, issued a river, that for several
miles was seen to meander through an amazing variety of meadows and
woods, till it emptied itself into the sea, with a large arm of which . . .
the prospect closed.

The view on one side terminates in a ruined abbey, ivy-covered,
and on the other in a ridge of wild mountains. With this
picture we suspect that Hagley, seat of Fielding's friend and
patron, Lyttelton, had something to do.

Peregrine Pickle (1751) goes for an evening walk with Miss
Emy "through a variety of little copses and lawns, watered by
a most romantic stream, that quite enchanted the imagination
of Peregrine." Aside from this, Smollett leaves picturesque
scenery alone until he comes to *Humphry Clinker* (1771).[7]
Matthew Bramble is a critic of landscape painting (the pictures of Mr. T. at Bath), of landscape gardening (the pleasure
grounds in Scotland are not so well laid out "according to the
genius loci as those in England, where the trees are thrown
into irregular groupes, with intervening glades"), and of picturesque views. He has seen the Italian lakes and Lake Geneva,
but Loch Lomond surpasses them all. "The prospect terminates in the high mountains. . . . Every thing is romantic beyond imagination. This country is justly styled the Arcadia
of Scotland." He finds "an ideal of truth, in an agreeable landscape taken from nature" which pleases him more "than the
gayest fiction which the most luxuriant fancy can display."
Drumlaurig, the Duke of Queensberry's seat, is "an instance of
the sublime in magnificence." Miss Laetitia finds Vauxhall "a
wonderful assemblage of the most picturesque and striking objects, . . . groves, grottoes, lawns, temples, and cascades."
Edinburgh to Jerry Melford is "very romantic." Pretentious
and ill-judged attempts at landscape gardening are ridiculed in

[7] He has some satire to fling at the ignorant chatter about painting, in
his Mr. Pallet, *Peregrine Pickle*, Chapters XLII, LXII, and LXIV, the
virtuoso's cabinet. Ferdinand Fathom becomes (Chap. XXXII) a connoisseur, who is consulted by persons of fashion "in every thing relating
to taste and pictures." The *Travels* (1766) have considerable to say about
scenery, as previously noticed.

the account of Mrs. Baynard's enterprise. When Lismahago escapes from the supposed fire, Sir Thomas Bulford cries out, "*O che roba!* — O what a subject! — O! what *caricatura!* O for a Rosa, a Rembrandt, a Schalken!"

Sterne, though he wrote to Eliza of returning "from a delicious walk of Romance," of "a most Romantic Situation," and of "as sweet a set of romantic apartments as you ever beheld," did not let his pleasure in romantic views or objects stray into his fictions. He thought well of himself as a painter, judging by his letters, and attempted landscape, though the specimens available to us show but the vaguest generalization. One has a temple resembling that of Tivoli.[8] Doubtless it is to his practice of the art that we owe his comic imitation of De Piles' Scale in the dedication of *Tristram Shandy,* and the gibe at the connoisseur: " The *corregioscity* of *Coregio* — the learning of *Poussin,* — the airs of *Guido,* — the taste of the *Carrachi's* — or the grand contour of *Angelo.* — Grant me patience, just heaven! — of all the cants in this canting world, though the cant of hypocrites may be the worst, — the cant of criticism is the most tormenting!"

The Life of John Buncle, by Thomas Amory, was the most picturesque novel which had yet appeared, even by the time of its final volumes (1750–1766). It is notable for pleasure in wild scenery, especially for its early accounts of the Lake Country. The author is truly picturesque in his vision. " The mountains, the rocky precipices, the woods and water, appeared in various striking situations, every mile I travelled on, and formed the most astonishing points of view." "A silent unfrequented glade, that was finely adorned with streams and trees. . . . The woods, the meadows, and the water . . . formed the most delightful scenes." " I came as the sun was rising, to a valley. . . . It was green and flowery, had clumps of oaks in several spots, and from the hovering top of a precipice at the end of the glin, a river falls ingulphed in rifted rocks. It is a fine rural scene." He is fond of sunrise and sunset pictures, and has also a liking for the Salvatorial: "A vast craggy precipice, that . . . by its gloomy and tremendous air, strikes the mind with a horror that has something pleasing in it";

[8] *Letters,* ed. Cross, II, 210.

" a wilder and more romantic country than I had ever before seen . . . an amazing mixture of the terrible and the beautiful." On one occasion he shows the characteristic eighteenth century overlaying of the native scene with the scenery of Italy: " A vast valley, enclosed by mountains whose tops were above the clouds . . . a country that is wilder than the *campagna* of *Rome,* or the uncultivated vales of the *Alps* and the *Apennines.* Warm with a classical enthusiasm I journeyed on, and in fancy's eye beheld the *rural divinities* in those sacred woods and groves, which shaded the sides of many of the vast surrounding fells, and the shores and promontories of many lovely lakes and bright running streams."

The lady novelists, who soon began to appear in force, usually showed a taste for scenery. Mrs. Brooke's *Lady Julia Mandeville* (1763) provides a fine seat, with prospect including mountains, a foaming cascade, and meandering streams. " The gardens and park . . . are romantick beyond the wantonness of Imagination; and the whole adjoining country diversify'd with hills, valleys, woods, rivers, plains and every charm of lovely unadorned nature." In *The History of Emily Montague* (1769) she uses the Canadian setting which she knew, " bold, picturesque, romantic." " Sublimity is the characteristic of this western world; . . . a landscape-painter might here expand his imagination, and find ideas which he will seek in vain in our comparatively little world." The prolific Mrs. Griffiths, Welsh by birth, illustrates what was a general habit (does not Jane Austen give way to it?) of making her heroine visit one or more of the British regions famed for picturesque touring. " I honour your Taste, for dropping Tears, at the Lake of Killarney," writes the hero of her interminable epistolary novel, *A Series of Letters between Henry and Frances* (1757). Wales presents amazing transitions from sublime to beautiful. " I am persuaded that all the inhabitants of Wales must be romantic:— there never was any place appeared so like enchanted ground," writes an ecstatic heroine. Mrs. Griffiths has a tendency common in the novels of the next thirty years: to describe grounds, sometimes actual places, and to ridicule the false taste of some improvers. " Such an improver as this would introduce the wildness of a wood into a parterre, plant a willow pendant over

a fish-pond, and build a pavilion resembling a ruin. An architect of this persuasion will erect an Italian palace in Scotland;
nay, I have seen portico's in Ireland built to the north."

In Henry Mackenzie's *Man of Feeling* (1771) appears "an
old broken soldier," as Goldsmith would call him, against a
sunset in a hollow vale:

> He was one of those figures which Salvator would have drawn; nor
> was the surrounding scenery unlike the wildness of that painter's back-
> grounds. The banks on each side were covered with fantastic shrub-
> wood, and at a little distance, on the top of one of them, stood a finger-
> post, to mark the directions of two roads. . . . A rock, with some
> dangling wild flowers, jutted out above where the soldier lay; on which
> grew the stump of a large tree, white with age, and a single twisted
> branch shaded his face as he slept.
> "Father!" said Harley (who by this time found the romantic en-
> thusiasm rising within him).

In the vein of *The Deserted Village* (which had appeared the
year before) is a lament for the old schoolhouse demolished
because it stood in the way of the squire's prospects.[9]

Village Memoirs (1774) by Goldsmith's friend Cradock gave
part of its slight substance to satire of the professional improver. Cradock, a gentleman gardener, did not admire Brown,
whom he satirizes as the Mr. Lay-out, who destroys old scenes,
and makes extravagant plans for changes.

The friend of Shenstone, Richard Graves, had reason to be
especially interesting in gardening. In that lively anti-Metho-
dist novel, *The Spiritual Quixote* (1773), he ridicules the artificial ruin, through the mouth of an indignant antiquarian who
takes Lord Bathurst's specimen for genuine, and being unde-
ceived expostulates, on the ground that, like the use of Roman
costume for pictures of living Britons, it misrepresents to pos-
terity the habits and customs of the age. Graves' novel is
closely topographical; and he brings in both Hagley and the
Leasowes, with Shenstone in person (dead ten years before) to
point out the beauties of the cascades.

Columella; or, the Distressed Anchorite (1779), which has
landscape gardening as a leading theme, is manifestly the pic-

[9] In *Julie de Roubigné* are several descriptions of landscape, notably in
Letter xxvi.

FRONTISPIECE OF COLUMELLA, 1779.

Drawn by C. W. Bampfield, amateur artist and gardener.

ture of Shenstone. The grounds of Columella are laid out in imitation of Claude Lorrain, as the view from the grotto, or hermitage, shows:

The fore ground of this landscape was broken by some tufts of oaks, and other forest trees, on the verge of the lawn; beyond which, on each side of the valley, several little hills, covered with hanging woods, rose in beautiful perspective, the tops or sides of which Columella had ornamented with several striking objects.

On the brow of one hill appear'd the Sibyl's temple, ruinated like that at Tivoli; a pediment, supported by Ionic columns, rose at the foot of another; the venerable gothic tower of a parish church was discovered at a distance among the tufted trees; and the whole was terminated by some blue mountains in the horizon, and enlivened by a considerable stream, which ran winding down the valley; over which an old bridge of three arches made a picturesque appearance; and as the sun was now setting behind the western hills, it gave a glowing warmth to the landscape, which would have foiled the pencil of B[amp]-f[iel]d, G[ains]b[oroug]h, or even of Claude Lorraine himself.[10]

The frontispiece of the first volume attempts to show this scene, in a caricature of Claude by Bampfield. Viewing with distaste a naked hill adjoining his grounds, Columella remarks to his visiting friends that it would be best adorned by a gibbet. " I think I have seen it introduced by Salvator Rosa, or some great painter," says Hortensius, " with good effect, to heighten the idea of a wild, unfrequented country; the usual scene of action of those lawless banditti." But Columella is actuated in this instance not by picturesqueness, but by revenge; for the owner of the hill, having sold him his grounds, refuses to sell the hill which has a bad effect on his garden pictures. Columella's difficulty is no doubt copied from Shenstone's; and this too:

His man Peter . . . told Columella that the farmer's heifers were got into the young plantation at the bottom of *Aaron's well*.

"Aaron's well! you blockhead," says Columella, " Arno's Vale, you mean."

" Nay, nay," quoth Peter, " I know as how the right name of it is Tadpole Bottom."

The friends visit Stourhead, which introduces a disquisition on the over-crowding of many grounds with buildings of all ages

[10] *Columella,* . . . A Colloquial Tale, 1779, I, 46–48. Bampfield was a gentleman who painted landscapes and also designed them on his grounds. Graves has several poems to him in *Euphrosyne.*

and nations. "The taste of the time, tho' more natural as well as elegant than ever prevailed in England before, yet for want of some fixed principles, a luxurious fancy is in danger . . . of relapsing again into Gothicism and absurdities. In the justly celebrated gardens of Stowe, we are led from an hermitage to a temple of Venus, and from St. Augustine's cave to the temple of Bacchus, and thence to a Saxon temple, and so on. *Quelle melange!*" Graves ridicules also the artificial hermit, such as Charles Hamilton employed at Pains Hill. A candidate for the position presents himself to Columella,

a very venerable figure, with a long white beard, a bald head, and dressed in a long brown coat almost to his ancles; he had two sticks nailed across in his hand, by way of a crucifix, and a string of issue-peas for a rosary of beads. . . .

Columella asked him whence he came? He said, he had lived four years in that capacity with the late Sir Humphry Whimwham. But that when Sir Humphry died, his son had insisted upon his doing a great deal more work than he had agreed for with Sir Humphry; which was only to keep his hermitage clean, and to sit at the door with a book in his hand when any company came, and such like.

It turns out that he had been dismissed for misconduct with the dairy-maid, and for being caught too often with pipe and jug of ale instead of book and beads. Graves of course has a fling at the vulgar *cit*, who, in the person of Mr. Nonsuch, makes absurdly unpicturesque comments on Columella's grounds, and exhibits in his own portion of an acre " every individual article of modern taste," including " a barn-end converted into a Gothic spire," to make an effect from the garden. The ladies connected with trade show more picturesque feeling. "How did the ladies like your master's place?" one of the friends asks of Columella's housekeeper. " O! perdigiously," says Mrs. Betty; " they said it was so rural, and so gothic! Miss was quite in *exotics*, and repeated plays, and poetry,— the lady said she could sit in that grotto and *sympathize* by the hour."

Fanny Burney shows no interest in prospects or gardens; " Green trees and fat cows! what do they tell one? " she seems to say, with Mr. Meadows, in *Cecilia*. Other women novelists of the period, however, enter into description with zest. One is the Scottish Susanna Harvey Keir, whose *History of Miss Gre-*

ville (1787) is rural and romantic in high degree. The heroine takes a picturesque walk, and coming to " a height commanding one of the grandest prospects " she had ever beheld, pulls from her pocket a volume of Thomson (she is by no means the only heroine of this era thus equipped) and finds therein " a lively description of the surrounding scenery." She goes with one of her lovers to view a cascade in a setting " remarkably wild and picturesque, and finely suited to the sublime ideas which, in such a place, one is naturally led to indulge." They behold a genteel young woman who stood "leaning against one of the rocks, and, with a pencil and small book in her hand, appeared to be taking some sketches of the surrounding landscape, which indeed was suited to the genius of a Salvator."

Charlotte Smith was a pupil of the highly-regarded George Smith of Chichester. To support herself and her children, the unfortunate lady turned out novels at the rate of about one a year. Though she never went any nearer to the south of France than Normandy (where she and her husband lived for a time to escape importunate creditors) she had recourse to its scenes for her first novel, *Emmeline, the Orphan of the Castle* (1788), which preceded Mrs. Radcliffe's adventures in the adjacent regions by more than a year. Emmeline is a great admirer of scenery; impressed by that between Marseilles and Toulon, she thinks of her lover; "she knew nobody but Godolphin who had taste and enthusiasm enough to enjoy it." Congenial enjoyment of scenery is frequently a bond, in the novels. *Ethelinde, or The Recluse of the Lake* (1789) opens at Grasmere; the heroine goes forth at sunset to sit beside the lake, bearing with her "that volume of the works of Gray" in which he describes it. *Celestina* (1791) dwells in a castle in the Pyrenees, in " a sublimely beautiful landscape." *The Old Manor House* (1793), her best, abounds in scenery; moonlight scenes, " a sunset with ruins," as the title of a Claudian picture might read. The hero, Orlando, sighs for the presence of Monimia, the heroine: " But never am I allowed to point out to her these lovely prospects, never permitted to cultivate that pure and elegant taste she has received from nature." Such a scene as this, from *The Wanderings of Warwick* (1794), shows a Claudian pattern:

The hills suddenly sinking into a long tract of meadow, made a passage for the river, which there made its way to the sea, distinctly visible at about seven miles distance, where the passing sail was frequently seen glittering in the sun, and then disappearing behind the opposite hills.

She has wearied of so much castle-building, as she says in *The Banished Man* (1794),[11] and is perhaps a little resentful of the successes of Mrs. Radcliffe, to whom she had manifestly shown the way. In *The Letters of a Solitary Wanderer* (1799) she expresses a novelist's view of art: "It is undoubtedly true, that the rudest and wildest sketch of Salvator is more precious than the most laboured piece of the correctest Flemish master." Resentment at Mrs. Radcliffe is perhaps responsible for a bit of satire:

> You must not be displeased at having perpetual description, little narration, and still less character. My hills will boldly swell, my woods wave over as many nightingales as I can collect, my castles frown, and my streams fall, or murmur, or glitter, as luxuriously and as frequently, as if I were the wandering and persecuted heroine of a modern novel in the very newest taste. You may be assured, that should I meet with either ghost or banditti, I will not fail to engage them to
>
> > "Deepen the horror of the falling floods,
> > And breathe a browner horror on the woods."

In *Rural Walks* (1800), "Dialogues intended for the use of young persons," she urges the value of a sense of the picturesque, though she considers "the affectation of being in rapture at prospects" often "tiresome cant." But to view objects with a painter's eye enhances their charms; and drawing will be a resource for amusement, and perhaps against adversity.

Charlotte Smith's more successful rival, Mrs. Radcliffe, "the Shakespeare of romance," carried landscape decoration of the

---

11 *The Banished Man*, second ed., 1795, II, iii-iv. "I find that Mowbray Castle, Grasmere Abbey, the castle of Roche Mort, the castle of Hauteville, and Raglan Hall, have taken so many of my materials to construct, that I have hardly a watch-tower, a Gothic arch, a cedar parlour, or a long gallery, an illuminated window, or a ruined chapel left to help myself. . . . My ingenious cotemporaries have so fully possessed themselves of every bastion and buttress, of every tower and turret, of every gallery and gateway, together with all their furniture of ivy mantles, and mossy battlements; tapestry and old pictures; owls, bats, and ravens, that I had some doubts whether . . . it would not have been better to have *earthed* my hero."

novel much further. "To the wild landscape of Salvator Rosa," so a critic of her own time said, she "added the softer graces of a Claude." [12]   For a generation admiringly familiar with these artists, her pictures constituted no slight part of the popularity of her fictions; though an occasional complaint at her excesses of description is heard.   She enlarges description as she proceeds.   Her first slight tale, *The Castles of Athlin and Dunbayne* (1789), "a Highland story," makes little use of the scenic opportunities of its setting; in *A Sicilian Romance* (1790) there are more pictures; *The Romance of the Forest* (1791), has still more; while in her two best novels, *The Mysteries of Udolpho* (1794) and *The Italian* (1797), this last written after her visit to the Rhine, and to the Lakes, in 1793, the landscapes are elaborate and numerous to a degree which wearies the modern reader, who fails to find in them the delights of recognition which readers of the earlier day discovered.[13]   Her pictures are manifestly taken from the painters' landscapes, not from nature.   She had not indeed travelled farther south than part way down the Rhine; but what was the need?   The pictures of Claude and Salvator gave her precisely what she required. Her literary enjoyment of a Claude is shown in some remarks which she makes on a picture of Lord Eardley's:

An evening view, perhaps over the Campagna of Rome.   The sight of this picture imparted much of the luxurious repose and satisfaction, which we derive from contemplating the finest scenes of Nature.   Here was the poet, as well as the painter, touching the imagination, and making you see more than the picture contained.   You saw the real light of the sun, you breathed the air of the country, you felt all the circumstances of a luxurious climate and the most serene and beautiful landscape; and, the mind thus softened, you almost fancied you heard Italian music on the air, — the music of Paisiello.[14]

Two words often recur in her descriptions.   One is *romantic,* suggesting that subjective treatment of nature, so frequent with

[12] Nathan Drake, *Literary Hours,* third ed. I, 261.

[13] *Gaston de Blondeville,* which she left unpublished, lacks the abundant descriptions, besides being otherwise inferior.

[14] *Memoir, in Gaston de Blondeville,* 1826, I, 65.   "She knew how to paint Italian Scenery which she could only have seen in the pictures of Claude or Poussin," says Scott; and he remarks that some of her descriptions "approach more nearly to the style of Salvator Rosa."   Scott's *Life of Mrs. Ann Radcliffe.*

her, and certainly encouraged by the artists she admired; for if ever two temperaments, vastly different, to be sure, were mirrored in the painted scene, so were mirrored the temperaments of Claude and Salvator. In her first novel, Ossian seems chiefly the inspiration of her scenery. "He loved to wander among the romantic scenes of the Highlands, where the wild variety of nature inspired him with all the enthusiasm of his favourite art [i.e., poetry]," she says of her hero. "He delighted in the terrible and in the grand, more than in the softer landscape." Later heroes and heroines are still more impressionable. In *The Italian* the heroine looks out on the mountains purple in the sunset light, and "the silence and repose of the vast scene, promoted the tender melancholy that prevailed in her heart." Again, borne away in captivity, she reflects among peaks and precipices, "If I am condemned to misery, surely I could endure it with more fortitude in scenes like these, than amidst the tamer landscapes of nature! Here, the objects seem to impart something of their own force, their own sublimity, to the soul." The hero finds the scenery about him in harmony with himself: "Disappointment had subdued the wilder energy of the passions, and produced a solemn and lofty state of feeling; he viewed with pleasing sadness the dark rocks and precipices, the gloomy mountains and vast solitudes, that spread around him."

Another word which is frequent, and expressive of her elaborate, artificial, yet beautifully ordered and effective compositions, is *picturesque*. She describes a picture, not a natural scene; though she will sometimes throw in a conventional phrase, such as "magic scenes . . . no pencil could do justice to," or "more terrific than the pencil could describe." She borrows many of the hints for her designs from the painters, such as the dark foreground, the strong chiaroscuro, as in these from *The Italian*:

To the south a small opening led the eye to a glimpse of the landscape below, which, seen beyond the dark jaws of the cliff, appeared free, and light, and gaily coloured, melting away into blue and distant mountains.

One of the supporting cliffs, with part of the bridge, was in deep shade, but the other, feathered with foliage, and the rising surges at its foot, were strongly illumined; and many a thicket wet with spray, sparkled in contrast to the dark rock it overhung. Beyond the arch, the longdrawn prospect faded into misty light.

From Claude she borrows sunset scenes, far horizons, like these just cited, edged with dim mountains, or with the sea, castles and ruins crowning the cliffs and wooded hills, pastoral scenes, seaports, with buildings and ships, and light dancing on the tips of the waves, — " sunshine landscapes and blue distances ":

A natural vista would yield a view of the country, terminated by hills which retiring in distance, faded into the blue horizon.

She viewed the flowery luxuriance of the turf, and the tender green of the trees, or caught, betwixt the opening banks, a glimpse of the varied landscape, thick with wood, and fading into blue and distant mountains.

These from *The Italian;* and from the *Sicilian Romance:*

There appeared on a point of rock, impending over the valley, the reliques of a palace, whose beauty time had impaired only to heighten its sublimity. An arch of singular magnificence remained almost entire, beyond which appeared wild cliffs, retiring in grand perspective. The sun, which was now setting, threw a trembling lustre upon the ruins and gave a finishing effect to the scene.

The lawn, which was on each side bounded by hanging woods, descended in gentle declivity to a fine lake. . . . Beyond appeared the distant country, rising on the left with bold romantic mountains, and on the right, exhibiting a soft and glowing landscape, whose tranquil beauty formed a striking contrast to the wild sublimity of the opposite craggy heights. The blue and distant ocean terminated the view.

For all these, the appropriate illustrations could be selected from the *Liber Veritatis,* without difficulty. So too of the seaports, as in *The Italian,* though the extreme magnificence of the Claudian architecture is lacking; but even the groups of figures are traceable to the pictures.

The ruined villa on some bold point, peeping through the trees . . . the dancing figures on the strand, . . . the sea trembling with a long line of radiance.

The sea fluctuating beneath the setting sun, the long mole and its light-house tipped with the last rays, fishermen reposing in the shade, little boats skimming over the smooth waters.

The strong effulgence, which a setting sun threw over the sea . . . the Roman tower that terminated the mole below, touched as it was with the slanting rays; and the various figures of fishermen, who lay smoking beneath its walls, in the long shadow, or who stood in sunshine on the beach.

The long mole and the lighthouse are like some of Salvator's seaports, too. But from him she derives chiefly a taste for banditti, caves, cliffs and torrents, oaks and gigantic chestnuts, precipices and chasms. She loves to paint a party of banditti or gypsies seated around a fire, with fine chiaroscuro. Once she erects a gibbet in a wild landscape of barren crags and precipices; an object which, as Graves testifies in *Columella*, was esteemed peculiarly Salvatorial.[15] Her vast granite precipices are " shagged with larch, and frequently darkened by lines of gigantic pine bending along the rocky ledges." The nightmare quality of her scenery shows well in this from *The Sicilian Romance:*

A group of wild and grotesque rocks rose in a semi-circular form, and their fantastic shapes exhibited Nature in her most sublime and striking attitudes. Here her vast magnificence elevated the mind of the beholder to enthusiasm. Fancy caught the thrilling sensation, and at her touch the towering steeps became shaded with unreal glooms; the caves more darkly frowned — the projecting cliffs assumed a more terrific aspect, and the wild overhanging shrubs waved to the gale in deeper murmurs. . . . The last dying gleams of day tinted the rocks and shone upon the waters.

How strong was the impress of Salvator on her mind is shown by her venturing close to a conscious anachronism in *Udolpho,* to introduce his name:

The scene of barrenness was here and there interrupted by the spreading branches of the larch and cedar, which threw their gloom over the cliff, or athwart the torrent that rolled in the vale. . . . This was such a scene as Salvator would have chosen, had he then existed, for his canvass. St. Aubert, impressed by the romantic character of the place, almost expected to see banditti start from behind some projecting rock.

In other words, though Salvator will not be painting his landscapes for sixty years to come (the novel is laid in the year

---

[15] *Udolpho,* I, 143–144. Chap. v. I have never seen a picture of Salvator's with this adornment; but the association is so frequent that there must have been some, or some attributed to him.

Salvator Rosa *pinx.* Published by A. April Field 1744. *In the Collection of* Wm *Kent* Esqr J. Wood. *Sculp*

LANDSCAPE WITH CAVE, BY SALVATOR ROSA.

In the Collection of William Kent. Engraved by John Wood, 1744.

1584) St. Aubert feels in advance the association Salvator is to create between wild mountainous scenes and banditti.

Mrs. Radcliffe's most characteristic scenes are composed of a union of the savage and the soft, Salvator and Claude: "tremendous precipices . . . contrasted by the soft green of the pastures and wood." After a vivid account of a mountain torrent, thundering through the chasm which is its bed, and the gloom and vastness of the rocks which overhang it, she loves to come

> . . . to extensive prospects over plains and toward distant mountains, . . . the sunshine landscape, which had so long appeared to bound this shadowy pass. The transition was as the passage through the vale of death to the bliss of eternity.[16]

> The evening sun, shooting athwart a clear expanse of water, lighted up all the towns and villages, and towered castles, and spiry convents, that enriched the rising shores; . . . and coloured with beamy purple the mountains, which on every side formed the majestic background of the landscape. . . .
> How sweetly the banks and undulating plains repose at the feet of the mountains; what an image of beauty and elegance they oppose to the awful grandeur that overlooks and guards them.

> Woods and pastures, and mingled towns and hamlets, stretched toward the sea . . . while over the whole scene was diffused the purple glow of evening. This landscape, with the surrounding Alps, did indeed present a perfect picture of the lovely and the sublime, . . . of "beauty sleeping on the lap of horror."[17]

Mrs. Radcliffe is less given to gardening than many of the novelists of her time; but it is noteworthy that when she wants a garden in *The Italian* she transfers one in the English manner to Italy:

> The style of the gardens, where lawns, and groves, and woods, varied the undulating surface, was that of England, and of the present day, rather than of Italy; except "where a long alley peeping on the main" exhibited such gigantic loftiness of shade, and grandeur of perspective, as characterize the Italian taste.

No other novelist is so closely a follower of painted scenery. Indeed, the names of the painters somewhat rarely appear. In

[16] *Italian*, Bk. I, Chap. VI.

[17] *Udolpho*, Bk. I, Chap. v. The phrase is presumably borrowed from Helen Maria Williams, whose *Julia* will be noticed later.

the pretended *Love-Letters* of Hackman and his victim, Martha Reay, by Croft (1777), " If Salvator Rosa, or Poussin, wanted to draw a particular character, I am their man," says Hackman; and later imagines a painting of Augustus, Antony, and Lepidus meeting on a desolate island; " Salvator Rosa would not make me quarrel with him for doing the background." [18]

Julia (1790), by Helen Maria Williams, that person of intense sensibilities and friend of the Revolution, has a phrase which Mrs. Radcliffe borrowed, without improving. After a lyric description of the broken crags and rocky promontories of a lake, and the sound of a neighbouring cataract, she adds: " The contrast between this cultivated valley, and its savage boundaries, was so striking, that it seemed like Beauty reposing in the arms of Horror." She has a splendid sunset scene over the lake, and a moonrise following. Another lady of more romance than discretion, Mrs. Robinson — Perdita — goes to Italy for the setting of *Vancenza* (1792), — " towering precipices from whose giddy height the fearful shepherd gazes with terror and astonishment." " A picture so exquisitely sublime " has marked effect on the hero; " Dal Vero, fascinated with delight, forgot for a moment even the graces of Elvira. ' All beauteous Nature! ' exclaimed he, ' how extensive, how luxuriant are her enchantments! ' "

In *The Monk* (1796), Lewis confines his landscape to the catastrophic close:

> The disorder of his imagination was increased by the influence of the surrounding scenery; . . . the gloomy caverns and steep rocks, rising above each other, and dividing the passing clouds; solitary clusters of trees scattered here and there, among whose thick twined branches the wind of night sighed hoarsely and mournfully; . . . the stunning roar of torrents, as swelled by late rains they rushed violently down tremendous precipices; and the dark waters of a silent sluggish stream, which faintly reflected the moonbeams, and bathed the rock's base on which Ambrose stood.

Bits of landscape are frequent decorations of the Minerva Press, and those other ephemeral volumes which appeared in great num-

---

[18] Dr. John Moore in *Zeluco*, 1786, (Chaps. xxiv, xliv), has something to say of the impositions practiced by unscrupulous dealers in pictures, but makes no adequate use of the scenery his Italian setting afforded.

bers, feeble followers of the school of Terror or Wonder. One of the most conscious example is in *The Wanderer of the Alps* (1796), which opens its volumes with a pair of companion pieces like those numerous Evenings and Mornings of the painters. In Volume I " The sun had just sunk beneath the craggy summit of a gloomy rock, that shot its brown spires above the waving tops of the tall pines," and in II " The sun had just risen above the eastern hills, and cast his dazzling lustre over the immense forest . . . hanging from the projecting sides of the precipices, or crowding the deep sunk vallies with the vegetable progeny."

Landscape gardening is a frequent topic; useful to show true taste, or false, or fashionable folly, or parvenu ineptitude. Johnstone, in *Chrysal* (1760), tells of the church built by Dashwood at Medmenham for " the double purpose of convincing the populace of his regard to religion, and of making a beautiful termination to a vista which he had cut through a wood in his park." The ladies of *Milennium Hall* (1762), written by Sarah Scott, sister of Mrs. Elizabeth Montagu, design their own grounds. " On an eminence, ' bosomed high in tufted trees,' is a temple dedicated to solitude. The structure is an exquisite piece of architecture, the prospect from it noble and extensive." Moore, in *Edward* (1796), depicts a mulatto nabob whose grounds change with the taste of his successive mistresses.

Ridiculous aspects of the gardening fashion are satirized by the dramatists also. Arthur Murphy's *Three Weeks after Marriage* (1764) borrows outright from Pope's essay in *The Guardian,* to describe the clipped trees of his Drugget. Garrick and Colman show Sterling, in *The Clandestine Marriage* (1766), advanced to the point of serpentining; (" Ay, here's none of your straight lines here — but all taste — zig-zag — crinkum-crankum — in and out — right and left — so and again — twisting and turning like a worm ") ; a cascade, an artificial spire, and ruins which cost a hundred and fifty pounds to repair. Garrick was himself an ornamentor of grounds. Sheridan makes Puff, in *The Critic,* speak as a literary Brown: " to insinuate obsequious rivulets into visionary groves," etc.

The novelists' ornamented grounds of fine taste, though frequent, are rather vaguely described. They are sure to have a meandering stream ; and either nature inevitably seems the work

of art or art the work of nature.[19] Capability Brown and the improvers in general are referred to in tones both humourous and
admiring. " Lady Frances sent for Mr. Brown, who found great
Capabilities in the situation; "[20] " Nothing ever pleased me so
thoroughly as the figure, physiognomy, and behaviour, of the person who came down (in his own carriage) to me in the capacity of
schemer. . . . He no sooner examined the ground than he pro-
tested it was *capable of every thing."*[21] A full description of
the Brownesque landscape is given in *Melissa and Marcia*
(1788):

> From the eminence on which the house was placed, as far as the eye
> could reach, it traced a silver meandering stream. — In the distribution
> of the grounds, the hand of Brown had assisted, but not forced nature;
> . . . A velvet lawn gently sloped from the house down to the river, and
> served for pasture to some hundreds of sheep. . . . A rising wood
> stretched itself to a considerable distance on the East. — On the West,
> the eye wandered over an immense Park; the ground was beautifully
> irregular; wild, and diversified with scattered herds of deer and cattle;
> groups of trees with here and there a spire or a steeple peeping over
> their heads, and the view was terminated by rising hills.

" Mr. Outline, a most capital improver " comes down to arrange
the grounds of a lady of fashion, in *A Tale of the Times*, by
Jane West (1789); he creates cascades, replaces walls by ha-has,
and erects ruins in abundance. Another seat is described, belonging to persons of taste. " I have set up temples and alcoves out
of number," says the lady; " some are for solitary musings,
others for social parties. There is one . . . formed upon a plan
. . . [taken] from a beautiful ruin on Campania." In Holcroft's
Anna St. Ives (1792) improvement of grounds is an important
interest, furnishing nearly all the humor, in the vanity of Sir
Arthur and the illiteracy of his steward and superintent, Abi-
melech Henly, apparently a first cousin of Smollett's Winifred
Jenkins. " There is the temple beside a the new plantation,

[19] Among the many examples are: *Barford Abbey*, by Mrs. Gunning,
second ed., 1771, I, 15-16; *Agnes de Courci*, by Mrs. Bennet, Bath, 1784, I,
110-111; *The Progress of Love or The History of Stephen Elliott*, 1789.
I, 10-12; *The Younger Brother*, by Mr. Dibdin, 1793, I, 8; *Adeline de
Courcy*, 1797, II, 25; *Munster Abbey*, by Sir Samuel Egerton Leigh, Edinburgh, 1797, I, 25-26.

[20] *Munster Village.*

[21] *Shenstone-Green*, 1779, I, 59.

of a witch your onnur has so long bin a talkin of a buildin of,"
he writes to Sir Arthur; "and then there is the extension
and ogmenshun of the new ruins." Sir Arthur enjoys showing
his grounds: " Nobody can suspect so many temples, and groves,
and terraces, and ascents, and descents, and clumps, and shrub-
beries, and vistas and glades, and dells and canals, and statues,
and rocks, and ruins are in existence, till they are in the very
midst of them." Maria Edgeworth, in *Castle Rackrent* (1798),
makes one of that reckless line a spendthrift on improvements;
and in *The Absentee* (1812) shows the folly of the vulgar Mrs.
Rafferty, whose " happy moving termination," an artificial fisherman on a Chinese bridge, tumbles over as the visitors approach,
to the lady's dismay.

The heroines of novels are often employed with the pencil,
depicting " the soft features of the landscape." One suspects
that they insert castles, or ruins, and group peasants, " or any
thing that will make it unlike the original," as the fashionable
lady in Jane West's *Infidel Father* (1792) recommends. Jane
Austen's Emma, we remember, painted unsuccessful portraits and
presumably landscapes; the sensible Eleanor Dashwood in *Sense
and Sensibility* was skilled in the art, and her devoted sister
found the lukewarmness toward it of Edward Ferrars almost
damning.

Jane Austen's world is much interested in grounds. John
Dashwood improved his; and Cleveland, the Palmers' place,
offers to Marianne Dashwood a Grecian temple on an eminence,
from which she may survey the prospect toward the horizon hills.
In *Emma* we hear from Mrs. Elton of Maple Grove, — an instance of the vulgarian imitation of the gentry; and Knightley's
Abbey is situated charmingly beside the usual curving river with
wooded banks of some abruptness. Lady Catherine de Bourgh
has grounds, but not to compare with her nephew's, which,
Elizabeth Bennet intimates very reasonably, caused her to soften
her prejudices toward their owner. " She had never seen a
place for which nature had done more, or where natural beauty
had been so little counteracted by an awkward taste. . . . The
hill crowned with wood, from which they had descended, was
a beautiful object. Every disposition of the ground was good,
and she looked at the whole scene, the river, the trees scattered

on its banks, and the windings of the valley as far as she could trace it, with delight." Mr. Rushworth, in *Mansfield Park*, is a foolish victim of the rage for improvement. He will engage Mr. Repton at five guineas a day. "Smith's place is the admiration of all the country; and it was a mere nothing before Repton took it in hand. I think I shall have Repton." Edward Bertram "would rather have an inferior degree of beauty," of his own choice, than the beauties of the professional improver. Henry Crawford, a man of taste, is ready to give amateur advice; which Rushworth is equally ready to accept. The scene, intended though it is to reveal individual traits, is also one of Jane Austen's few general satires on a contemporary folly. Yet the general fashion is worked into the individual character most cleverly. "That iron gate, that ha-ha, give me a feeling of restraint and hardship," says Miss Bertram; "I cannot get out, as the starling said."

As to the picturesque, though Jane Austen laughs at the excesses of its devotees we feel that she was one herself in some degree, so sympathetic is she, and so abundant are her references. Of her most delightful heroines only Catherine Morland is without a native taste for views; and she acquires one with suspicious ease and readiness. She goes walking with the Tilneys, and hears them talking a language strange to her ears.

> They were viewing the country with the eyes of persons accustomed to drawing; and deciding on its capability of being formed into pictures, with all the eagerness of real taste. . . . It seemed as if a good view were no longer to be taken from the top of a high hill, and that a clear blue sky was no longer a proof of a fine day. . . . A lecture on the picturesque immediately followed, in which his instructions were so clear that she soon began to see beauty in every thing admired by him; and her attention was so earnest that he became perfectly satisfied of her having a great deal of natural taste. He talked of foregrounds, distances, and second distances; side-screens and perspectives; lights and shades; — and Catherine was so hopeful a scholar, that when they gained the top of Beechen Cliff, she voluntarily rejected the whole city of Bath, as unworthy to make part of a landscape.

Marianne Dashwood is an ardent follower of Gilpin. Edward enrages her with his insensibility.

> "I have no knowledge of the picturesque," [he admits shamelessly] "I shall call hills steep, which ought to be bold; surfaces strange and

uncouth, which ought to be irregular and rugged; and distant objects out of sight, which ought only to be indistinct through the soft medium of a hazy atmosphere. . . . It exactly suits my idea of a fine country, because it unites beauty with utility — and I daresay it is a picturesque one too, because you admire it; I can easily believe it to be full of rocks and promontories, grey moss and brushwood, but these are all lost on me. I know nothing of the picturesque."

Eleanor attempts to calm her sister's agitation at this heresy by suggesting that Edward is affecting indifference because of the affectations of admiration on the part of the crowd. " It is very true," Marianne replies, " that admiration of landscape scenery has become a mere jargon. Everybody pretends to feel and tries to describe with the taste and elegance of him who first defined what picturesque beauty really was." To which Edward adds,

" I like a fine prospect, but not on picturesque principles. I do not like crooked, twisted, blasted trees. I admire them much more if they are tall, straight and flourishing. I do not like ruined, tattered cottages. I am not fond of nettles, or thistles, or heath blossoms. I have more pleasure in a snug farm-house than a watch-tower, and a troop of tidy, happy villagers please me better than the finest banditti in the world."

Marianne looked with amazement at Edward, with compassion at her sister.

Elizabeth Bennet knows the principles of Mr. Gilpin. " You are charmingly grouped," she answers Darcy's attempt to include her in the walking party in the garden; " the picturesque would be spoiled by a fourth." She is moved to raptures at the thought of a visit to the Lakes: " What are men to rocks and mountains? " She and the Gardiners, people of taste (though citizens), visit Derbyshire with enthusiasm, and Pemberley with felicity. Sweet Anne Elliott repeats poetry as she looks at the autumn landscape, and the encomiums of Captain Wentworth on Lyme send the whole party thither on a scenic visit. But the description of " a scene so wonderful and lovely . . . as may more than equal any of the resembling scenes of the far-famed Isle of Wight " is in the words of Jane Austen herself.

Maria Edgeworth and Jane Austen represent so decidedly the eighteenth-century standpoint towards nature that though with them we move out of the eighteenth and into the nineteenth century, their testimony may fairly be claimed. There is even need to pursue the subjects of the picturesque and of gardening a little further. The improver especially continues to haunt the novel for several years. The views of the novelists are coloured by Price and Knight; they ridicule Repton. " The artist with his curling-tongs and comb, had dressed out the landscape with as much wild irregularity as the ' disposition of the place ' was perceptible of," says *Men and Women* (1807). Lucille, in Hannah More's *Coelebs* (1809), is " the little Repton of the valley." A chapter of *Flim-Flams!* (1805) by Isaac D'Israeli, is given to a distortion of the controversy between Repton, and Price and Knight; Mr. Contour, the hero, tries to make his grounds look like a picture.

"The Improver," closing with great composure his Red-Book, observed that Gaspar Poussin could do any thing in three yards of canvass — we work with different materials. The earth is no canvass, the spade is no pencil, the foliage are no tints that mingle to the hues we wish, — except in the verses of the Garden Poets.

Peacock was another satirist of the improver, taking Price's side against Repton. He treated the subject in his farce, *The Dilettanti*, written about 1809,[22] and carried over from it some of the characters. Marmaduke Milestone is Repton, Sir Patrick O'Prism is Price; in *Headlong Hall* (1816), Peacock's first novel, Milestone arrives at Headlong Hall, portfolio under arm, and observes " that there were great capabilities in the scenery, but it wanted shaving and polishing." He has an argument with Sir Patrick, in which phrases from their works fly about. The romantic Miss Tenorina admires a cascade in its natural state. " Beautiful, Miss Tenorina! " exclaims the improver. " Hideous. Base, common, and popular. Such a thing you may see any-where in wild mountainous regions."

The picturesque is frequent. William Godwin has much of it. *Fleetwood: or The New Man of Feeling* (1805) derives a good deal of his excess of feeling from Wales. " I sat for hours on the edge of a precipice, and considered in quiet the grand and savage objects of nature," he says. Oxfordshire makes a paltry showing beside North Wales. " Wales was nature in the vigour and animation of youth; she sported in a thousand wild and ad-

22 Carl Van Doren, *Life*, 1911, p. 75.

mirable freaks; she displayed a master-hand; every stroke of her majestic pencil was clear, and bold, and free." We meet a young woman in this novel " who applied herself to the art of design; she drew, and even painted in oil; and her landscapes in particular had an excellence which to speak moderately of them, reminded the beholder of the style of Claude Lorraine." " There is a lady in the Romance of the Highlands," (I quote from *The Heroine,* a satirical novel of 1813) " who . . . when dying, and . . . about to disclose the circumstances of a horrid murder, . . . unfortunately expended her last breath in a beautiful description of the verdant hills, rising sun, all nature smiling, and a few streaks of purple in the east." In *Melincourt* (1817) Peacock makes frequent reference to the picturesque, to the " everlasting talkers about taste and beauty, who see in the starving beggar only the picturesqueness of his rags, and in the ruined cottage only the harmonizing tints of moss, mildew and stonecrop." A picturesque tourist is discovered sketching " a scene of magnificent beauty," including lake, precipices, and woods. That engaging hero, the silent Sir Oran Utan, " after looking at the picture, then at the landscape, then at the picture, then at the landscape again, at length expressed his delight in a very loud and very singular shout." The later *Crotchet Castle* (1831) is especially notable for scenery; as is of course *The Adventures of Elphin* (1829).

In *Waverley* (1814) is a true Salvatorial scene with the appropriate tree:

> The path, which was extremely steep and rugged, winded up a chasm between two tremendous rocks, following the passage which a foaming stream, that brawled far below, appeared to have worn for itself in the course of ages. A few slanting beams of the sun, which was now setting, reached the water in its darksome bed, and showed it partially, chafed by a hundred rocks, and broken by a hundred falls. The descent from the path to the stream was a mere precipice, with here and there a projecting fragment of granite, or a scathed tree, which had warped its twisted roots into the fissures of the rock.

When Waverley meets Donald Bean Lean, he finds him not as expected:

> The profession which he followed — the wilderness in which he dwelt, — the wild warrior forms that surrounded him, were all calculated to

inspire terror. From such accompaniments, Waverley prepared himself to meet a stern, gigantic, ferocious figure, such as Salvator would have chosen to be the central figure of a group of banditti.

References to Claude and Salvator continue to appear for some time. Mrs. Burdett blames Claude for the idealization of Italy by the English. " To the almost cloudless skies of Claude we join in perspective the harmonious green of English verdure." [23] G. P. R. James has a robber band in *Richelieu* (1829) meeting by torchlight which " glared upon features which Salvator might have loved to trace." Lady Charlotte Bury describes the scenery near Volterra as bearing " all the characteristick features of Salvator Rosa's wildest pencil. That painter is said to have studied in this neighbourhood three years." [24] A lady speaks of the Alps, in Godwin's *Deloraine* (1833): " In her description it was as if the pencil of Claude or of Gaspar Poussin had passed over the landscape, and brought forth at one point and another hidden beauties, which but for their inspiration would never have been revealed."

More thorough search would doubtless produce many more such references, but these are sufficient to show how the influence of the Italian landscape school was extended well into the nineteenth century. For landscape description in the English novel up to about 1825, these painters are largely responsible. From that time, the description became more realistic, and the pictures of Claude, Salvator, and Gaspar were soon an antiquated mode, discarded and, after Ruskin's attacks, discredited.

[23] *English Fashionables Abroad*, 1828, I, 103.
[24] *Journal of the Heart, New Brit. Nov.*, x, 24.

IX

ITALIAN LANDSCAPE AND ROMANTICISM

THROUGHOUT the preceding chapters I have carefully avoided that nebulous word *romantic*, except in frequent quotations; and that equally nebulous term, *romanticism*, I have not used till now. But now it is desirable to emphasize that no definition of that term can fairly exclude the feelings with which the English in the eighteenth century regarded the landscapes of Claude Lorrain, Gaspar Poussin, Salvator Rosa, Jan Both, Hermann Swanevelt, Richard Wilson, and all the rest who painted remote and extravagant Italian scenes, — surely a world of dreams and romance. And if the attempts to reproduce on English ground these visions of the distant and ideal Italy may not be accounted romantic, I do not know what more fairly may. Nor was this devotion to the imaginary landscapes of Italy a growth of the late century only, or dependent in any way on Jean Jacques Rousseau for its origin. It appears as early as the *Spectator* advertisements, in 1711; indeed, Dryden's *Ode on the Death of Mistress Anne Killigrew* implies that in 1686 it had already begun. To be sure, it was shared in the early half of the century only by the comparative few who were privileged by fortune to have glimpses of the pictures at home or abroad; but the few included leaders of taste, such as Shaftesbury, Lady Betty Germaine,[1] Dr. Mead, Thomas Coke, Horace Walpole. Never, as I have spent time in telling, was understanding of art, or pretence of understanding it, so essential for the well-bred English person as from 1740 on through the opening of the nineteenth century; and the new art of landscape painting occupied a position of increasing importance.

It is hard for us today to realize the importance of the print in determining the mode in which the eighteenth century regarded nature. The large scrapbooks which polite society examined in leisure hours, the framed prints which adorned the

[1] Graves, *Art Sales*, 1918. See under *Claude;* also under *Salvator Rosa.*

rooms of intimate association (how often in the account of great houses we are told of the dressing-rooms hung with landscape prints), the little prints which ladies and gentlemen took as models for their amateur paintings, were of a world removed noticeably from the world of reality. Indeed, this detachment from reality, we apprehend, made much of the charm of the pictures for the eighteenth century. We have to remember that at no other time or place were excellent engravers of landscape so abundant as in England through the last sixty years of the eighteenth century and the opening of the nineteenth. More often than not, the references to Claude and the others are based not on the paintings but on the work of Vivares, Woollett, Goupy, Mason, and their fellows. Those large and impressive, beautifully wrought plates are what John Scott, for example, is thinking of in his *Essay on Painting*; so he says, in the footnotes to a passage which itself shows well the romance which the pictures represented:

> When CLAUDE's bright morn on Mola's precinct dawns,
> What sweet quiescence marks the groves and lawns!
> How calm his herds amongst the ruins graze!
> How calm his curious peasant stands to gaze!
> When bold SALVATOR under turbid skies
> Bids his scath'd hills and blasted trees arise,
> Behind wild rocks bids his wild stream be lost,
> And from vast cliffs shews broken fragments tost. . . .

Unless we realize to some degree the place held in the eighteenth century by the "fair visionary world" of the print, we cannot understand the poetry or the thought of the century. The prints gave entrance to a world almost as fanciful as that of the *Arcadia*, or of *Otranto*; and the pleasure which the folk of the eighteenth century took in them was similar to that which the folk of any age will take in a playhouse which gives refuge from the always unsatisfactory reality.

The romantic generation of the closing eighteenth and the opening nineteenth century found much stimulus in the Italian landscape painters. The world of letters clung still to the distant and visionary at a time when Constable and Crome were taking the path of a beautiful realism. Even Wordsworth, who, like Cowper, is exceptional in this regard, refers to Salvator as a standard for wild landscape; and according to *The Prelude*, found pleasure in the panorama of

> . . . the Falls
> Of Tivoli; and high upon that steep,
> The Sibyl's mouldering Temple.

There are suggestions of Claude in Coleridge's *Reflections on Having Left a Place of Retirement* (1796), and in *Religious Musings* (1794). Scott manifestly admired both Claude and Salvator. He picked from *Childe Harold's Pilgrimage*, reviewing Part IV in the *Quarterly*, the stanzas on Clitumnus, as presenting "the outlines of a picture as pure and brilliant as those of Claude Lorraine." It is indeed one of the rare instances in Byron of such close copying, or so it seems, of pictures. For pictures we are assured by his friends, Byron had little taste; but here he seems to be arranging a really Claudian design of river, nymph, and milk-white steer, in foreground, and in the background

> . . . a temple still,
> Of small and elegant proportions, keeps
> Upon a small declivity of hill
> Its memory of thee. . . .

Hazlitt in his view of both artists is typical of many:

I used to walk out at this time [1809] . . . of an evening, to look at the Claude Lorrain skies. . . . I was at that time an enthusiastic admirer of Claude, and could dwell for ever on one or two of the finest prints from him hung around my little room: the fleecy flocks, the bending trees, the winding streams, the groves, the nodding temples, the air-wove hills, and distant sunny vales.

As for Salvator Rosa, Hazlitt regards him as "the most *romantic* of landscape painters." "Salvator Rosa — never was man so blest in a name!" cries Hartley Coleridge.

I once did see a landscape of Salvator's which taught me what an imaginative thing a landscape may be. . . . Such shaggy rocks, — such dark and ruinous caves, — such spectre-eyed, serpent-headed trees, wreathed and contorted into hideous mimicry of human shape, as if by the struggles of human spirits incarcerated in their trunks, — such horrid depths of shade, — such fearful visitations of strange light, — such horrid likenesses

Of all the misshaped half-human thoughts
That solitary nature feeds

were surely never congregated in any local spot.

" The magnificent imagination of Salvator Rosa," is the phrase
of Sir Egerton Brydges; who compares him with Byron.[2] Peacock, in *The Philosophy of Melancholy* (1812), unites the contrasted painters to the romantic gloom that is his theme:

> In Claude's soft touch thy tenderest image reigns.
> His evening vallies, and his weed-twined fanes.
> Salvator's hand thy darkest grandeur caught . . .
> Piled the black rock, and grasped the Alpine storm.

In the letter to Reynolds (1818) we have witness to the day-
dreaming uses to which Keats turned the glimpses of Claude
gained from the British Institution:

> You know the Enchanted Castle, it doth stand
> Upon a rock, on the border of a Lake,
> Nested in trees. . . .
>
> See what is coming from the distance dim!
> A golden galley all in silken trim. . . .
>
> . . . From the Postern gate
> An echo of sweet music doth create
> A fear in the poor Herdsman, who doth bring
> His beasts to trouble the enchanted spring. . . .
>
> O that our dreamings all, of sleep or wake,
> Would all their colours from the sunset take. . . .[3]

How the persons of Claude and Salvator were taken as ex-
emplars of the worship of nature, we find in some of the minor
poets of the same period. So in a poem, *The Painter*, the Reverend George Croly depicts Claude as the lone gazer on sunrises and sunsets.[4] William Sotheby, going to Italy in 1816,
makes much of the painters in his *Italy:*

---

[2] *Recollections*, 1825, I, 30, 75.

[3] Keats was a picturesque tourist: " I put down Mountains, Rivers, Lakes,
dells, glens, Rocks and Clouds, with beautiful, enchanting, Gothic, picturesque."
Letters, ed. Forman, p. 157. " I have been *werry* romantic indeed among
these Mountains and Lakes." P. 198. " My Scotch journey gave me a dose
of the Picturesque with which I ought to be contented for some time." P.
277.

[4] *Catiline . . . With Other Poems*, 1812, pp. 212–213.

From the surrounding scene a Poussin drew
His rich and mellow hue:
And Claude there taught his pencil how to trace
The soft aerial grace
That sooth'd the westering sun, whose orb of light
Like molten gold, on the proud temple shone. . . .

That rocky crest, where oft Lorraine was found . . .
And from the shapings of his fancy gave
To tow'r, or palace, or hoar monument . . .
Some height'ning touch, some new embellishment,
Such as th' enchanted spirit might adore,
And lovelier make the scene that loveliest seem'd before. . . .

   . . . Where was Salvator found,
When all the air a bursting sea became,
Deluging Earth? — On Terni's cliff he stood,
The tempest sweeping round.

Alaric Watts, chief creator of the Annual, is another admirer of

Claude's bright rippling wave and sunset sky,
Salvator's storm-rent rock and mountain brow,
And Poussin's classic glooms,

and also of George Barret, two of whose very Italian landscapes
adorn the sumptuous *Lyrics of the Heart* (1851), and to whom
Watts addresses a memorial poem:

   . . . Thou shouldst have lived
Where sunny Claude his inspiration drew,
Or learned Poussin neath th' umbrageous oaks
Of some old forest. . . .

In the Annuals Italian landscape lingers on for years. There
were even Landscape Annuals, from 1830 to 1839, for which
Prout and Harding designed charming pictures, — a last faint
efflorescence of the romantic delights of distant Italian scenes,
and faint shadow of Claude and his companions, doomed, with
Ruskin's heavy sarcasms in *Modern Painters*, to pass into dis-
repute and eclipse.

So in the Age of Victoria the conventions of landscape which
had prevailed in England since the Age of Anne were at last
discarded. Entering England with the support of history painting, to which their subjects often made them akin, the Italian

landscapes had been more and more admired, by travellers who delighted to recognize scenes they had visited, and by readers who found the appeal of Italy and classic ruins and names irresistible. Established by the leaders of fashion as the correct patterns, these landscapes had been taken as models by poet, painter, and even gardener, and had laid the rules of picturesque beauty for the observer of nature. Multiplied by the engravers and the imitators, they were present in almost every English home of means or culture. If at the last of the century — beginning with Cowper — there came poets and painters who cast aside the Claude-glass and found beauty in hedge-rows and corn-fields, and in Hampstead and Mousehold Heaths, it was because of a long training in seeing landscape pictorially, — a training which of necessity began with the most elaborate and heightened forms of landscape, with the richest and most obvious appeal, and on the most vast and impressive scale. Polite eyes were shocked by Salvator Rosa into recognition of the " beauty and fierceness " of wild and mountainous scenery.[5] An age which valued conscious form found satisfaction in the superb and unreal forms of Claude's landscape; but that same landscape was the inspiration of Constable and Keats.

[5] Letter of Edward Rolle, from the Alps, 1753. Spence's *Anecdotes*, p. 444.

INDEX

A

Addison, Joseph: painting, 10, 11, 16; gardening, 124–126; picturesque, 10, 11, 124, 169
Aikin, John, 163, 199
Akenside, Mark, 111, 112
Albano, 22, 65, 90, 132, 142, 144
Algarotti, Count, 36 n.
Alison, Archibald, iii, 162, 198
Allen, Ralph, 137, 204
Alps. *See* Mountains
Amateur artist: in society, 8, 12, 87, 89, 90, 91, 92, 171; in world of letters, 90, 91, 92, 93, 96, 206; represented in fiction, 211, 221, 222, 225; instruction, 14, 86–89, 94; etchers, 90; designers of gardens, 127, 128, 134–136, 140, 143, 145, 153, 155, 156, 159, 208–210, 219, 222
Amory, Thomas, 110, 206, 207
Amphitheatre, 11, 101, 105, 124, 127, 146, 175, 180, 181, 194
Ancients, landscape of the, iii, 10, 21
André, Major, 177
Anglo-Chinese garden, 121. *See* Chambers, Sir William; Landscape gardening
Annuals, 231
Apennines. *See* Mountains
Arblay, Mme. d', 210
Art. *See* Engraving, Print, Painting; Landscape gardening
Art, instructive, 23, 90
Art, interest in, iii, v, 7–10, 12, 14–34, 35–56, *et passim*
Artificial hermit, 155, 210
Artificial ruins. *See* Ruins, artificial
Auctions. *See* Picture sales
Austen, Jane, 87, 91, 221–223
Avenues, 122, 123, 140, 154, 163

B

Babbitt, Irving, *Rousseau and Romanticism*, iv

Bacon, Lord, 152
Baker, Henry, *Universal Spectator*, 27
Baldinucci, 36, 44
Bampfield, C. W., 93, 94, 209
Barbauld, Anna Laetitia, 114
Barnard, Edward, 166
Barret, George (elder), 42, 73, 75
Barret, George (younger), 75
Barrière, Dominique, 79
Barrington, Daines, 153
Barry, James, 23, 30, 42, 71
Bartsch, Adam von, *Anleitung*, 80
Beattie, James, 112, 113
Beauclerk, Lady Diana, 90
Beaumont, Sir George, 16, 36, 42, 70, 89, 98 n.
Beauty and sublimity. *See* Sublime and beautiful
Beckford, William, 67, 91
Beckham, George, 132 n.
Belgium, English garden in, 165
Bell's *Fugitive Poetry*, 132 n., 133 n.
Bellamy, Daniel, 116
Berghem, 69, 70, 71, 72, 78, 187, 196
Berkeley, Bishop, 12, 92
Berkeley, George Monck, 50 n.
Beyle, Henri, 167
Bishop, Samuel, 94
Blake, William, 119
Blenheim, 132, 140, 141, 146, 165
Bloem, Hans von, 69
Blunt, Reginald, *Mrs. Montagu*, 141 n.
Borgognone, Il, 10, 24, 69
Boswell, James, 31; picturesque, 156, 190, 191
Both, Jan, 35, 69, 70, 74, 78, 79, 83
Boul, Philip, 8
Bourdon, Sebastian, 68
Bowles, William Lisle, 115
Bramston, J., 27 n., 129
Bray, William, 195
Breval, John, 64
Bridgeman, Charles, 109, 125, 126
Bril, Paul, v, 10, 57, 63, 65, 69, 79, 83
British Magazine, 176

233